RETREAT RESOURCES

DESIGNS AND STRATEGIES FOR SPIRITUAL GROWTH

RETREAT RESOURCES

DESIGNS AND STRATEGIES FOR SPIRITUAL GROWTH

Volume One:

Retreats for Clergy and Religious

GENERAL EDITOR:
MAURY SMITH, O. F. M., D. MIN.

ASSISTANT EDITOR:
E. JACKIE KENNEY

PAULIST PRESS
NEW YORK, N.Y., PARAMUS, N.J., TORONTO, CANADA

Published by Paulist Press
Editorial Office: 1865 Broadway, New York, New York 10023
Business Office: 400 Sette Drive, Paramus, New Jersey 07652

Printed and bound in the United States of America

Library of Congress Catalogue Card Number: 74-83719

ISBN: 0-8091-1850-5

Designed by Joanne Cossa

ACKNOWLEDGMENTS

God Is Here—Let's Celebrate by Leslie Grant. Copyright 1969 by Concordia Publishing House. Used with permission.

Introduction to Christianity by Joseph Ratzinger. Published by Herder and Herder, New York, 1970. Used with permission.

No Exit and The Flies by Jean-Paul Sartre. New York, Alfred A. Knopf, 1947. Used with permission.

Flight from Woman by Karl Stern. New York, Farrar, Straus and Giroux, Inc. Used with permission.

The Divine Milieu by Pierre Teilhard de Chardin, translated by Bernard Wall. New York, Harper & Row; London, William Collins Sons & Co., 1960. Used with permission.

A Handbook of Structured Experiences for Human Relations Training, Vol. I, edited by J. W. Pfeiffer and J. E. Jones. Iowa City, University Associates, 1969. Reprinted by permission.

Christian Spirituality by Bernard Cooke. Chicago, Argus Communications. Used with permission.

English translations of the Eucharistic Prayers and selected Alleluia verses from the Lectionary. Copyright © 1969, International Committee on English in the Liturgy, Inc. All rights reserved.

Catholic Digest. St. Paul, Minn. Material used with permission.

Of the City of God, edited by J.W.C. Wand. New York, Oxford University Press, 1963. Used with permission.

The Diary of a Country Priest by Georges Bernanos. New York, Macmillian; London, William Collins Sons & Co., 1937. Used with permission.

"Berry's World." Reprinted by permission of Newspaper Enterprise Association.

"No Prayer Unanswered" by Margery Finn Brown. Reprinted from *Redbook* Magazine, December 1960. Copyright © 1960 by The McCall Publishing Company. Used with permission.

"Christian Faith and Today's Man" by Jean Danielou. *Our Sunday Visitor*, April 19, 1970. Reprinted with permission.

McCall's Magazine, article by Henry Ehrlich. Copyright *McCall's Magazine*, September 1970. Used with permission.

"On Love" and "On Friendship." Reprinted from *The Prophet* by Kahlil Gibran with permission of the publisher, Alfred A. Knopf, Inc. Copyright 1923 by Kahlil Gibran; renewal copyright 1951 by Administrators C.T.A. of the Kahlil Gibran Estate and Mary G. Gibran.

Homiletic and Pastoral Review, November, 1969. Material reprinted with permission.

Prayer Book For Religious by F.X. Lasance. New York, Benziger Bros., Inc., 1934. Used with permission.

Meditations and Prayers for the Sick, Aging and Homebound. Franciscan Mission Associates, Mount Vernon, New York, 1973. Used with permission.

DEDICATION

In Memory Of
Rev. Germain R. Schwab 1916-1969
Provincial of Midwest Franciscans

and

Rev. Francis Leo Madsen 1920-1968
Vicar Provincial of Midwest Franciscans

Both of these priests were committed to the preaching apostolate.

SPECIAL THANKS

The editor wishes to thank all who participated in making this resource materials an actuality. Special thanks go to Jackie Kenney who did the indexing and organization of the materials; to the Franciscan Community who encouraged and supported me: Charles Bloss, Paul Schullian, and Donald Betz. There were several typists but I wish to thank Pauline Dossman who did most of the typing and to our secretary Jean Wawrzyniak who was always there in an emergency. Finally, I would like to thank my friends, the Alperns, Banet and Kleins; who have not seen much of me the last six months but have been patient and supportive of this work.

CONTENTS

PART ONE:

GENERAL INTRODUCTORY MATERIALS

A. INTRODUCTION:

So you've been asked to give a retreat! If you have little experience, then this probably has raised your anxieties about what you will be able to do. The purpose of these resource materials is to provide you with ideas and structures that will help you to give a successful retreat. From the beginning, the editors of these resource materials wish to emphasize the importance of your not merely taking them as they are and reading them to your participants. Their purpose is to provide you with models and ideas of what you can do with men and women religious.

You as a person are the most important asset that you have as a retreat master. This is not to belittle the importance of good content, good presentation, and good administrative procedures. It is important that you do have good content and have really worked through your ideas so that you are clear. It is important that you have a style of presentation that is interesting and appealing to your audience. And it is important that you organize your retreat in such a way that the structure helps the person to grow in his spiritual life. However, what is most important is you as a person and a Christian: your enthusiasm, your sincerity, your goodness, your interest in the people you are working with in the retreat, your willingness to share yourself and your relationship with God and other people with the audience, your willingness to mix among the retreatants and letting them get to know you and you trying to get to know them. You as a person and Christian are much more important than the content, presentation, or organization of the retreat. The behavioral sciences and psychology have "discovered" that man grows in relationship with his fellow humans. A person responds to a person who shows openness, understanding, a willingness to listen deeply, empathy and positive regard. People are helped by being in contact with persons who are congruent. Congruence is when a person's feelings and thinking are clear to him, and he is able to express them clearly and openly to another person. The other person experiences his feeling/thinking as matching his expression of his feeling/thinking. Or, to put it in popular terms, the person is not putting on a front.

The behavioral sciences have also affirmed the basic goodness of man. In fact, many of the experiential and humanistic psychologies held that man has an energy that moves him toward self-actualization. For this reason a person should trust his organismic responses to life situations.

Although the terminology is somewhat different, what the behavioral sciences have been "discovering" about man correlates with the scriptural understanding of man. In the Scriptures man is seen as a composite unity of body-soul-spirit. Christ taught that we are to love our neighbor, which can be behaviorally defined in terms of listening, understanding, empathy and positive regard. The beatitudes describe the characteristics of the Christian lover: to be poor in spirit means you know you need others and God; to mourn means to empathize with others; to be meek is to be gentle and accepting; to be just is to be set on doing God's will; to show mercy is a compassionate love; to be pure means to be sincere; to be a peacemaker; and to be able to endure suffering. Those qualities are the same qualities of personhood that psychology encourages people to grow in. These are the qualities that any Christian should be striving toward and especially any retreat master or spiritual leader.

Granted that you are dedicated and enthusiastic about growing in your relationship with Christ and are willing to share this with people, then hopefully these resource materials can be of help to you in suggesting content as well as modes and styles of presentation, and also in providing you with models for organizing a retreat.

Reflect on your past experience. You have a lot going for you. If you are a priest, you have a great deal of experience in speaking to groups. If you are a layman, you may well have experience in giving talks and working with people. No doubt you have done a great deal of reading and thinking about the current situation of the Church in the world today. You have many ideas and attitudes about how the Church might accomplish its mission of continuing Christ's work of love in the world today.

Most of the modern styles of communication and preaching, stress the importance of a personal, informal type of communication. I'm referring here to the style with which you speak to a group. You do not have to be a great stage orator. Rather, what is encouraged is a presentation in which you talk to the people in as personal a way as possible insofar as tone of voice, inflection, and attitude. Your sincerity is the most important quality you have.

You will find in this general introduction a number of suggestions and ideas that will be of help to you in organizing your retreat. For example, there is a section on scheduling procedures, on how to choose the content for your retreat, on administration procedures, direction procedures, follow-up to the retreat, and evaluation procedures for the retreat you give.

The following two organizations may be of help to you: Christian Preaching Conference, 3015 Fourth St., Washington, D.C., 20017 and Retreats International, Donaldson Road, Erlanger, Kentucky, 41018.

B. CONTENT CHOOSING PROCEDURES

Frequently the hardest part of giving a retreat is deciding what you will talk about and what activities you may include. Set yourself a specific deadline for deciding and then force yourself to do it.

One way you can do this is by perusing the type of retreat you are interested in. These resource materials have basically four audiences: retreats for religious, adult retreats, married couples retreats, youth retreats. Write down the talks that look interesting to you that you would like to talk on. Keep your audience in mind as you do this. Read the list of talks you have selected. After reading them, rank order them from first to last according to how you evaluated them as fitting what you want to do.

Another approach would be to select a theme and seven topics under that theme that you would like to talk on. Then go through the index and see if you can find talks that are on the topics you want. Do not hesitate to adapt talks to your audience. For instance, you may want to talk to married couples about faith and adapt the talk on Faith from the Christ Among Us adult retreat.

Whatever you do it is important that you absorb, integrate and adapt any of the materials here so that they are part of you. At no time under any kind of excuse should you merely read these talks to a group. You will simply be boring and ineffective. If you are too busy to prepare for a retreat, then you are too busy to give one. A good retreat master who is researching and writing a new retreat from scratch spends approximately two months reading, reflecting, writing, editing, and practicing.

If you do decide to use one of these programs as it is; you must make the material your own. First read over the talks a few times. Then add some of your own ideas and approaches and edit anything that you do not agree with. Next make some outlines of your own to talk from. Then practice delivering what has become your own talk. This process will take about ten days. For most priests, they will have to find about two hours a day to assimilate the material and make their own outlines.

AN EXAMPLE:

For example, one of the local high schools asked for a day of renewal for its junior class. The class teacher was asked to poll the class and find out what issues or topics and what it was that they were interested in doing that day that would be important to them. The response was in the area of: getting along with others; overcoming the apathy in the class; how do you grow in friendship; how could we build class spirit.

On the basis of these responses we chose the following materials: The film and the value clarification sheet called "Is it Always Right to be Right" was chosen because of its emphasis on interdependence among people. This exercise was from Charles Bloss' Youth Retreat. The Win as Much as You Can exercise was chosen from Ken Keiffer's retreat to show how mistrust and uncooperativeness destroy a group's spirit. The "Evaluating My Attitudes" based on the Beatitudes was adapted from Chuck Tobin's youth retreat, because the beatitudes describe the qualities necessary to build a Christian Community which also applies to a class spirit.

The day was then designed in such a way that there would be unity between these three sessions. After the film on interdependence the teenagers were asked to write a few paragraphs on whether they agreed with the film or not. After the exercise, Win as Much as You Can, they were asked to write a few paragraphs on what their reaction to this exercise was. Then, after they filled out the sheet on the film, they were asked to compare what they had written about the film and the exercise. They were challenged with the question: Did you agree intellectually with the film on interdependence and say that you believed in interdependence and then in the exercise actually behave in a mistrustful and uncooperative manner? Or did you act the way you say you believe?

The schedule for this day was as follows:

8:30 AM. Register.

8:45. Film: "Is it Always Right to be Right" Write whether you agree or disagree with the film.

9:15. Exercise: Win as Much as You Can. After exercise: write your reactions to the exercise.

10:00. Value Clarification Sheet on film.

10:15. At this point ask the teenagers to compare what they wrote immediately after the film with what they wrote immediately after the exercise.

10:20. Discussion on the Value Clarification Sheet on the film.

11:00. Shift the focus of the discussion: In the light of the film on interdependence and the exercise on trust and mistrust what are the changes you would like to make to build a class spirit?

11:30. Have a member from each group report. The class secretary records. Meet with the class officers during lunch to help them plan a follow-up to the ideas expressed by the class.

12:00 PM. Lunch.

12:45. The sheet on the Beatitudes. Give them five minutes to evaluate themselves and then to discuss.

1:15. Eucharist with the theme of love and Community.

C. HOW TO DESIGN A RETREAT

1. Know the people. Meet with a committee of the group. If that is not possible, talk to similar people. For example, if they are teenagers in another town, meet with some teenagers nearby. Find out what is currently on their minds. Discover their spiritual needs. Confer General Introduction.

2. Pick a theme and then break it down into six or eight talks. Or let the group pick the topics.

3. Design the liturgies and prayer service to fit your theme. It is best to involve the participants in this when feasible.

4. Decide on films, slides, projects, outlines, etc.

5. Get your schedule formed in detail. Confer schedule procedures.

6. Check on administrative details. Confer administrative procedures.

7. Decide on a follow-up. Confer follow-up procedures.

8. Evaluate your first draft. Confer evaluation procedures. Have a talk with someone who has given retreats. If that is not possible, talk to a friend about your ideas.

9. As a general rule, do what you do best. Talk about what you believe in and have experienced. Adapt any of these resource materials to fit your style and personality.

D. SCHEDULING PROCEDURES

In this section we have eleven examples of various kinds of schedules for adults, married couples, young people, sisters' retreat, and even one in for a parent/teenager week-end. These are presented as possible models that you may devise your own schedule from. From perusing these schedules, it should be very evident to you that a schedule is a very subjective item. Retreat masters who think that people need a lot of input, and information will tend to have a very heavy and full schedule. On the other hand, retreat masters who feel that one of the most important parts of the retreat is time for the individual to reflect and pray will give the participants a great deal of time to themselves.

There are certain basic ingredients that go into any retreat: namely the meals, the talks, confession, the Eucharist, and some prayer services. These can be scheduled in any manner that you wish, as you will see from these example schedules. Generally speaking, I think most retreat masters do follow a pattern of having a talk and then having some kind of prayer service or such as the rosary, stations, scriptures service, or communal celebration of Penance, and then another talk. In other words they try not to run several talks in a row, but try to break up the conferences with some activities in between.

In general, I would think that most retreat masters nowadays give a talk that lasts from 20 to 30 minutes. Long talks are a rarity nowadays. People who are involved in group dynamics and experiential learning will tend to schedule two hour sessions. The break down of such a schedule might well be a 15 minute introduction, one half hour to do the project, and then approximately an hour to discuss the project.

Those who take a discussion approach to retreats tend to schedule sessions of an hour and a half long so that there is ample time to discuss. Frequently they will begin with a short 10 or 15 minute talk and then open the meeting for a discussion of the particular topics that they have talked about.

By the time you look through the examples that we have in this section plus the schedules of the retreats that are contributed here, hopefully you will see that what you should do is make a schedule that fits into your purpose and to your personality.

Schedule one is a modern discussion week-end that blends some conferences with some short talks and discussions. If you look at the overall schedule you will see that it begins with three conferences, in which there is no discussion, and then there is a project Saturday afternoon, with a discussion. The rest of the retreat is scheduled in such a manner that there are hour and a half periods for a short talk and conference.

Some retreat leaders put the emphasis on discussion and simply schedule a short talk and discussion for every session. In the first half of the retreat the discussions are of a short duration of only about an hour. Towards the later part of the retreat, time is allowed for an hour and a half discussion. The rationale for this is that groups need time to get started, need time to get to know one another, and also need input, before they are stimulated to discussion.

Schedule number two is a modern schedule that was designed by a group of laymen for their particular organization. You will notice that they like the idea of a film and discussion each evening. The retreat began on Saturday with having four talks. Discussions began Saturday afternoon and then more time was allowed for talk and discussion during the rest of the retreat. There was a discussion and recreation Saturday evening. The better half of Sunday morning was given over to the individuals so that they could rise when they wanted and have time for rest, reading, prayer, and reflection. And then there was a talk and discussion on the latter part of Sunday afternoon.

Schedule number three is a traditional schedule. On the whole there are not many people who follow this heavy a schedule anymore, but it is good to look at it to see what has been done in the past.

Schedule number four is a modified traditional; the basic ingredients are the conferences, the stations, the rosary, time for confession and the Eucharist. Note that it is also permissible that on Saturday evenings there is to be a film and discussion, a question and answer period or a discussion with the retreatants. The people who come for a traditional retreat do enjoy and like to have an opportunity to sit with the priest and to ask the questions that are on their minds.

An option to schedule number four is to drop some of the conferences and/or activities to give the retreatants more individual time. A retreat master who emphasizes prayer would allow plenty of time for the individual to reflect and pray.

Schedule number five is a modern day of renewal. There is really nothing unique, it all depends on how much time can be given. Frequently a group can only come in for example from 9:00 to 2:00, and so one of the talks and discussions would have to be dropped. It might well be that this is rather a full schedule. The load could be lightened by dropping one of the conferences and discussions and having a period of reflection and quiet for the members.

Schedule number six is a traditional day of renewal. Again this will depend on the amount of time that the people have to stay, whether they can stay a full day or only three quarters of a day. This schedule can simply be adjusted by dropping conferences or by only having the rosary or the stations. You simply fit the schedule to the time the group has.

Example number seven is an example of a modern evening of renewal. It is very simple in design. You do not necessarily even have to celebrate the Eucharist although in general groups do like this. If they have more time then there can be two talks or a longer discussion period. Instead of the scripture service you could have a communal service of Penance, if you so desired.

Example number eight is a traditional evening of recollection. This is a very heavy schedule. You could drop one of the conferences and give the people time to have prayer and reflection.

Example number nine is a modern discussion week-end for married couples. On the whole this follows the same format as any modern week-end. The one uniqueness about this schedule is that during the after lunch periods, the couples are encouraged to spend that time by themselves as a couple. Another feature of this that is different is the votive nuptial mass at the closing with a renewal of marriage vows. Generally speaking, married couples who make a spiritual retreat together like to have this renewal of their marriage vows. The priest can simply make an adaptation of the marriage ceremony itself.

Example number ten is a unique schedule of a father-son or mother-daughter week-end. Some of the features of this particular design are that in the first evening (say it is a father-son week-end) the fathers and sons gather together and the retreat facilitator discovers what their interests are, what their expectations are, and what are the topics that they wish to cover during the week-end. After the celebration of the Eucharist the spiritual leader should meet with the teenagers and let them do the talking, but simply be with them and let them get to know him. The schedule begins on Saturday morning, by meeting with the teenagers and again finding out what they are thinking. The reason why the spiritual leader is meeting twice with the teenagers is because it takes teenagers longer to feel comfortable in his presence and to be open with him. Also he is spending more time with them initially because they are afraid to talk in front of their fathers. He spends this time with them getting to know them and letting them get to know him and feel comfortable in his presence.

In the latter part of Saturday morning, the spiritual leader meets with the fathers and talks with them about the psychological dynamics of the teenagers. He encourages them to listen to their teenage sons. He also listens to the problems and issues that they feel are important. The parent and teenager are encouraged to spend time with each other after lunch breaks. During this program the particular topics that they choose are the ones that are discussed.

Example number eleven is an example of a youth retreat. One of the features you will notice here is that there are two full days, but only one evening at the center. Through our experience we have discovered that this is the best schedule for teenagers as far as we are concerned. Generally speaking, it is usually the second evening at a place when the teenagers begin to get into problems. You will notice that this retreat is filled with a lot of projects and experiential learning exercises. We use a lot of crayons and pictures, etc. to help keep them active.

Also notice that there are two large periods in the afternoon for the kids to either play football or baseball, according to the season. Generally it is important to keep the teenagers busy and to keep them occupied. They are full of energy. Let them have a hootenanny in the evening. The one discipline rule we ask is that they be in bed by twelve. We do not try to enforce silence in a modern youth retreat. Frequently, the youths themselves ask for a period of silence, so that they can have time to think, reflect, and pray. We usually let this suggestion come from them, because then they will much more willingly keep it and benefit from it, than if it is merely forced upon them.

Besides these examples of schedules you have the schedules of each of the programs that have been contributed in this resource kit.

I. MODERN DISCUSSION WEEKEND

This schedule blends some conferences and short talks with time for discussion.

FRIDAY

8:00	P.M.	Registration
9:00	P.M.	Introduction (living room)
9:30	P.M.	Celebration of Eucharist (mass)
10:45	P.M.	Opening Conference

SATURDAY

7:30	A.M.	Rise
8:00	A.M.	Breakfast
9:00	A.M.	Conference (chapel)
9:30	A.M.	Reflection
10:00	A.M.	Conference (living room)
11:00	A.M.	Scripture Reading and Discussion (chapel)
12:00	noon	Lunch
12:30	P.M.	Time for Reading, Private Confession or Conference
2:00	P.M.	Discussion, use of project.
4:00	P.M.	Prayer Service in Chapel
4:30	P.M.	Confessions
5:00	P.M.	Celebration of Eucharist
6:00	P.M.	Supper
7:30	P.M.	Conference - Discussion
9:00	P.M.	Film: "The Eucharist"

SUNDAY

7:30	A.M.	Rise
8:00	A.M.	Breakfast
9:00	A.M.	Meditation
9:30	A.M.	Reflection
10:30	A.M.	Questions and Issues
12:00	noon	Lunch
1:30	P.M.	Closing Conference
2:30	P.M.	Eucharist - Rededication to Christ

Father is available for private conferences. Feel free to ask to speak with them. His office is on the second floor.

Please move any discussion group to the downstairs room after 10:00 P.M. so that the sleeping quarters are quiet for reading and sleeping.

II. MODERN PROGRAM SCHEDULE

This is an example of a schedule that a committee of laymen designed for their group.

FRIDAY

7:30 P.M.	Registration
8:00 P.M.	Mass
9:00 P.M.	Film: "Eucharist"
9:15 P.M.	Talk: "The Christian Today"

SATURDAY

7:30 A.M.	Rising
8:00 A.M.	Breakfast (continental)
9:00 A.M.	Talk: "The Catholic Family Today"
10:00 A.M.	Talk: "Confession Today"
11:00 A.M.	Talk: "Authority and the Church"
12:00 P.M.	Lunch
12:30 P.M.	Recreation
2:00 P.M.	Talk: "The Christian working with all men of good will"
3:30 P.M.	Time for Confession
4:00 P.M.	Mass Homily: "Meaning of the New Liturgy"
5:00 P.M.	Social Hour
6:00 P.M.	Dinner
6:30 P.M.	Recreation
7:30 P.M.	Talk and Discussion: "The Christian in the Changing Church"
9:00 P.M.	Film: "Workout"
9:30 P.M.	Optional: Discussion or recreation or retire

SUNDAY

Rise when you please

8:00-10:00 A.M.

Breakfast (continental). This is time designed to be used as you see fit in rest, reading, prayer and reflection. A charitable quiet atmosphere is desired.

10:30 A.M.	Talk and Discussion: "Morality Today"
12:00 P.M.	Dinner
12:30 P.M.	Recreation
1:00 P.M.	Talk: "The Christian Tomorrow"
2:30 P.M.	Mass Homily: "Christ is with us"
3:30 P.M.	Departure

III. A TRADITIONAL SCHEDULE

This is an example of a heavy schedule.

FRIDAY	9:00 P.M.	Beginning of Grand Silence
		Benediction or Mass
		Opening Conference
		Evening Prayers
SATURDAY	7:00 A.M.	Rising
	7:20 A.M.	Morning Prayers
		Angelus
		Holy Mass
		Breakfast
	9:00 A.M.	Conference
	10:00 A.M.	Rosary
	11:00 A.M.	Conference
	11:50 A.M.	Angelus
	12:00 noon	Dinner
	2:00 P.M.	Stations of the Cross
	3:00 P.M.	Conference
	4:00 P.M.	Eucharistic Devotion
	5:00 P.M.	Conference
	5:50 P.M.	Examination of Conscience
		Angelus
	6:00 P.M.	Supper
	7:00 P.M.	Confessions
	8:30 P.M.	Conference
		Benediction
SUNDAY	7:00 A.M.	Rising
	7:20 A.M.	Morning Prayers
		Angelus
		Holy Mass
		Breakfast
	9:00 A.M.	Conference
	10:00 A.M.	Rosary
	11:00 A.M.	Conference
	11:55 A.M.	Angelus
	12:00 noon	Dinner
	1:15 P.M.	Open Forum (Question Box)
	2:30 P.M.	Stations of the Cross
	3:00 P.M.	Blessing of Religious Articles
		Closing Remarks
		Renewal of Baptismal Promises
		Papal Blessing and Benediction
		Angelus

IV. A TRADITIONAL SCHEDULE

This example tries to blend both input in the way of a conference and yet allows some time for the individual.

FRIDAY	8:00 P.M.	Registration
	9:00 P.M.	Mass
	10:00 P.M.	Conference
SATURDAY	7:30 A.M.	Rising
	8:00 A.M.	Morning prayers (chapel)
		Breakfast
	9:00 A.M.	Conference
	10:00 A.M.	Rosary
	11:00 A.M.	Conference
	12:00 noon	Lunch
	2:00 P.M.	Conference
	3:00 P.M.	Stations
	4:00 P.M.	Conference
	4:30 P.M.	Confessions
	5:00 P.M.	Mass
	6:00 P.M.	Supper
	7:30 P.M.	Conference
	8:00 P.M.	Film and discussion

SUNDAY   Schedule for Sunday morning is the same as on Saturday morning.

	1:30 P.M.	Conference
		Blessing of religious articles
	2:30 P.M.	Mass and closing
	3:15 P.M.	Departure

LET SILENCE PREVAIL DURING THE RETREAT.

V. MODERN

One Day of Renewal

8:30	A.M.	Arrive
9:00	A.M.	Conference
10:00	A.M.	Scripture Service
11:00	A.M.	Conference and Discussion
12:00	P.M.	Lunch

Time for Prayer and Reading

2:00	P.M.	Talk and Discussion
4:00	P.M.	Communal Celebration of Penance
5:00	P.M.	Eucharist

VI. TRADITIONAL

One Day of Renewal

8:30	A.M.	Arrive
9:00	A.M.	Opening Conference
10:00	A.M.	Rosary
11:00	A.M.	Conference
12:00	P.M.	Lunch

Time for prayer, reading or private conference with priest.

2:00	P.M.	Conference
3:00	P.M.	Stations
4:00	P.M.	Conference
4:30	P.M.	Confessions
5:00	P.M.	Mass

VII. MODERN

Evening of Renewal

6:30 P.M.	Arrive
7:00 P.M.	Scripture Service
7:30 P.M.	Talk and Discussion
9:00 P.M.	Eucharist

VIII. TRADITIONAL

Evening of Recollection

6:30 P.M.	Arrive
7:00 P.M.	Mass
8:00 P.M.	Conference
8:45 P.M.	Rosary or Stations
9:15 P.M.	Conference
10:00 P.M.	Closing Prayers

E. ADMINISTRATION PROCEDURES

Check List One

How many people?

What kind of people: adults, teenagers, married couples, age, social status, interests.

Where will the retreat be held? Address: Directions.

When start and end?

What kind of facilities are available: chapel, large discussion room, moveable chairs, tables, chalkboard or easel with newsprint.

What equipment is available: stereo, tape recorder, film projector, overhead projector, art materials, old magazines, paper, pencils, organ, piano.

Will you use a film? Which? Where can you get it?

Do you need to make copies of anything: schedule, liturgies, scripture services, outlines, reading suggestions, projects, etc.

Are you taking care of the details above or is there a chairman who will handle some of these for you?

How much do you wish to charge the group or are you going to accept a donation stipend?

What will be the cost of room and board at the retreat center or place?

Who collects the money?

Does the retreat center have set meal times?

Chaperons for kids' retreats, suggest one adult per ten kids.

What kind of prayer service do you desire?

What kind of liturgies do you have planned?

Check List Two

I. If you are going as a retreat master to a retreat center, you should:

Let the retreat director know when you will arrive and leave.

Try to bring your own materials and equipment, such as, schedules, outlines, paper, pencils, art materials, etc.

If you are organizing the whole retreat, then go over the check list with the retreat director.

Generally speaking, you will find retreat directors very helpful and they will help you get all the details lined up.

If there is any item you want, check with the retreat director whether they supply it or whether you must bring it.

Whatever other mistakes you might make, by all means get your group to meals on time. Allow fifteen minutes between the last talk or event and meal time. The larger the group, the slower they move.

II. If you are not going to a retreat house, then you will need a full-time co-ordinator to organize things for you: You should be available for private conferences during the retreat workshop. Get someone from the group to be a chairman who takes care of details.

F. EVALUATION PROCEDURES

I. Introduction:

Here are some check lists and questions that will help you evaluate your content and remind you of important aspects of presentation. Also included are some evaluation questions you could ask your participants. Encourage the participants to be honest with you so that you can learn.

II. Checklist for evaluating your own talks:

Do you have a theme for the retreat?
In a one-half hour talk there should be only about three ideas clearly illustrated.
What needs of the audience are you addressing yourself to?
Do you know your audience?
Do your talks focus on one issue or are you merely rambling?
Have you translated technical theological language into plain English?
Do you have stories, quotes, examples, life experiences that can clarify your topic?
Do you have an interesting beginning?
How clear and understandable is your talk?
Would your talk be instructional, inspiring or motivating?
Can you state your idea in one clear simple sentence?
What example is there that will clarify your ideas?
Are you making practical applications?
Do you have a conclusion?

III. Check list for evaluating your presentation:

Who are you talking to:
    1. The clock
    2. The ceiling
    3. Your notes
    4. Persons

What is your attitude toward the audience:
I am: 1. Friendly
       2. Aloof
       3. Angry
       4. Interested

How do you think you will sound to your audience:
    1. "Fatherly"
    2. Authoritarian
    3. Permissive
    4. Fellow Christian

Tape record one of your talks and listen to see if you are using:
    1. Slang
    2. eh-eh
    3. Slurring
    4. Clear enunciation

How would you rate your speaking style:
    1. Academic professor: use technical vocabulary
    2. Shakesperian: use too formal a language
    3. Impersonal: use "it", "this," "that", etc. too much
    4. Natural spoken style: informal personal attitude

How does your voice sound:
    1. Loud
    2. Dramatic
    3. Sing-Song
    4. Pleasant

What do you do to make your talk clearer:
    1. Gestures
    2. Blackboard
    3. Outlines
    4. Slides

The bias in this check list is toward the presentation being with a friendly attitude toward your fellow Christians. Try to develop a pleasant voice with a natural style of delivery. Take advantage of audio-visuals to aid the clarity of your presentation.

IV. *Some questions to ask yourself about your talk and presentation*

Are you enthusiastic about what you are talking about?
Do you believe what you are saying to the point that you act on that idea?
Are you talking from experience?
Is what you are saying interesting to others?
If you have said that several times before, do you have a fresh way to present it?
Is what you are talking about something recent?
How well are you manifesting an understanding and empathy for people?
Is your audience tuned in to you or have they become restless or fallen asleep?
How important a life issue are you talking about?
Can you put your idea in one clear phrase?
How logical are the connections between your ideas?
Are you showing your mind or your heart?
Are you dealing with issues that are important to these people, at this time, at their age and background?
Have you given the participants an opportunity to give input on topics they want?
Are you giving the participants an opportunity to respond and to ask questions at least one session?

V. *Evaluation by the Participants Sheet*

Date_____Occupation_____Schooling_____Age_____

1. Did the talks on the Gospels help you understand them? Why? Why not?

2. Rank these in the order from one to six according to which they were the most helpful; comment on what you thought of the technique:
   ____reading and discussing together
   ____rewriting paragraphs in your own language
   ____finding music that expressed an idea in the Gospel
   ____acting out a parable or story in the Gospel
   ____relating a theme in the Gospel to a film you have seen
   ____making a poster or collage.

3. Were the talks and discussions related to your life and practical for you?

4. List at least three things you disliked about this program:

5. What did you like about this program?

6. What are the ideas, insights, experiences, inspirations that you think you will carry with you? List as many as you can.

VI. *Retreat Questionnaire*

1. What did you like about this retreat?
2. What did you dislike about this retreat?
3. What suggestions would you have for restructuring a retreat of this type in the future?

G. BIBLIOGRAPHY ON PREACHING

I. Professional Journal

PREACHING TODAY, Magazine of the Christian Preaching Conference, 3015 Fourth Street, Washington, D.C., 20017. There are many helpful and valuable articles in back issues.

II. Sermon Preparations

Baillargeon, Anatole, O.M.I. (ed.), *HANDBOOK FOR SPECIAL PREACHING*, New York: Herder and Herder, 1965.

Baillargeon, Anatole, O.M.I., *NEW MEDIA: NEW FORMS*, Franciscan Herald Press, Chicago, 1967.

Baumann, J. Daniel, *AN INTRODUCTION TO CONTEMPORARY PREACHING*, Grand Rapids, Michigan: Baker Book House, 1972.

Dubay, Thomas M., S.M. *SISTERS' RETREATS*, Westminister, Newman Press, 1963.

Kahlefeld, Heinrich, *PARABLES AND INSTRUCTIONS IN THE GOSPELS*, S. S. Herder and Herder, New York, 1966.

Lee, Charlotte, *ORAL INTERPRETATION*, Second Edition: Boston: Houghton-Mifflin, 1959.

MacNutt, Francis S., O.P., Madden, Dalmatius, O.P., *TEACH US TO LOVE: SISTERS' CONFERENCE NEEDS*, St. Louis, B. Herder Book Company, 1963.

MacNutt, Sylvester, *GAUGING SERMON EFFECTIVENESS*, Priory Press, 1963.

MacLennan, David A. (ed.), *REVELL'S MINISTER'S ANNUAL 1966*, Westwood, New Jersey, Fleming H. Revell Company, 1965.

Maertens, Thierry, O.S.B., *BIBLE THEMES: A SOURCE BOOK*, Burges, Biblica, 1964.

Mead, Frank S. (ed.), *THE ENCYCLOPEDIA OF RELIGIOUS QUOTATIONS*, Westwood, New Jersey, Fleming H. Revell Company, 1965.

Miller, Charles E., Miller, Oscar J., and Roebert, Michael, *ANNOUNCING THE GOOD NEWS*, Staten Island: Alba House, 1971.

Miller, Charles E. and Miller, Oscar J., *COMMUNICATING CHRIST*, New York: Joseph Wagner, 1970.

Rice, Charles L., *INTERPRETATION AND IMAGINATION*, ''The Preacher and Contemporary Literature'', Philadelphia, Fortress Press, 1970.

Sangster, William, *THE CRAFT OF SERMON CONSTRUCTION*, Grand Rapids, Michigan: Baker Book House, 1972.

Sleeth, Ronald, *PROCLAIMING THE WORD*, New York: Abingdon Press, 1964.

Thompson, William D. and Bennet, Gordon C., *DIALOGUE PREACHING: THE SHARED SERMON*, Valley Forge, Pennsylvania: The Judson Press, 1969.

III. Theology of Preaching

Drury, Roman, (ed.), *PREACHING*, New York: Sheed and Ward, 1962.

Hitz, Paul, *TO PREACH THE GOSPEL*, New York: Sheed and Ward, 1963.

Jungmann, Josef A., S.J., *ANNOUNCING THE WORD OF GOD*, Herder and Herder, New York, 1967.

Murphy-O'Connor, O.P., *PAUL ON PREACHING*, New York: Sheed and Ward, 1964.

Rahner, Karl (ed.), *THE WORD, READINGS IN THEOLOGY*, compiled at the Canisianum, Innsbruck, New York, P.J. Kennedy and Sons, 1964.

Semmelroth, Otto, S.J., *THE PREACHING WORD: ON THE THEOLOGY OF PROCLAMATION*, New York: Herder and Herder, 1965.

IV. Speaking and Communications

Brack, Harold A., and Hance, Kenneth G., *PUBLIC SPEAKING AND DISCUSSION FOR RELIGIOUS LEADERS*, Prentice-Hall, Inc., Englewood Cliffs, New Jersey, 1961.

Jackson, B. F., Jr., *TELEVISION—RADIO—FILM FOR CHURCHMEN*, New York, New York: Abingdon Press, 1969.

Reid, Clyde, *THE EMPTY PULPIT: A STUDY IN PREACHING AS COMMUNICATION*, New York: Harper and Row, 1967.

Roxburg, Gilbert E., O.P. (ed.), *Clergy is Communication*, Homiletic Service, Ottawa, Canada, Novalis, 1971.

V. Selected Books on Group Dynamics

Casteel, John, *CREATIVE ROLE OF INTERPERSONAL GROUPS IN THE CHURCH TODAY*, New York: Association Press, 1968. A variety of "How to" use groups in the Church. Worth Reading.

Clinebell, Jr., Heard J., *THE PEOPLE DYNAMIC, CHANGING SELF IN SOCIETY THROUGH GROWTH GROUPS*, New York: Harper and Row, 1972.

Doherty, Sr., Michael, *DYNAMIC APPROACHES TO TEACHING HIGH SCHOOL RELIGION*, New York: Alba House, 1969. Applies group dynamics to high school teaching.

Dow, Robert A., *LEARNING THROUGH ENCOUNTER*, Valley Forge: Judson Press, 1971. Best solid introduction on the market for a clergyman.

Egan, Gerard, *ENCOUNTER: GROUP PROCESSES FOR INTERPERSONAL GROWTH*, Belmont: Brooks/Cole, 1970. Highly technical and systematic synthesis of group theory. Contract theory of groups. Worth Reading.

Flynn, Elizabeth and LaFaso, John, *GROUP DISCUSSION AS LEARNING PROCESS*, New York: Paulist Press, 1972. An excellent summary of group discussion findings by the behavioral sciences from a sociological standpoint.

Hall, Brian, *VALUE CLARIFICATION AS A LEARNING PROCESS: A SEARCH INTO THE CHOICES, COMMITMENTS AND CELEBRATION OF MODERN MAN*, A Sourcebook, New York: Paulist Press, 1973.

Hall, Brian and Smith, Maury, *VALUE CLARIFICATION AS A LEARNING PROCESS: A GUIDEBOOK*, New York: Paulist Press, 1973.

Hall, Brian and Smith, Maury, *VALUE CLARIFICATION AS A LEARNING PROCESS: A HANDBOOK FOR CHRISTIAN EDUCATORS*, New York: Paulist Press, 1973.

Howe, Reuel, L., *THE MIRACLE OF DIALOGUE*, New York: Seabury Press, 1963.

Jackson, Edgar, *GROUP COUNSELING: DYNAMIC POSSIBILITIES OF SMALL GROUPS*, Philadelphia: Pilgrim Press, 1969. Very elementary. Deals with working with young people.

Knowles, Joseph, *GROUP COUNSELING*, Philadelphia: Fortress Press, 1964. Good elementary introduction. Theology of groups. Very brief.

Leslie, Robert, *SHARING GROUPS IN THE CHURCH*, Nashville: Abingdon Press, 1971.

Meissner, W. W., *GROUP DYNAMICS IN THE RELIGIOUS LIFE*, Notre Dame: University of Notre Dame Press, 1966.

Pfieffer, C. Wm. and Jones, J. E., *ANNUAL HANDBOOK FOR GROUP FACILITATORS*, Iowa City, Iowa, University of Associate Press, 1973.

Raths, Louis E., Harmen, Merrill, and Simon, Sidney B., *VALUES IN TEACHING: WORKING WITH VALUES IN THE CLASSROOM*, Columbus, Ohio: Charles E. Merrill Publishing Company, 1966.

Reid, Clyde, *GROUPS ALIVE—CHURCH ALIVE*, New York: Harper and Row,

1969. Brief introductory treatment of the use of groups in the Church. Good.

Rogers, Carl, *CARL ROGERS ON ENCOUNTER GROUPS*, New York: Harper and Row, 1970. A very popular presentation of Rogers' thinking on groups.

Rogers, Carl, *FREEDOM TO LEARN*, Columbus, Ohio: Charles E. Merrill Publishing Company, 1969. Rogers' views on education and pupil-centered learning.

Shostrom, Everett, *MAN, THE MANIPULATOR*, New York: Bantam Book, 1967. Good introduction to humanistic and existential psychology and communication theory.

Seifert, Harvey and Clinebell, Howard J., *PERSONAL GROWTH AND SOCIAL CHANCE*, Philadelphia: Westminster Press, 1969.

Simons, Joseph, *RETREAT DYNAMICS*, Notre Dame: Fides, 1967. Applies encounter group techniques to retreat and shows how the encounter group achieves the traditional goals of the retreat better than the traditional retreat.

H. FOLLOW-UP PROCEDURES

Put them on your mailing list if you send out a newsletter. Especially if you have a spiritual article in it.

Plan a day of renewal or an evening of renewal six months later. Set a definite date, time and place while the group is together.

Have them write a memo postcard saying that they plan to attend a evening of renewal three or six months later. Mail it to them a month ahead of time.

Have them write a letter to themselves which you mail to them 4 to 6 months later.

The focus of this letter can be: A decision they have made, what they think is important from the retreat, what they will have hoped to accomplish in that time, etc.

In a workshop type spiritual renewal plan one of the last sessions to be a back home applications session where the participants can make decisions and get ideas from each other about follow-up.

Ask the participants to keep a personal journal or to take notes. Give them outlines or full copies of your talks to take with them.

Give a bibliography on spiritual reading to the participants.

PART TWO:

RETREATS FOR RELIGIOUS WOMEN

I. MODIFIED TRADITIONAL

BY OSCAR J. MILLER, C.M.

A. THEME PARTICIPANTS

1. DEFINITION

This retreat is intended for Sisters with vows, living a more or less traditional form of community life. Experiences are drawn from retreats given by the author to the Daughters of Charity of St. Vincent de Paul in the United States. The basic approach is modified traditional.

2. THEME

"Relationship with Almighty God"

This theme is treated on three levels, forming the three areas of discussion during the retreat.

I. The Human Level—We are first of all human beings.

II. The Christian Level—Then, we are baptized human beings.

III. The Professed Religious Level—Finally, we are "religious."

Each of these levels is divided into four parts, forming the twelve presentations (conferences). In the six days of retreat two days are devoted to each level.

3. OBJECTIVES

The main objective of this retreat is to renew our relationship with God and fellowman. This renewal involves an examination of the past, an evaluation of the present, and an orientation to the future. The specific purposes of each retreat can be made more particular and unique to the retreat by the use of the "Expectations" questionnaire, a copy of which is appended.

B. OUTLINE/SCHEDULE

1. PRESENTATIONS

The term "Presentation" is preferred to "Conference" to distinguish between the more formal, "all-talk" type and the more informal, "audio-visualized" type.

PRESENTATION I—The Human Dimension of Our Relationship with God, Part A—The Need for Salvation

PRESENTATION II—The Human Dimension of Our Relationship with God, Part B—The Saving God is Creator

PRESENTATION III—The Human Dimension of Our Relationship with God, Part C—The Saving, Creating God, is Conserver

PRESENTATION IV—The Human Dimension of Our Relationship with God, Part D—This God Saves through Us

PRESENTATION V—The Christian Dimension of Our Relationship with God, Part A—This Saving God Became Man

PRESENTATION VI—The Christian Dimension of Our Relationship with God, Part B—This Saving Man Is God

PRESENTATION VII—The Christian Dimension of Our Relationship with God, Part C—Our Salvation Is Accomplished through Redemption

PRESENTATION VIII—The Christian Dimension of Our Relationship with God, Part D—Salvation Is Applied Through the Sacraments, as Initiated in Baptism

PRESENTATION IX—The Religious Dimension of Our Relationship with God, Part A—Manifested in Prayer

PRESENTATION X—The Religious Dimension of Our Relationship with God, Part B—Perfected in the Vows

PRESENTATION XI—The Religious Dimension of Our Relationship with God, Part C—Practiced toward Christ

PRESENTATION XII—The Religious Dimension of Our Relationship with God, Part D—In Service to the Neighbor

First Day

9:00 a.m.	Morning Prayer: Creative Lauds. Bulletin: "I Am Who Am".
9:45	Presentation I
10:15	Coffee Break
10:30	General Discussion on Presentation I
11:05	Preparation for the Liturgy
11:15	Mass of the Eucharist.
Noon	Lunch
12:30 p.m.	Recreation or Rest Period
3:00	Presentation II
3:30	General Discussion on Presentation II
3:45	Small Group Discussions
4:45	General Recapitulation
5:15	Small Group Prayer
6:00	Dinner
7:00	"Free Time". Program constructed by the Sisters.

Second Day

9:00 a.m.	Morning Prayer: Creative Rosary, The Joyful Mysteries
9:30	Preparation for the Liturgy
9:40	Mass of the Holy Trinity
10:30	Coffee Break
11:00	Presentation III
11:30	General Discussion on Presentation III
Noon	Lunch
12:30 p.m.	Recreation or Rest Period
3:00	Presentation IV
3:30	General Discussion on Presentation IV

	4:00	Small Group Discussions
	4:45	General Recapitulation
	5:15	Small Group Prayer
	6:00	Dinner
	7:00	"Free Time". Program constructed by the Sisters.
Third Day	9:00 a.m.	Morning Prayer: Dialogue Meditation.
	9:45	Presentation V
	10:15	Coffee Break
	10:45	Small Group Discussions
	11:45	Shared Prayer
	Noon	Lunch
	12:30 p.m.	Recreation or Rest Period
	3:00	Preparation for the Liturgy
	3:10	Mass for the Sick
	4:15	Presentation VI
	4:45	General Discussion on Presentations V and VI
	5:30	Private Meditation
	6:00	Dinner
	7:00	"Free Time". Program constructed by the Sisters.
Fourth Day	9:00 a.m.	Morning Prayer: "The Way of the Cross" from *Prayers* by Michael Quoist
	9:45	Presentation VII
	10:15	Coffee Break
	10:30	Small Group Discussions
	11:05	Preparation for the Liturgy
	11:15	Mass in Honor of the Baptism of our Lord
	Noon	Lunch
	12:30 p.m.	Recreation or Rest Period
	3:00	Presentation VIII
	3:30	Small Group Discussions
	4:15	Recapitulation and General Discussion on Presentations VII and VIII.
	5:00	Explanation of "Penance Day" (Fifth of the retreat) and Communal Celebration of the Sacrament.
	6:00	Dinner
	7:00	"Free Time". Program constructed by the Sisters.
Fifth Day	9:00 a.m.	Morning Prayer: Meditation on the Sacrament of Penance
	9:45	Presentation IX
	10:15	Coffee Break
	10:45	Small Group Discussions
	11:30	General Recapitulation
	Noon	Lunch
	12:30 p.m.	Recreation or Rest Period
	3:00	Presentation X
	3:30	Break
	4:00	Communal Celebration of the Sacrament of Penance, followed by the Celebration of the Eucharistic Liturgy, Mass for the Forgiveness of Sins.
	6:00	Dinner
	7:00	"Free Time". Constructed by the Sisters.
Sixth Day	9:00 a.m.	Morning Prayer. "Candle and Salt" Service.
	9:30	Presentation XI
	10:00	Coffee Break
	10:30	General Discussion of Vows
	11:30	Small Group Prayer
	Noon	Dinner
	12:30 p.m.	Recreation or Rest Period
	3:00	Presentation XII
	3:30	Private Meditation
	4:00	Mass of Religious Profession
	5:00	Retreat is concluded.

C. GUIDELINES

1. STRUCTURE

This retreat is constructed on the basis of six full days, beginning the morning of the first day and ending the evening of the sixth day. The topics are so arranged that the length of the retreat can be shortened to a three-day retreat, or extended to the traditional eight-day retreat.

The basic informational and motivational material is given in twelve conferences, called Presentations. Clarification of the issues can be handled during the question and answer periods, and in the time for general and small group discussions. Individual personal problems can be discussed during times for confession and private interviews. Periods of prayers are both public and private, centering in the daily Liturgy and with offshoots into private prayer, both communal and individual.

Aids to assist the retreat master will be found in the leadership of individual Sisters and groups of Sisters, constructing and leading the Liturgy, group prayer and group discussions. Further aids are those found under the general title of Audio-Visuals: Banners, Posters, Music, Films, Film Strips, Slides, and Tapes.

2. STAGE DIRECTIONS

1. Well in advance of the actual retreat starting date make sure all proposals for the retreat (topics, style, methods, etc.) are cleared with the proper authorities, including whatever diocesan permissions are necessary, e.g., times of liturgy, communal celebration of sacrament of penance, etc. Request the equipment you will need.

2. Allow four or five hours before the retreat begins to test the equipment, evaluate the places for presentations, conferences, interviews, etc. Make sure the ventilation, lighting, seating, sound etc., is suitable and convenient. Check the provisions for darkening the room during movies and slides and filmstrips. Appoint two or three competent Sisters to help with the audio-visuals.

3. Prepare in advance, or have the retreat house do so, lists of names of the retreatants, name tags, "Expectations" and "Evaluation" sheets, copies of the Order of the Day (preferably a copy for each retreatant), copies of materials for the various morning prayers, copies of materials for the Communal Celebration of the Sacrament of Penance, copies of materials for The Way of the Cross, copies of topics and questions for discussions, and a sheet for days and times for private interviews.

4. Before the retreat begins, in addition to the Sisters who will help with the audio-visuals, appoint several teams of two or three to construct the liturgy of the mass for each day, select leaders for the Small Group Discussions (not more than ten Sisters to a group), and suitable leaders for the Small Prayer Groups.

5. If feasible, perhaps a month before the retreat is to begin, have mailed to each prospective retreatant a copy of the "Order of the Day" and a copy of "Expectations". It is quite helpful if the Retreat Master has an opportunity to look over the "Expectations" before the retreat begins.

6. Be on time for each exercise, adhere to the scheduled times, without being absolutely rigid. Be prepared.

7. Before each presentation, morning prayer, and liturgy check materials required, e.g., films, papers, room, and make sure that everything is in order. This is especially necessary in the use of the audio-visuals, so that the presentation is smooth and unobtrusive. Give clear and precise directions to your assistants.

8. To promote responses to the presentations you may want to use a question box.

9. Begin each presentation with a prayer. Suitable prayers are found in the missal and the breviary.

10. Your communication will be better if you stand rather than sit, and if you use notes meagerly.

3. CONFESSIONS

The Retreat Master should make some times available each day for individual confession, according to the needs of each individual. It seems a good idea to reserve the Communal Celebration of the Sacrament of Penance to the fifth day of the retreat, and this should be explained early in the retreat. A suitable format is appended. It is also desirable to obtain the assistance of other confessors, especially during the Communal Celebration.

4. PRIVATE INTERVIEWS

Here again the Retreat Master should make times available each day for those who wish to confer with him privately, or even in small groups. A sheet of paper with days and times, usually one-half hour periods, indicating when the Retreat Master is available, simplifies the making of appointments. When one of the times is checked off (it is better not to have them sign names or use initials), then the Retreat Master and other retreatants know that this time is occupied.

5. AUDIO-VISUALS

(These suggested aids are used in the Presentations.)

I. Films—16 mm. Motion Pictures
1. TeleSPOT: "Can I Talk to You, Dad?" A teenage boy, in need of advice, is frustrated by his father's preoccupied, non-attentive listening. Time: 1 minute. Color.
2. TeleSPOT: "The Puzzle". A man takes time to help a little boy pick up the pieces of a puzzle. Time: 1 minute. Color.
3. TeleSPOT: "Signs of Love". A couple, upset by the news of pregnancy, finds their unacceptance of the fact resolved by the attitude of their young daughter. Time: 1 minute. Color.
4. TeleSPOT: "Masks of Man". Children make paper masks, which dissolve into malicious masks of violence that distort the human image. Time: 1 minute. Color.
5. TeleKETICS: "Eucharist: Sacrament of Life". An experience in sight and sound. This free-flowing film invites the viewer himself to recreate the meaning of the Eucharistic Mystery. Time: 10 minutes. Color.
6. TeleKETICS: "Search". Six one-minute spots which depict the encounter of Faith as the discovery of God in human experience and in prayer.
   a) A group attempt to define God verbally is followed by a series of still photos emphasizing God's presence in all who suffer.
   b) A very rapid sequence of still photos reveals Christ's redemptive action in every aspect of life.
   c) A woman on her way to church learns to find God in persons of racial or economic backgrounds other than her own.
   d) A series of man-on-the-street interviews illustrates various responses to the query "Do You Ever Talk to God?"
   e) The rhythm and motion of surfing, with quotations from psalm 139, illustrate God's presence in a person's life.
   f) Phrases of an ancient prayer in the Book of Daniel against fast-paced images of concrete, steel and neon reveal God's continued act of creation.
   TeleSPOT and TeleKETICS Films are produced by The Franciscan Communication Center, 1229 South Santee St., Los Angeles, Calif. 90015.
7. STORY LINE: "Afraid of the Storm". Line drawings illustrate the calming of the storm at sea as described in Luke 8. Drawings by Anne Vallotton. American Bible Society, Media Relations, Education and Information Department, 1865 Broadway, New York, N.Y. 10023.

II. 2 X 2 Slides
8. "Baptism: The Sacrament of Faith." A set of sixty colored slides with taped commentary and musical background. This set of slides was conceived as an aid in communicating the message that children are baptized in the faith of their parents, who constitute for their children the primary link with the Christian community. Time: Ten minutes. Produced by Novalis, 1 Stewart St., Ottawa, Canada.

9. "Marriage, the Sacrament of Love". A set of forty colored slides with taped commentary and musical background. This set of slides explores and emphasizes the meaning of Christian marriage. Time: Six minutes. Produced by Novalis, 1 Stewart St., Ottawa, Canada.

10. "Ad Lib" Slides of the religious community to whom the retreat is being given. Slides of the Sisters at various activities (Prayer, Mass, Recreation, Teaching, Social Work, Visiting, Hospital, etc.) are needed to make pertinent and relevant the general material.

III. Filmstrips

11. "Listen Christian". A series of photos and captions illustrative of "As long as you did it to one of these, the least of my brethren, you did it to me." Time: Approx. 5 minutes. Color. Geo. A. Pflaum, 38 W. Fifth St., Dayton, Ohio 45402.

12. "The Beginnings of Man". A series of excellent drawings depicting creation. Life Filmstrips, Time & Life Bldg., Rockefeller Center, New York, N.Y. 10020.

IV. Posters

13. Excellent large black and white posters from photographs which can illustrate and emphasize the theme of this retreat. Especially recommended are the posters on "The Way of the Cross" and "The Beatitudes". Geo. A. Pflaum, 38 W. Fifth St., Dayton, Ohio 45402.

V. Banners

14. It is suggested that the making of banners suitable to the theme of this retreat be turned over to the Sisters.

VI. Music

15. It is suggested that the music for the liturgy, as well as that for background in meditations, readings, etc., also be turned over to the Sisters.

VII. Bulletins

16. The three bulletins used in this retreat can be obtained from the Franciscan Communication Center, Los Angeles.

VIII. Equipment

17. 16 mm motion picture projector, with sound, and external speaker.
18. 2 X 2 Slide projector with remote control switch.
19. Filmstrip projector with remote control switch.
20. Record player.
21. Tape players, reel-to-reel and cassette.
22. Cassette tape recorder and a blank cassette (C-60) for each presentation, and possibly for each general discussion.
23. Materials for making banners and posters.
24. Pencils and paper for retreatants.
25. Name tags.
26. Public address system, if necessary.

D. TALKS/EXERCISES

1. The Human Dimension of Our Relationship With God

PRESENTATION I—The Need for Salvation

OPENING PRAYER

Psalm 121

(Note: Version used throughout is "The New American Bible" published by P.J. Kenedy & Sons, New York.)

In the name of the Father, and of the Son, and of the Holy Spirit. Amen.
I lift up my eyes toward the mountains;
    whence shall help come to me?
My help is from the LORD,
    who made heaven and earth.
May he not suffer your foot to slip;
    may he slumber not who guards you:
Indeed he neither slumbers nor sleeps,
    the guardian of Israel.
The LORD is your guardian; the LORD is your shade;
    he is beside you at your right hand.
The sun shall not harm you by day,
    nor the moon by night.
The LORD will guard you from all evil;
    he will guard your life.
The LORD will guard your coming
    and your going,
    both now and forever.

GREETING

Good morning, Sisters. My name is _____. God is very good in giving us this opportunity to come together to devote these days to the renewal of our relationship to Himself and to our fellowman. We should enter into these days with a great feeling of joy. It is God who, through his Church, calls us to this renewal. In the Decree on the Appropriate Renewal of the Religious Life we read in section one: "A life consecrated by a profession of the counsels is of surpassing value. Such a life has a necessary role to play in the circumstances of the present age. That this kind of life and its contemporary role may achieve greater good for the Church, this sacred Synod issues the following decrees". Then, as you know, the document goes on to spell out its recommendations. A retreat can be a wonderful time during which to consider the renewal of our relationship with God and those with whom we live our lives. May these days be a wonderfully joyous time for all of us. "God is love, and he who abides in love abides in God, and God in him. Our love is brought to perfection in this, that we should have confidence on the day of judgement; for our relation to this world is just like his. Love has no room for fear; rather, perfect love casts out all fear. And since fear has to do with punishment, love is not yet perfect in one who is afraid. We, for our part, love because he first loved us" (1 Jn. 4:16-19).

TERESA OF AVILA

Perhaps we can take a hint from Teresa of Avila concerning the joy we can have in serving God. This is the way Phyllis McGinley writes about Teresa: "Now and then one comes across a character so ebullient that it can not be stifled by the dreariest historian. Teresa of Avila, irrepressible as a volcano, unsinkable as balsa wood, never fitted for a moment into a pious strait jacket. 'From silly devotions and sour-faced saints, good Lord deliver us!' she protested . . . Teresa could not live with pomposity. Self-importance was a balloon she pricked whenever she saw it bobbing along. I relish her advice to a young nun who came to her with tales of exaggerated temptation and who boasted of being a very great sinner. 'Now, Sister,' Teresa said deflatingly, 'Remember, none of us is perfect. Just make sure those sins of yours don't turn into bad habits.' " (From an article in Catholic Digest, August 1962.)

PURPOSE

In joyfully renewing our relationship with God and fellowman we will consider ourselves from three different levels or viewpoints. Before anything else we are human beings, so we will look at the relationship established by God between himself and his human creatures. However, most of us were quickly raised to the supernatural level by baptism, and so as baptized human beings we examine ourselves at the Christian level. Finally, we have dedicated ourselves in a special way to the service of Christ and his members, so that viewing ourselves at the present time, we find that we are human beings, who have been baptized, and have dedicated ourselves to the life of a professed religious. An evaluation of our response to God's call on these three levels will hopefully lead us into a consideration of ways and means whereby we can effect improvement in our relationship to God, to ourselves, and to those whom God has called us to live with and serve.

EXPECTATIONS

So far we have seen the general objectives of this retreat. However, we come to this retreat as individuals, unique objects of God's wonderful love. In order to get some idea of your own particular expectations from this retreat, I ask you to fill out the sheet of paper titled "Expectations" and hand it in to me before noon today. As much as possible I will try to fulfill these expectations, either in the conferences, or in private interviews, or in the homilies at mass. Opportunities for private interviews and confessions are offered all during the retreat. For private interviews please check off a convenient time on the paper attached to the door of my office. There is no need to sign your name or initials, just a check mark to let others know that the time is taken. I will be in the chapel before mass each day for confessions, or at any other time you wish. On the fifth day of the retreat we will have a communal celebration of the sacrament of penance, which I will explain a little later. If at the end of a conference, which I call "Presentations", you wish to pose questions or enter into a discussion, please feel free to do so. However, this part of the retreat will be one of several voluntary attendance exercises.

PRAYER

Obviously prayer is one of the means of establishing relationship with God. And during a retreat we should have the opportunity, as well as the assistance, to develop a deeper sensitivity to God, so that, hopefully, our communication with Him will improve. Our most important prayer each day will be the Liturgy of the Mass. Surrounding our great prayer with Christ through the Spirit will be our Morning Prayer, vocal prayers throughout the day, and prayer entered into by freely formed small groups.

PIVOTAL POINT

In our times the pivotal point of God's revelation is the Eucharistic Liturgy. It is here that God's word is authentically interpreted for us and the application to daily living made. In the liturgy of the sacrifice Jesus Christ once again exercises his priestly office, and, under the species of bread and wine, offers loving reparation to our heavenly Father. In the Constitution on the Sacred Liturgy (section 7), the Bishops of the Second Vatican Council state: "From this it follows that every liturgical celebration, because it is an action of Christ the priest and of His Body the Church, is a sacred action surpassing all others. No other action of the Church can match its claim to efficacy, nor equal the degree of it." In each mass we are not only reminded of our need for salvation, but our redemption is effectively promoted. All other modes of redemption have to find their value in the redemptive act of Christ. Prayer, reading, study, meditation, works of service and mercy, consultation, discussion, retreats, workshops, recreation, rest, and whatever goes to make up our lives must find its redemptive value in the ever-renewed sacrificial act of Calvary. "Every time, then, you eat this bread and drink this cup, you proclaim the death of the Lord until he comes" (1 Cor. 11).

NEED OF SAVIOR

When we participate in the mass our action tells anyone who wishes to know that we admit the need for salvation. The very purpose of our presence is beautifully expressed in the acclamation just before the Lord's Prayer. "Through him, in him, with him, all glory and honor is yours, Almighty Father, forever and ever. Amen." The first facet of being a human being comes to us when we face up to the necessity of being saved. Unless this characteristic of humanity is admitted and understood, I really do not truly know who and what I am. So, we participate in the mass not to do God a favor, but because we desperately need to be saved. And the need is a continuous one. For we are ever changing and consequently, renewal, that is, salvation, must be an on-going process. What a wonderful thing that we can hear in the consecration of each mass: "Take this, all of you, and drink from it: this is the cup of my blood, the blood of the new and everlasting covenant. It will be shed for you and for all men, so that sins may be forgiven. Do this in memory of me." "Will be shed . . .", once in a bloody manner, but also every day in an unbloody manner; "for you and for all men, so that sins may be forgiven." Yes, because of our sinfulness we need continuing redemption. Otherwise, we cannot have the life, and life in its fulness as promised to us by Christ. "I came that they might have life and have it to the full" (Jn. 10:10). Our daily communion is not only a sign of our redemption, but also continually effects it. Jesus said: "Just as the Father who has life sent me and I have life because of the Father, so the man who feeds on me will have life because of me" (Jn. 6:57).

EUCHARIST: SACRAMENT OF LIFE

(16mm. motion picture film)

In the Constitution on the Sacred Liturgy, Chapter II, these four statements accentuate the mystery of the eucharist which is—
"a memorial of Christ's death and resurrection"
"a sacrament of love"
"a sign of unity, a bond of charity"
"a pledge of future glory given to us."
In the brochure explaining the motion picture I want you to experience in a few minutes, the Franciscan Communication Center, producers of the film, give explanations of the above statements by modern theologians.

—"a memorial of Christ's death and resurrection" means that "the one redeeming act, totally present in what Christ himself did at the very beginning, continues to find expression through the lives and activity of today's Christians as they share in the act of Eucharistic sacrifice." (B. Cooke)

—"a sacrament of love" means that the Eucharist sustains the "community of Christians joined in love where Christ achieves His most dynamic and real presence in the world." (A. McBride)

—"a sign of unity, a bond of charity" means that the Eucharist "is a consistant reminder that no one stands alone in the Church, that all are responsible to and for one another." (J. Powers)

—"a pledge of future glory given to us" means that the Eucharist signifies that "the people of a Christian community have a faith-vision of human existence . . . They are gathered together in the name of Jesus. They are a people who see the Father's saving love in joy. They are a people who see the Father's saving love in sorrow. They come together to express the full meaning which the present moment, situation, or event has for them. In a word, they come together to profess their faith." (S. Marsili)

Reflecting all these various dimensions of the Sacrament, the film, Eucharist: Sacrament of Life, seeks to demonstrate that the mystery of the resurrection is not something that happens to Christ in isolation from the rest of mankind; it is a proclamation that in all times and all places the Spirit of God-LIFE is forming the family of man into the People of God.

(Note to the Retreat Master: Now show the film. If, at the conclusion of this presentation, you wish to lead a discussion, helpful directions are found in the brochure accompanying the film. After the film allow some minutes for silent reflection before you continue your comments.)

MYSTERY   We have just experienced an attempt to enter into a mystery. The film is keynoted by the celebrant's words at the beginning, "Let us proclaim the mystery of Faith." Marcel van Caster has outlined the relationships as follows (see the film brochure):

General meaning: A mystery is a reality existing beyond man but realized and expressed in a human reality.

Particular meanings: 1. Historical: a mystery is an event, a supernatural intervention of God in human history.
2. Liturgical: it is a symbolic action in which an encounter with God is effected and expressed.
3. Doctrinal: a mystery is a truth beyond human understanding but expressed in human ways and language.

For example, the paschal mystery is realized historically in the biblical event. It is rendered actively present today in the Eucharist in which we participate. There is a truth in the paschal mystery which we do not perfectly understand, but which the practice of our faith helps us to understand more and more. In our daily life, we have to live according to this whole mystery, in all its different meanings.

SIGNS OF LIFE   Perhaps the most stark contrast in the film is that between death and life. The symbolic death of Jesus in the separate consecration of the bread and wine is the turning point in the film from death to life. After the medical corpsman has given first aid to the wounded soldier, we see the helicopter approaching to carry the soldier to the base hospital for further treatment and nursing back to health. The spiritual death of hatred between white and black is resolved in the words of play, "Pass it around" juxtaposed to the liturgical phrase "Cup of my Blood". The dullness and stagnation of old age is suddenly shocked into a lively happiness by the vitality and fun of the little girl. The desperation engendered by hunger becomes cheerful hope as the father enters carrying the box of groceries. These and other signs of life in the film point up the various ways in which we as humans need salvation. Certainly we are children of God, created in his own image and likeness. But, if we are going to understand who and what we are, then we must realize that we are children in need of a savior. Only then can we go the next step in renewing our relationship with God. Our Father is revealed to us, first of all, as Savior. And in our times this revelation is made present to us in each eucharistic sacrifice, both in word and in sacrament.

CONCLUSION   Let us conclude this presentation at this point. If any of you would like to ask questions or enter into a discussion on the points I have presented, we have time to do so after our concluding prayer.

Let us pray. God grant us your saving grace, so that as the birth of the Virgin Mary marked the beginning of the time of salvation, our devotion to her may be the means of our continuing redemption. We ask this through Christ our Lord. Amen.

OPENING PRAYER

Come, let us bow down in worship;
    let us kneel before the Lord who made us.
For he is our God,
    and we are the people he shepherds, the flock he guides. (Ps. 95:6,7)
Thus says the Lord, Israel's King
    and redeemer, the Lord of hosts:
I am the first and I am the last;
    There is no God but me. (Is. 44:6)
I say that my plan shall stand,
    I accomplish my every purpose. (Is. 46:10)

(Note to the Retreat Master. Be sure to ask for and collect the "Expectations".)

BEGINNING AT THE END

Almost everyone likes to read a mystery story. Do you have the tendency to impatiently look to the end of the story to see how it comes out? Well, we began a mystery story this morning, the mystery of our relationship with God and fellowman. And we very quickly got to the end, not really solving the mystery, but at least shedding some light on it. For the Eucharist in our times is the sign of God's mysterious love for us. In the Eucharist, above all other signs, one can find the answer to the gnawing questions: Is there a God? If so, what is he like? What is my relationship to him? Look for just one minute at a film illustration of a group of modern people struggling with these questions. (Note: Show the first segment of the 16mm film, "The Search", produced by the Franciscan Communication Center.)

ANCIENT MAN

Many modern people have not done any better in discovering God, and consequently themselves, than did ancient people. Our advantage is not truly appreciated until we perceive the discovery of God in its historical perspective. The epistle to the Hebrews begins on this note. "In times past, God spoke in fragmentary and varied ways to our fathers through the prophets; in this, the final age, he has spoken to us through his Son, whom he has made heir of all things and through whom he first created the universe" (Heb. 1:1,2). A comparative study of ancient religions shows us that there existed a common denominator in the recognition of some superior being who would reward good deeds and punish bad ones. A reflection of this common belief is summarized in the Book of Sirach. "For mercy and anger are alike with him who remits and forgives, though on the wicked alights his wrath. Great as his mercy is his punishment; he judges men, each according to his deeds." (16:11,12) St. Paul in writing to the Romans refers to the common belief of all men, or at least the possibility, even responsibility, of arriving at the recognition of a superior being. "The wrath of God is being revealed from heaven against the irreligious and perverse spirit of men, who, in this perversity of theirs, hinder the truth. In fact, whatever can be known about God is clear to them; he himself made it so. Since the creation of the world, invisible realities, God's eternal power and divinity, have become visible, recognized through the things he has made. Therefore these men are inexcusable. They certainly had knowledge of God, yet they did not glorify him as God or give him thanks; they stultified themselves to no purpose, and their senseless hearts were darkened. They claimed to be wise, but turned into fools instead; they exchanged the glory of the immortal God for images representing mortal man, birds, beasts, and snakes. In consequence, God delivered them up in their lusts to unclean practices; they engaged in the mutual degradation of their bodies, these men who exchanged the truth of God for a lie and worshipped and served the creature rather than the Creator—blessed be he forever, amen!" (Rom. 1:18-25). The footnote to this passage in The American Bible explains St. Paul's reaction to the pagan religions of his day as follows. "The conversion of the Gentiles through the gospel preaching constituted the divine indictment against paganism, which error had benighted and moral depravity had corrupted. It was the evil will of the pagan world that provoked the divine anger and abandonment. Contrary to nature itself which provides evidence of God's existence, power, and divinity through creation, pagan society misread the evidence, fashioned gods of its own that could not exert any moral restraint, and freely indulged its perverse desires through every kind of wickedness." Ancient man's problem had even before St. Paul been summarized by the author of the Book of Wisdom. "For all men were by nature foolish who were in ignorance of God, and who from the good things seen did not succeed in knowing him who is, and from studying the works did not discern the artisan; but either fire, or wind, or the swift air, or the circuit of the stars, or the mighty water, or the luminaries of heaven, the governors of the world, they considered gods." (13:1,2).

BIBLICAL GOD

On the surface it seems that the Bible offers man a complete and simple definition of God. "God, simply as God, does not exist in the Bible." This statement is made by Father Carroll Stuhlmueller, C.P., in an unpublished talk addressed to Serra International. For the next few minutes I would like to follow his approach to the problem of knowing who God is. "In the scriptures God comes to us as savior, as redeemer, as brother, as spouse of Israel and of the Church. God never comes to us simply as God. This distinction is not making a great to-do over something unimportant. It matters a great deal whether we consider God simply as God Almighty, or whether we consider God first as savior, as a personal God speaking and relating with us, as a God, merciful, kind and forgiving as a brother. Just how we intuit God, just how we understand the mystery of God, and what qualities about God we put first, second and third, can make all the difference between a rationalist and a person of sturdy faith. The Old Testament intuition of God determined how men approached God, not just in Old Testament times, but, also, in the New Testament days, and today. God is living today in the Old Testament.

FATHER

"It is important which attribute of God is put first, whether we first consider God as Almighty Creator, or look upon Him as a merciful savior. For instance, in a family the holiness and psychological peace of children depends on how they look upon their father. Do they look upon him first as that man who makes the money and brings home the food? Do they look upon him as the man employed at a factory, or working in a store? Do they look upon their father as someone who simply keeps order in the home? Or do they look upon that man as *their father*? If they put first their father, second the man who works, then the man who keeps order, there is a proper perspective. But, if they put first a man who makes the money, then they are not going to love their father nearly as much as they could. They will deprive themselves, and their father, of joy and peace in their hearts and in their homes."

SAVIOR

The motif in the symphony of God's revelations in the Old Testament that is heard the strongest and most persistently is the motif of hope. This is so because in the Old Testament God is understood first of all as Savior. Because of the arrangements of the chapters in the Book of Genesis, this motif does not come through strongly until chapter twelve. A more accurate beginning of God revealing himself is made at this chapter rather than at chapter one. When Moses was compiling the oral traditions of a people who were searching for their identity after four hundred years of Egyptian slavery, the first note was that they were children of Abraham. Only after they began questioning their origins did the account of creation take on meaning. But first they found themselves a people, and a people in need, mostly in need of redemption from slavery. They needed a savior. And in the person of Moses God provided that savior. Not only a savior from their physical woes, but even more importantly, they needed someone to save them from the obscurity and impersonalism of ancestors born and reared in captivity. The heritage of slavery is not something to boast about, at least, not until you are free and have established an identity of which you can be proud.

ABRAHAM

After a youngster begins to know a little something about himself he wonders where he came from, that is, who his ancestors were. The family tree takes on a new interest. If in their background they discover someone who was really great, then the relationship becomes a point of pride. "My grandfather was a navy captain in World War II", one boy may say to another. Or earlier generations will take pride in someone who fought in the Civil War. And, if you can trace an ancestor back to the Revolutionary War, or even better to the landing at Plymouth Rock, then the pride level rises accordingly. And so the constant boasting in the Bible: "We are the children of Abraham" (Jn. 8:33). Abraham had become the popular hero, the founding father of a great nation. If you begin the reading of the Bible with Chapter Twelve of the Book of Genesis, you will feel more strongly the notion of God as Savior coming through.

"The Lord said to Abraham: 'Go forth from the land of your kinfolk and from
your father's house to a land that I will show you.
I will make of you a great nation,
and I will bless you;
I will make your name great,
so that you will be a blessing.
I will bless those who bless you
and curse those who curse you.
All the communities of the earth
shall find blessing in you.'
Abraham went as the Lord directed him . . ." (12:1-4)

So, a nation tracing back it's beginnings starts with a man leaving his home country and going into a foreign land to establish his family there. Furthermore, he receives a promise from God that he will be the father of a great nation.

THE SAVIOR INTERVENES

From this point on in the traditional history of the Hebrew people we find that God constantly and repeatedly intervenes as Savior. For a while it looks as if the promise of God to establish a nation through Abraham is going to go by default. For, Abraham and his wife Sarah have not yet had even one child from whom a nation could spring. Yet, God intervenes as savior of the situation and Isaac is born. The biblical accounts of Jacob and Esau, of Joseph and Benjamin, of the slavery in Egypt, of Moses and the trek to the promise land, of the establishment of a nation in the land of Palestine, of David the king and his successors, all these and many other accounts point up the intervening power of God as Savior. All of this history of God's chosen people was handed down mostly by word of mouth. The written format with which we are familiar was solidified some five or six hundred years before the coming of Christ.

EZRA-NEHEMIAH

One very outstanding example of the pattern of a people learning about God is contained in the Old Testament Books of Ezra-Nehemiah. This title, "Ezra-Nehemiah has been taken from the two persons who figure most prominently in the narrative and who are responsible for much of the material that has gone into it." (Booklet: "The Books of Ezra-Nehemiah" with a Commentary by Bruce Vawter, C.M., Paulist Press, New York, c1971.) The year 587 B.C. brought disaster to the Israelite kingdom of Judah in Palestine. The Chaldean King Nebuchadnezzar II deported all the Israelites to Mesopotamia. Thus began the time of exile foretold by the prophet Jeremiah. After about fifty years God intervened in the lives of these Israelites. Salvation, that is, liberation from exile and slavery, came in the person of Cyrus, leader of the new Persian empire which had conquered the Babylonians. The Books of Ezra-Nehemiah recount the return of these people to Palestine and the rebuilding of the city of Jerusalem and its temple. It was this city and its temple that existed in the time of Christ, and therefore stood as symbols of God's intervening mercy for the sake of his chosen people. So, in effect they told Christ: "We are the children of Abraham. God is our savior. Just as he saved our nation in times past, so will he again do so by freeing us from the yoke of the Romans." Acceptance of Christ as Savior hinged on his leading God's people in a successful revolt against the Roman domination. When Christ explained that his kingdom was not of this world, they rejected him. All through their history, the Chosen People fluctuated between the need for God saving them and their pride in being self-sufficient. Christ was rejected because the Jewish leaders did not want the kind of salvation he offered. The plotting against Nehemiah were prophetic of the later plots against the life of Christ. And so the prayer of Nehemiah as recorded in the first chapter of "The Book of Nehemiah" stands as a summary of the need of God as a Savior.

PRAYER OF NEHEMIAH

"The words of Nehemiah, the son of Hacaliah. In the month of Chislev of the twentieth year, I was in the citadel of Susa, when Hanani, one of my brothers, came with other men from Judah. I asked them about the Jews, the remnant preserved after the captivity, and about Jerusalem, and they answered me: 'The survivors of the captivity there in the province are in great distress and under reproach. Also, the wall of Jerusalem lies breached, and its gates have been gutted with fire.' When I heard this report, I began to weep and continued mourning for several days; I fasted and prayed before the God of heaven. I prayed: 'O Lord, God of heaven, great and awesome God, you who preserve your covenant of mercy toward those who love you and keep your commandments, may your ear be attentive and your eyes open, to heed the prayer which I, your servant, now offer in your presence day and night for your servants the Israelites, confessing the sins which we of Israel have committed against you, I and my father's house included. Grievously have we offended you, not keeping the commandments, the statutes, and the ordinances which you committed to your servant Moses. But remember, I pray, the promise which you gave through Moses, your servant, when you said: Should you prove faithless, I will scatter you among the nations; but should you return to me and carefully keep my commandments, even though your outcasts have been driven to the farthest corner of the world, I will gather them from there, and bring them back to the place which I have chosen as the dwelling place for my name.' They are your servants, your people, whom you freed by your great might and your strong hand. O Lord, may your ear be attentive to my prayer and that of all your willing servants who revere your name. Grant success to your servants this day, and let him find favor with this man'—for I was cupbearer to the king.' " (verses 1-11)

PEOPLE OF HOPE

Notice the hope in Nehemiah's prayer. He recalls the glories of the past, but he also looks forward to something better. This promise is enshrined in the very Hebrew word for God, "Yahweh", which can be translated as, "He who is always there." Father Stuhlmueller sums up his remarks on God as Savior in this way: "In the Bible God is primarily understood as Savior, not as creator God. That fact has overwhelming repercussions upon the spirituality of each one of us. If God were understood primarily as creator we would always look back to the golden age, that first wonderful moment of paradise in creation and all our efforts would be to try, in some way, to snatch something of the past for today. All of our prayer and good works would be an attempt to piece together the parts broken apart by sins. That would have happened if God, in the Old Testament, was known primarily as a creator. But, no, he is known primarily as savior and redeemer. This means that we look forward to paradise, that we are looking ahead to the perfect age, that our endeavor in religion is not to snatch something from the past, is not to be looking with nostalgia to the days long ago. We are men of hope, we are men who look ahead, we are men who expect our paradise."

THE SAVING GOD IS A PERSON

Our hope is to live with God forever, with the God who has saved us. A word that can be added is "personally"—God who has saved us personally. For this Saving God is a Personal God. Page after page of the Old Testament tells us that our God is not like other gods, which are man made. No, in those pages this God speaks to his people, he answers their cries, he is someone who can think and feel. In fact, in the twelfth chapter of the Book of Jeremiah, the prophet, we find him to be one with whom the prophet can argue. "You would be in the right, O Lord, if I should dispute with you; even so, I must discuss the case with you. Why does the way of the godless prosper, why live all the treacherous in contentment?" (verse 1). God saves his people, and us, and all men, personally, by enabling us to ponder, to think, to pray, to become a person who can look eye-to-eye with God.

THIS PERSONAL SAVING GOD IS CREATOR

Once the notion that God, a Person, saves us, then the mind can come to grips with the existence of all things, including man himself. That the God in whom we believe is the Creator of all things is evident enough in the Bible, in nature, in the teachings of almost all religions, and in the general concensus of mankind. In fact, our traditional approach to the consideration of God was that of Creator, rather than that of the Bible's approach to see him first of all as Savior. And, so, in this presentation we have dwelt at length on God in his attribute as Savior.

SUGGESTED MEDITATION

For the purposes of meditation on God as our Savior, let us regard ourselves as creatures, human beings, yes, but creatures in need of salvation. For this time I would ask you to restrict your prayerful thinking and feeling to the aspect of yourself as a human being. Hold back on the considerations of yourself as a Christian and Professed Religious for later in the retreat. At the present moment we need to look at ourselves in the common denominator of humanity which we share with all other men and women. It is imperative that we recognize our need for God, totally. Only few individuals feel that they need God, or anyone else, in no aspect of their lives. Most of us realize the need for salvation, at least in some area. We may be up against a serious decision. Obviously, one would call upon God's help at such a time. But for the minor things, such as to stand or sit, we can get along by ourselves. Let me suggest that we need God every single moment for every single thing in our lives. As human beings we are not self-sufficient in anything. Each of us needs to say something like this to herself: "I need God if I am going to relate to this particular Sister who annoys the living daylights out of me. I need God if I am going to be able to do what he is asking of me. I need God if I am going to give some consolation to this poor sick person who is facing death and is scared, scared to death. I need God if the decision I make at this particular moment is going to be one that he will be pleased with, both now and in eternity." Our lives, for the most part, are miniature reflections of the history of the Chosen People: salvation by God, adherence to God, prosperity, rejection of God, punishment, sorrowful return to God, reinstatement in his saving love through another saving act of his mercy. Our first and always stance toward God must always be one of humility. Oh, my saving God, I need you desperately every single moment of my life.

CONCLUDING PRAYER

God, through the fruitful virginity of Mary you bestowed the blessings of eternal salvation on all mankind. Grant that we may enjoy her intercession, for through her we received your Son. Amen. (Prayer of Christians, p. 164)

PRESENTATION III—The Saving, Creating God, Is Conserver

OPENING PRAYER

"O God, the morning comes all too soon for those of us who sleep well; let me not forget those who cannot sleep.
I am glad that as I go out I shall find myself today surrounded
By more loyal people than disloyal;
By more generous people than mean;
By more gracious people than rude;
By more happy people than the newspaper headlines might lead me to think.
I bless you for
The countless happily-married people I know who never get their names in print;
The countless unselfish people who never look first for praise;

The countless courageous ones who might long ago have given up but for you;
The countless people in unexpected places who translate Christianity into daily living.
Give me the will to join them today. For Christ's sake. Amen."
("A Woman's Book of Prayers" by Rita Snowden. Fontana Books, London, c1968)

DREAMS

"I have spread my dreams under your feet. Tread softly because you tread on my dreams" (Yeats). These words could have been spoken by God Himself. Yesterday we meditated on the fact that the God who created us and all things, revealed himself first of all as a saving God. It certainly was not out of a desire to make things that God created our universe and everything in it, including his human creatures. And since all things were the works of his hands, therefore his pride would compel him to continue them in existence. And not only to continue them, but to rejuvenate them as often as would be required. No, this is not the image the Bible gives us. Rather are we made acquainted with someone who is good; so loving, and so generous that he wants to share everything he has, even himself. And, so, we discover in the first chapters of the Book of Genesis Yahweh dreaming dreams. "In the beginning, when God created the heavens and the earth, the earth was a formless wasteland, and darkness covered the abyss, while a mighty wind swept over the waters" (v. 1). The dream matures with light, and sky, and land, and vegetation on the land and in the sea, and animals on the land and in the sea. And "God saw how good it was" (v. 25). And, then, the dream bursts into glory. "God created man in his image; in the divine image he created him; male and female he created them" (v. 27). Truly God has spread his dreams under our feet. Yes, let us tread softly because we tread on his dreams. It takes a good deal of awareness to be alert to the dreams youngsters dream; and, oh, so very much wisdom to help them interpret these dreams; and, please, let us have deep humility to avoid the presumption of experience and age that would crash a youthful dream before it ever has the chance to unfold.

DEPENDENCE

Yesterday we recalled how dependent the Bible says we are on God. Once again we saw it to be a total dependence. We made the effort to examine ourselves to see if we really put into practice the belief that we need God to be saving us at every moment of our lives. Perhaps we had to face up to the realization that we do sometimes feel that we can get along without God. Or, if we do not feel that way then we act as if we do. When we do not seek him as we should, when we do not begin a project asking his assistance, when we trust to our own capabilities to achieve a certain result, then, in practice, we have told God that we don't need him. At least, we give the impression that we do not need to bother him, at least right now. Maybe when things get a little sticky, or we find ourselves botching an assignment, then we start calling out for help. It's not only ridiculous to seek fulfillment without God, it is positively insane, if insanity is the inability to find and face the reality that is a human being. When God created man he dreamed that there would be a loving communication between himself and his creature. God and Adam are pictured together, working on the names of the animals (Gen. 2:19). This was after God had settled Adam in the garden to cultivate and care for it (Gen. 2:15). The definite impression one receives while reading this section of Genesis is one of a corporate effort; God granting freedom to man to act in Yahweh's name, but not independently of him. Is there not a similarity in the way superiors are asked to exercise their authority? Listen for a moment to the Bishops convened in the Sacred Council of Vatican II.

RENEWAL IN OBEDIENCE

"Therefore, in a spirit of faith and of love for God's will, let religious show humble obedience to their superiors in accord with the norms of rule and constitution. Realizing that they are giving service to the upbuilding of Christ's body according to God's design, let them bring to the execution of commands and to the discharge of assignments entrusted to them the resources of their minds and wills, and their gifts of nature and grace. Lived in this manner, religious obedience will not diminish the dignity of the human person but will rather lead it to maturity in consequence of that enlarged freedom which belongs to the sons of God." (#14) And the recommendations to superiors are no less pertinent. "For his part, as one who will render an account for the souls entrusted to him (cf. Heb. 13:17), each superior should himself be docile to God's will in the exercise of his office. Let him use his authority in a spirit of service for the brethren, and manifest thereby the charity with which God loves them. Governing his subjects as God's own sons, and with regard for their human personality, a superior will make it easier for them to obey gladly. Therefore he must make a special point of leaving them appropriately free with respect to the sacrament of penance and direction of conscience. Let him give the kind of leadership which will encourage religious to bring an active and responsible obedience to the offices they shoulder and the activities they undertake. Therefore a superior should listen willingly to his subjects and encourage them to make a personal contribution to the welfare of the community and of the Church. Not to be weakened, however, is the superior's authority to decide what must be done and to require the doing of it." (#14) In *THE NUN IN THE WORLD*, Cardinal Suenens made some comments which seem to be reflected in the decree of Vatican II on Obedience. He takes into full consideration the individuality of the human being. Awareness of the human dimension of our relationship with God makes the Cardinal's remarks quite convincing. "The central place of obedience in the religious life demands particularly careful training in it. Obedience must be lived as a positive virtue, a stimulus rather than an invitation to passiveness. If it is not properly understood, it will tend to inhibit missionary zeal; properly understood, it will guarantee its full freedom. Obedience does not mean lack of personality, initiative or responsibility, but giving to God one's deepest will in order the better to serve Him in the field which authority, His interpreter, indicates. Obedience cannot be productive unless there is openness, reciprocity and dialogue. Submission must not be confused with passivity. Real submission carries out loyally orders given after having, if necessary, raised the points which seem to favor another course. The most passive nun is not the most subject nor the most obedient."

CO-OPERATION

Perhaps the best word to express our relationship with God who conserves what he has created by continually saving it is co-operation. This story illustrates this point in a sort of reflex way. There was this man who moved into a small country area. He was able to find an old rundown farm which he bought for unpaid taxes. Nothing was in usable condition, not the land nor the buildings. However, this fellow, whom we shall call, "Mr. Jones", was very industrious. In the space of a year, working when he was free from his factory job in the nearby town, he had put up fences, repaired gulleys, rebuilt the house and the barn, and with his family moved onto the new homestead. Shortly after the family was settled, a deacon of the local church paid a visit. Mr. Jones and his family were delighted to have the deacon visit. Let us call the deacon, "Deacon Smith". After an improvised lunch, Mr. Jones invited the deacon to look around the property. Each time Mr. Jones showed Deacon Smith what he had done, for example, putting up the new fence, Deacon Smith would remark: "Mr. Jones, you and the Lord have certainly done a good thing." And so for each item of improvement: "Mr. Jones, you and the Lord have certainly done a good thing." Well, finally, they were at the front gate and Deacon Smith was just about to leave, when Mr. Jones remarked: "Deacon Smith, I surely do appreciate what you say about the Lord and me doing a good thing. But, really, you should have seen this place when the Lord had it all by himself." Now the point of the story is not that God could not take care of all his creation all by himself, but rather that he did not intend to do so. The writer of the Book of Genesis understood this, and so in his story of creation, he shows how "The Lord God then took the man and settled him in the garden of Eden, to cultivate and care for it." (Gen. 2:15) God asks us to cooperate with him in helping to save all mankind. So we pray in the fourth eucharistic prayer: "And that we might live no longer for ourselves but for him, he sent the Holy Spirit from you, Father, as his first gift to those who believe, to complete his work on earth and bring us the fullness of grace".

FULLNESS OF GRACE

Keep in mind that we are looking at our relationship with God from the human level. God does will the salvation of all men. But salvation does not mean merely getting pushed into heaven. It envisions a life here on earth that leads to a life hereafter of eternal happiness. But the fullness of grace depends on the completion of Christ's work here on earth. This is why God's creative, saving power is also a conserving power, an on-going manifestation of his love for all people at every moment of time. This thought seems to cross St. Paul's mind when he is writing to the Romans and considering the destiny of glory. "I consider the sufferings of the present to be as nothing compared with the glory to be revealed in us. Indeed, the whole created world eagerly awaits the revelation of the sons of God. Creation was made subject to futility, not of its own accord but by him who once subjected it; yet not without hope, because the world itself will be freed from its slavery to corruption and share in the glorious freedom of the children of God. Yes, we know that all creation groans and is in agony even until now. Not only that, but we ourselves, although we have the Spirit as first fruits, groan inwardly while we await the redemption of our bodies. In hope we were saved" (Rom. 8:18-24).

ACCOMPLISHING SALVATION

We must not make God into some kind of an energy force which, like a hydrogen bomb, does its work once and for all. We cannot apply this principle to God in his saving power. No, God is continually saving, conserving, if you wish to use the traditional term. God accomplishes salvation through a developing process, rightly called an evolutionary process, so that the effects of Christ's saving immolation of himself have come down to us, and through us will pass on to future generations. Obviously, God can use many and diverse instruments to manifest his love. The advances in science in the last fifty years, the medical discoveries in our twentieth century, the perfection of technologies, the opportunities for advanced education, all these and many more improvements in the material world are manifestations of God's love, even when men abuse these miracles for selfish purposes. The difficulty is not in the material advances in which we are engulfed, but in trying to substitute them for the Savior of the world. This is the lesson God repeats over and over again in the Old Testament. There is no other God than himself, and no power in heaven or on earth can save as he can save.

MASKS OF MAN

Let us pause for just a minute here to look at a film which will summarize the problem for us, and lead us into further considerations of God's place as Conserver of the universe. (Note: Show the TeleSPOT, "Masks of Man".)

GOD'S IMAGE

Every moment of history tells us that the image of God in man must be rejuvenated. One part of the problem we need to look at briefly is going to the wrong source of rejuvenation. The crisis of our society is in seeking salvation outside God. The crisis of our society is not war instead of peace; is not hate instead of love; is not starvation instead of filled bellies; is not inadequate housing, better school buildings, more superhighways. The crisis is in not seeking God as our savior. For those who believe in God, the problem is not in admitting that we need God, but in finding him and his help where he is, and where it is. God cannot see his image in us, until we are willing to see that image in one another. God really saves us, in Christ, through each other. We are his instruments for rejuvenating his image in each of his children.

ST. IGNATIUS OF LOYOLA

St. Ignatius, the founder of the Jesuits, equates God's conserving power, his salvific will, with the process of conversion. "True conversion," he says, "looks to one's relationship both to God and to the world he has made. It presupposes that one shall find God first by ordering one's attitudes and feelings toward created goods, and then by actively using those things which God wishes one to use in order to accomplish the particular task in salvation history which he has given each one to accomplish." ("Pentecostal Piety" by Donald L. Gelpi, S.J., Paulist Press, c1972.) One who truly seeks a deeper conversion to God must be willing to accept the following beliefs proposed by Ignatius: "(a) that man is in fact created for the praise, reverence, and service of God; (b) that every other creature exists in order to help man attain the end for which he was created; (c) that a man must use the things of this world which lead him to God and avoid those which do not; (d) that one must moderate one's use of every creature according to the effectiveness with which it leads one to God" ("Pentecostal Piety").

TREAD SOFTLY   We began this presentation looking at God spreading his dreams of the universe under our feet. Unfortunately, as we see history unfolding, we do not find a soft treading. Although not shattered, God's dreams for mankind's happiness were rudely abused. But such a loving God seeks to restore those dreams, and promises to bring them to greater reality. As we proceed through this retreat we will seek for the role that God asks each of us to play in helping to restore those dreams, in being the agents of his loving salvation. For this moment, let us realize more fully than ever before two things. First, as human beings we need God at every moment of our existence. Secondly, God is willing to make himself lovingly present to every person whom we meet; for this, God needs us.

LET US PRAY   *"For the simple things I so often take for granted, O God,*
I give you thanks now:
For the immensity of the sky,
For the fertility of the earth,
For water with reflections, dashing-smashing beauty, and always life-giving
powers;
For the songs of birds,
For the natural movement of wild creatures,
For crickets and grasshoppers, and the gauzy wings of dragonflies;
For the graceful curves of grass stalks,
For the changing colors of leaves,
For the cleansing, refreshing might of winds;
For the purity and challenge of mountain peaks,
For the awesomeness of thunder,
For the unceasing power and pull of the tides.
Above all these, I give thanks that you have placed in my personality secrets
whose issue is in eternity, power to worship you, to love you, and to serve you
now and always. Amen.
(A WOMAN'S BOOK OF PRAYERS)

PRESENTATION IV—This God Saves Through Us

OPENING PRAYER   "Please help me to achieve a little privacy, Lord. I'm tired of being squashed in with other people, of eating and sleeping and sharing everything with them. Dear as they are to me, they don't recognize my need for a little space between us.

"Please fire me with the determination and the ingenuity to achieve some privacy, Lord. And give me the will and the words to make my family understand. Please let them cooperate. Amen."

GOD ANSWERS HUMAN NEEDS   The prayer we just said is a shortened version of one which is printed in Woman's Day magazine for October 1971. It is by a devoted wife and mother named Marjorie Holmes. This prayer is the first in a series entitled, "A Woman's Conversations with God". The need for privacy is just one of many human needs. It is these needs that the God who loves us saves us from. But as we saw in the previous presentation, God asks each of us to cooperate with him in helping our fellow humans with their needs. In this presentation we wish to examine our role more completely and offer some points of examination. Before we do that, let's look for a few minutes longer at this need for privacy.

PRIVACY   In the longer version of this prayer by Mrs. Holmes she expands on this need for privacy. "It is as if they are all over me all the time—with their possessions and themselves. Even when they're out of the house their papers and books and toys and gear clutter every room—even my bedroom, my desk and the place where I sew.

"They not only drop things behind them, they raid my books and papers and possessions. They make off with my lipstick, my sweaters, my scissors, my portable typewriter, the magazines I wanted to read. I don't feel I really own a

46

thing in this house except maybe the iron and ironing board (they don't bother those!). Well, my toothbrush maybe—but I'm not always sure about that." All of us at one time or another have experienced this need for privacy. Even in community life, where many religious now have private rooms, and a door you can close and be with yourself alone for a little while. And yet, community life does demand our presence, not merely physically, but totally. It would be a good idea to ask ourselves two questions: (a) how much do I respect the need for privacy on the part of my fellow Sisters, and (b) do I achieve privacy for myself, while at the same time, giving myself totally to community?

LONELINESS

At the end of her prayer, Mrs. Holmes is struck by a thought that comes as a sort of sequel. "Now, having gotten this off my chest, let me also remember something: If I live long enough I'll have privacy, whether I want it or not! There are plenty of women who'd trade places with me in a minute. Women who've lost their husbands, whose children are gone. Privacy, complete privacy, comes all too soon. Thank you for that reminder, even as I struggle for a little privacy now." This is a very provocative thought offered by Mrs. Holmes. One would think that in community living there would not be too many hours of loneliness for aged Sisters. Yet, experience with those who have become incapacitated by illness or old age teaches us that many are truly lonely and feel forsaken. Again a human need for which we need salvation. Two questions present themselves: (a) am I aware of the loneliness of others and do I try to give of my time and myself to relieve this longing for companionship, and (b) in my loneliness do I resort to self pity and make unreasonable demands on the time and energy of others? Privacy and loneliness are only two of the many human needs demanding salvation.

MY HUMANITY

Religious who forget they are first of all human beings fail to realize their limitations, and consequently their need for God's saving power. God did not create us angels. When we push too far the idea that religious should lead an angelic life, we are setting ourselves up for failure. Then, because we fail to achieve an unrealistic goal, we begin to be filled with unreasonable guilt. The remark of St. Teresa of Avila quoted in the first presentation is worth repeating here. " 'From silly devotions and sour-faced saints, good Lord deliver us!' she protested . . . Teresa could not live with pomposity. Self-importance was a balloon she pricked whenever she saw it bobbing along. I relish her advice to a young nun who came to her with tales of exaggerated temptation and who boasted of being a very great sinner. 'Now, Sister,' Teresa said deflatingly, 'Remember, none of us is perfect. Just make sure those sins of yours don't turn into bad habits.' " The ability to laugh at ourselves is a genuine asset. Our humanity teaches us that there are two questions we must know the answers to, or at least, be striving to get the answers, if our love of God, of ourselves, and of our neighbors is going to balance.

TWO QUESTIONS

For a couple of minutes now I would like to draw on the remarks of clinical psychologist, Donald J. Tyrell, found in his book, "When Love Is Lost" published in 1972 by Word Books, Waco, Texas. Dr. Tyrell builds his approach to our humanness around these two questions: Who am I? and What should I do? Listen for a minute to his remarks on these two questions. "The second question cannot be answered without some knowledge of the first, and the first is a mere pipedream if not translated into the second. The disordered and aimless activity of contemporary society witnesses to a confused inability to offer answers to these questions. Man tends to avoid the challenges of everyday living that might help him come to understand himself . . . How a man behaves is a reflection of what he values, and his values in turn tell us who he is." These two questions of Dr. Tyrell's are, in actuality, the two questions that a retreat proposes to each retreatant. We are building our answer to "Who am I?" on the known fact that we have a relationship with God. And to better analyze that relationship we are considering it from the three aspects of our humanness, our Christianity, and our religious profession. Hopefully our meditations, examinations, liturgies, prayers, talks, and other exercises of the retreat will help us find answers to the second question of "What should I do?" Obviously, one cannot separate herself into three distinct persons, so no matter which of the three aspects of ourselves we are dealing with, the other two are always making their impact. At this point it might be helpful to offer a sort of summary that will help us focus on the answers we are seeking to the questions of "Who am I?" and "What should I do?" This summary is a result of my own personal reflections and should be regarded merely as that. Perhaps it will help you to formulate a similar summary for yourselves. It could be called a stance or position toward life.

STANCE

(Note: Retreat master might want to pass out copies of the following.)

1. God has given me life and intends that I should live it out, happily, for a certain number of years, with certain people, in certain situations.

2. Happiness in this life depends on seeking out, finding, and living according to the will of God, manifested to me through the people of my life and the circumstances in which I find myself.

3. Desires vary in individuals, and consequently individuals must be treated as individuals, so that they will be able to achieve their own happiness and contribute to the happiness of those with whom they live.

4. Self-fulfillment is a natural instinct implanted in us by Almighty God. He expects us to try to achieve that fulfillment without doing harm to ourselves or to anyone else. Each one should receive from those who make up his or her life situation, the support necessary to become the very best person that he or she is capable of. Meanwhile, each one should be giving mutual support to others.

5. Self-fulfillment can be achieved only in partial measure while we are here on this earth. The final and complete fulfillment will be ours only after death, but will last for eternity. My striving to become the person God intends I should be, must be earnest, enthusiastic, constant, well-balanced, and moderated according to circumstances. It is important to do this while I am living now, so that my capacity for total happiness and fulfillment hereafter will reach its full potential.

6. Decisions ought to be based on what I can recognize, as honestly as I can, as the will of God. God does not ask infallibility of me; only that I act as honestly as I know how. His will is that I fulfill to the best of my ability the responsibilities that have come into my life, either through my own choice, or through circumstances, some of which I may not have had any control over.

7. God does not ask the impossible of me. What may have been possible at one time may now be impossible; that which was impossible may now be possible. My life is in his hands and certainly he will give me whatever helps I need to do his will.

8. Persons and circumstances do change, and my life has to be regulated accordingly. Before I make a major change in my life situation, I should diligently try to determine what God is asking of me. Direction should be sought out through prayer, study, and consultation. When the decision is made let me pray that I will have the courage to act according to God's will.

9. What is advantageous and meaningful in life-style for one person may not be so for another. Freedom must be given to each person to be himself. In the process of fulfilling the law of charity, first to myself and then to my "neighbor" (all other persons), I must not unnecessarily injure another or interfere with his rights. Most of the time my living a full and happy life demands that I be willing to make agreements and compromises to whatever extent I can do so with a clear conscience.

10. Suffering of whatever kind is not a blessing in itself and should be avoided where this can reasonably be done. However, whatever suffering I must bear should produce positive results in my life, make me a better person. My experience with pain should help me to be more sympathetic of others in their sufferings. My attitude toward suffering can make me a happier person or more miserable. It all depends on how I understand and accept the refining process that suffering can be.

These ten propositions probably do not embrace every position I take toward God, myself, and my fellowman. But they do serve as pivotal points around which other proposition can be formulated. Sometime during this retreat draw up your own set of propositions. Examine them in the light of God's grace given during these days. Hopefully the human dimension of your relationship to God will be enhanced by this exercise.

THE PAST   As you look into your past, let me offer a caution and a recommendation. The caution is not to let the "if's" of our lives unduly rule the reality. The past does have a great influence on our lives. There are things we wish had never happened, some of which we feel personally guilty for. However, we cannot reverse these things. So, the effort must be made to utilize them constructively. It is true that if certain things had been different in the past, then our present lives would have been different, too. Would they necessarily have been better? To say, "If God has not let that accident happen . . . If I had had better opportunities . . . If I had been raised in a different neighborhood . . . If I had not become a religious". These are just a sampling of the thousand and one "if's" that we bog ourselves down with. This "ifing" does no good, unless we use the mistakes to learn for the present and the future. God gives us the present to live in. As long as we are humbly sorry he forgives us all the mistakes of the past. He promises us his help for a happier future, even though we may not be able to predict how this can come about. God expects us to build positively on the past, rather than wasting time and energy regretting it. Certainly he does not want us to waste ourselves planning vengeance on those who may be responsible for our past mistakes and the terrible consequences we are now living with. Our Father asks us to live each moment to the fullest.

CONNECTION   The title of this presentation is "This God Saves Through Us". You might be wondering what the title has to do with what we have been saying. The understanding of ourselves as human beings is necessary if we are to know how God is to save through us. However, God has directed our lives into the Christian and Religious Profession dimensions. Consequently, the saving acts that we perform in union with the Saving God will, in the practical order, be acts of a Christian who is also a woman who has dedicated herself to God's service in a religious community. Our effort in these first four presentations has been to look at ourselves at the basic level of our humanity. So, before we go into our Christian dimension tomorrow, let us look at three more aspects of our being human beings, especially those aspects which are necessary bases upon which our uniting with God in the salvation of mankind can rest.

ALIVENESS   Speaking about regretting things in the past, I have a humorous incident to ask you to listen to. If you have cooked for your community you probably have had a similar experience. A mother was baking some cookies, and while she had a batch in the oven, the telephone rang. A long conversation, and then she remembered her cookies, and rushed to the kitchen to find it filled with smoke, quickly removed the charred cookie sheet, and sat down utterly depressed. Suddenly, she felt the soft hand of her three-year old on her shoulder. A tiny voice said: "Don't feel bad mama. That's the best smelling smoke you ever made." Earlier I said that Our Father asks us to live each moment to the fullest. Not that each moment is going to be perfect. And we may have to be satisfied with making "the best smelling smoke" we ever made. Aliveness means that we just don't drag ourselves through life. It's almost impossible to share life with another if we do not have any zest for it ourselves. Aliveness means that we do not settle down into ruts of indifference, the just so-so reactions to the totality of God's creation. How can we admire the lilies of the field, the birds of the air, the fields ready for harvesting without being alive to these things? When will we experience the joyousness of young children, the sorrow of a widowed young mother, the anguish and then exultation of a father whose son is restored to him? The aliveness of the human Christ must be ours. Enthusiasm for living, and the manifestation of this verve, will vary somewhat in each individual. And certainly this is not an appeal for activism, running and going until one drops exhausted. The enthusiasm for life may be in a quiet meditation, or a time of silent relaxation, or just as truly in unspoken moments of just being with a beloved friend. It's all in the inner response to that which stimulates an individual, first in himself, then in relation to others, including God Himself, and finally in the things of God's creation. When I was a novice there was an elderly and partially crippled priest at our mother-house. At the annual bazaar he won a typewriter. He had never owned such a machine, and had never learned to type. All of us thought he would give the typewriter away, and maybe one of us novices would get it. Not on your life. Even at his advanced age he still had a zest for life, and so he determined he would learn to type. And he did before his death a short time later. During our lives here we must approach eternity with a zest for aliveness.

GROWTH AND DEVELOPMENT

The outcome of aliveness is growth and development. Becoming mature demands that we constantly enlarge our view of life. Otherwise we restrict God's saving power working through us to too narrow channels. Constant attention must be given to our values. Daily we must check and re-check our life-style, trying to improve it, getting rid of that which has become obsolete or even stagnant. We cannot remain exactly as we were last year, or the year before that, or before that, without suffering a decline. Otherwise we are led to stagnation, and a living kind of death, or a deathly kind of living, which can be called "mere existence". Each day should bring us new knowledge and new experiences. That which we gain through prayer, recreation, study, meditation, conversation, happenings, should be evaluated for its meaning and goodness. When we find that which has meaning for us, we should try to integrate it into our lives. "Our hope lies not in the man we put on the moon, but on the man we put on the cross." (Don Basham) However, to advance each day does demand undergoing the risk of becoming unsettled in the way we have been going. It can make us vulnerable to those who may accuse us of being unstable, always changing, immature. And this may be true in a certain sense. However, this changing helps us to arrive at a higher plateau. Climbing the mountain of life you go up, rest at a level place, but then go on up higher again. Because God has given us the freedom to change, we can grow and develop into the mature persons that he intends we should be here and for eternity. It's against the God-given instincts of the human spirit not to be allowed to soar to the heights. As we conclude, let me ask you to look for just one minute at the tragedy of a father not helping his son to grow, simply by not listening. (Note to Retreat Master: Show 16 mm film, "Can I Talk To You, Dad?")

CLOSING PRAYER

"O, Mary, you took the risk to say "Yes" to Our Father who asked you to help save the world. Obtain for us courage to say our "Yes" in the name of Christ, your Son. Amen."

2. The Christian Dimension of Our Relationship With God

PRESENTATION V—This Saving God Became Man

OPENING PRAYER

"O my God, I believe that you come close to us in your Son Jesus. I believe that he showed us how to live and that our only happiness comes in living as he did. I believe that it is in giving that we receive and in dying that we are born to a new life. I believe that you sustain us each day. I believe that you have made us a 'chosen race, a holy nation, a royal priesthood,' and that we are all the Body of your Son and our brother Jesus. I believe that we re-present him in this world when we love one another. I believe that you are ever with us and that all things work together unto the good of those who love God. I believe that you continue to speak to us in the community of believers which is your Church. I believe that you speak to me through the Spirit of Jesus dwelling within me. I believe that you are very close to me, Lord. Amen." (James Young, published in Large Type Prayerbook, Peters & Young, Paulist Press, N.Y. 1972)

TALK TO DAD

(Note to Retreat Master: Show once again the one minute spot film, "Can I Talk To You, Dad?" and after it is finished, have someone set up the one minute spot film, "Masks of Man", to be shown later in this presentation.)

(After the "Can I Talk To You, Dad?" film.) God has told us that he will not act toward us as did the father in this film we have just seen. I wanted to show it to you a second time, because it shows the necessity of a close relationship between the boy and his dad. Surely the dad loves his son. Yet, the inability to become involved in the son's problems, or perhaps the unwillingness to do so, spells possible disaster for the boy. God said that he will listen to us. In fact, he urges us to be persistent in our requests. "Ask and you shall receive, that your joy may be full," St. John quotes Jesus as saying at the Last Supper (Jn. 16:24). And Jesus himself gives us the encouragement to pray without giving up. "If one of you knows someone who comes to him in the middle of the night and says to him, 'Friend, lend me three loaves, for a friend of mine has come in from a journey and I have nothing to offer him'; and he from inside should reply, 'Leave me alone. The door is shut now and my children and I are in bed. I cannot get up to look after your needs'—I tell you, even though he does not get up and take care of the man because of friendship, he will do so because of his persistence, and give him as much as he needs" (Lk. 11:5-8). In the film the young man tries three times to get through to his dad, but even that persistence did not open the lines of communication. In the parable of the man in bed with his family, and in hundreds of other places in the old and new testaments the characteristics of a person come through. And, God in his efforts to make man realize this aspect of the Divine nature, includes in his teaching even those aspects of a person that would not make him immediately appealing. So, the man in the parable gets out of bed, not from friendship, but simply so he will not be pestered. It is necessary, therefore, that we cut through much of the material in the Bible and in the teaching of the Church to come to that aspect of God which we must know and understand, if relationship with him is going to have any meaning. This is especially true for the Christian, if he is going to understand his relationship with this Saving-Creating-Conserving God.

PERSONAL GOD

In revealing himself to Abram, later called Abraham, Yahweh shows himself to be a person in the full sense of that word. And also in a further sense, Yahweh reveals himself as the personal God of Abraham and all his descendants. In a word, it is a personal God who speaks personally to Abraham. "I will make of you a great nation, and I will bless you; I will make your name great, so that you will be a blessing. I will bless those who bless you and curse those who curse you. All the communities of the earth shall find blessings in you." (Gen. 12:2,3) This, then, is one of the hundreds of examples that occur in the scriptures letting us know the kind of God Yahweh is. Gradually there unfolded to the Hebrew mind the contrast between their God and the gods of their neighbors. In the fifth psalm that we recite in Sunday evening vespers, we have that long litany of what the non-Hebrew gods cannot do. "Their idols are silver and gold, the handiwork of men. They have mouths but speak not; they have eyes but see not; they have ears but hear not; they have noses but smell not; they have hands but feel not; they have feet but walk not; they utter no sound from their throat. Their makers shall be like them, everyone that trusts in them" (Ps. 115:5-8). In the Hebrew understanding of a person, these characteristics, or abilities, are marks of one who deals personally with another. To understand the relationship between two persons, we must understand the nature of the persons of that relationship. So, for the Christian to understand his relationship with God he must know a great deal about himself and also about God. It was necessary for us, therefore, to spend time the last two days in thinking about ourselves as we basically are, that is, as human beings. Now, with God's help, we can proceed to get a better glimpse of ourselves as Christians.

NEED FOR CHRIST

Obviously, God's attempt to reveal himself to his chosen people was only partially successful. Through thunder, lightning, hail, wind, rain, fire, sword;

planting, and growing, and harvesting; patriarchs, judges, kings, prophets, and rabbis, and many more agencies, God unfolded himself to a nation. But the notion of divinity that came through was so distorted that God seemed very far away, a fearsome force that had to be reckoned with here and hereafter. And, so, to prove that he was God of infinite mercy, compassion, and love, a God who saves because he loves, he, Yahweh, had to take on our human nature. Love is not born out of fear. But God is love. And so he comes to us as the child who will save us from our sins. A person, like us, in all things except sin. One of the responses to God become man that is most moving is that of reverence. The God of the Old Testament is reverenced, but there is such an element of fear present that the love of reverence does not get much chance. The first epistle of St. John, fourth chapter, verse 18, expresses it this way: "Love has no room for fear; rather, perfect love casts out all fear. And since fear has to do with punishment, love is not yet perfect in one who is afraid. We for our part, love because he first loved us." This entire fourth chapter gives the best explanation for God's reasons for becoming man. Listen to these pertinent verses. "Beloved, let us love one another because love is of God; everyone who loves is begotten of God and has knowledge of God. The man without love has known nothing of God, for God is love. God's love was revealed in our midst in this way: he sent his only Son to the world that we might have life through him. Love, then, consists in this: not that we have loved God, but that he has loved us and has sent his Son as an offering for our sins. Beloved, if God has loved us so, we must have the same love for one another. No one has ever seen God. Yet if we love one another God dwells in us, and his love is brought to perfection in us" (I Jn. 4:7-12). At the end of this presentation, I would like you to observe two one minute spot films which serve as cinematic interpretations of these passages from John. But before we leave John for this moment, let us hear his personal testimony to the presence of Christ in the Christian. "The way we know we remain in him and he in us is that he has given us of his Spirit. We have seen for ourselves, and can testify, that the Father has sent the Son as savior of the world" (I Jn. 4:13,14).

RESPECT

Did you notice the great reverence with which John speaks of the Father, and the Son, and the Spirit? This is a reverence that springs from love, not from fear. God revealed himself to us as a loving person, so that we would not need to fear him, but could love him fully. Listen to the story of a young girl as reported in Missionhurst Magazine for August-September 1972, published by the Immaculate Heart Missions. "When I was in secondary school I became restless and somewhat upset by many problems. I never had any inclination towards any kind of religion. I never fully doubted God's existence but I tried to find a solution for everything within myself. And then I came to the Catholic University. For the first time in my life I heard someone talk about God with great respect and deep interest. From the first religion classes I attended I knew that religion was something more than just superstition without any kind of foundation. I began going to church and I came into contact with young people who talked seriously about religion. I was more interested in them than in listening to sermons or private prayer, and joined them in trying to live a Christian life as a member of a group . . . Spiritual reading, however, and the practice of Christian life slowly introduced me to prayer . . . I had thousands of questions and my friends were surprised when I asked to be baptized . . . I can honestly say that I made the decision not because anyone encouraged me privately or because I wanted to be protected from harm or to be blessed . . . I took it because I believed. And I don't think I would ever have made it if I had not had the very solid instruction in a Catholic college." And what started her on the road to solid instruction? "For the first time in my life I heard someone talk about God with great respect and deep interest."

REVERENCE

"The person who leads a spiritual life has a profound attitude of reverence; he always tends to be respectful. The opposite attitude of life is one of violence." These two sentences are found on page thirteen of Father Adrian van Kaam's book, "Personality Fulfillment in the Spiritual Life". (Dimension Books, Wilkes-Barre, Pa. c1966) Let us follow Father van Kaam for a few minutes. He explains the first sentence I quoted—"The person who leads a spiritual life has a profound attitude of reverence; he always tends to be respectful"—in this way. We are incarnated spirits. "This means that I am truly involved in everyday endeavors while at the same time transcending them. To be a spirit is for a man to be beyond all things and yet in the midst of them. This life of the spirit is a life of presence inspired by the sacredness of people, of things, and of events in their deepest reality." Father van Kaam then goes on to give his notion of violence. "Violence is a refusal to revere people, nature, and things as they truly are. Violence may be described as a readiness to infringe upon the integrity or sacredness of reality. To the degree that I lose reverence, violence enters my life and expresses itself either in mild manifestations such as manipulation of myself and others, or in extreme forms such as discrimination against certain groups of the population or against people who profess a religion different from mine." Our society certainly needs to think a great deal about our attitudes toward reverence and violence. There is no need to amplify this statement. Newspapers, magazines, radio and television newscasts, and many other agencies constantly bombard our senses with accounts of crimes being contemplated, crimes in progress, and crimes already completed. Perhaps the motivation for the preservation of our natural environment and resources will spread its reverential awe to human life as well. (Note to Retreat Master: Show the one minute spot film, "Masks of Man" and after it is finished, have someone set up the second and third spots on the film, "Search", to be shown later in this presentation.)

RELIGIOUS PRESENCE

Two thousand years ago God presented himself to us in human form. As Jesus Christ he preached and exemplified a doctrine of love for God, his and our Father, a love for oneself, and for fellowman. Only when one forgets or ignores the Son of God becoming flesh can he perpetrate the crimes summarized in the film we just saw: discrimination, burglaries, war. Going back to Father van Kaam for just a minute, we find him reminding us that we must have a sense of religious presence. Let Father van Kaam explain. "Religious presence is a mysterious force in the core of my being. It can be the underlying and integrating principle of unity of my life . . . When my religious presence is concentrated and full, I perceive almost exclusively the sacred dimension of the people I encounter, the events I face, and the things I handle. Their profane aspects seem to recede in the background; only their relatedness to the Holy stands out in my perception. For example, instead of experiencing a flower as a decoration for my window sill, a specimen of plant life, or a gift for a friend who is celebrating his birthday, I experience it predominantly as a pointing to the mystery of creation, a tiding of the transcendent, a message of the beyond." All of us have at one time or another experienced the presence of God in ourselves, and in the people and things around us. In fact, in our novitiates we are encouraged to practice the "Presence of God" as a stimulus to the practice of virtue. But this is something more than the "Eye of God" watching me. It is a realization of the influence of the Redeeming Christ in all of creation. By his incarnation Christ has taken all of creation into himself. And so every person, all things, each event, every place is permeated with the religious presence of God become man.

PERSISTENCE OF RELIGIOUS PRESENCE

After describing the experience of religious presence in the flower, Father van Kaam goes on to explain the persistence of this religious presence. "Some moments later I may have to deal with this flower under many other practical aspects. I may have to prune it, to water it, to pack it carefully for my friend, or to find a place in my room where its beauty blends best with the surroundings. In those moments, the center of my attention is no longer the sacredness of the flower but a host of other purposes which emerge in the time and space of my daily existence. The interesting thing is that my former intensive experience of the Holy has not totally disappeared but somehow lingers on like a fine scent in a room after fragrant blossoms have been taken away. While it is true that I handle my flower in a functional way, it is also unmistakably true that the way in which I experience and handle my flower now is somewhat different from the way in which I did so before I experienced its sacred meaning. My practical approach seems somehow influenced by a newly gained reverence that reverberates in my attitude and action. In other words, there is a vital relationship between a concentrated experience of the Holy and my later experience of the same person, event, or thing on a different level."

PRESENCE OF CHRIST

It is a joyous thing that God has made his presence known to us in his Son, Jesus Christ. Our response should be one of exultant jubilation, and it is. But, then, we sometimes find it difficult to realize this presence of the Incarnated Son of God, and we look for him in many places, usually missing him where he obviously is. Perhaps, these two one minute spots with which we will conclude this presentation, will emphasize the point of jubilation, because "Emmanuel—God is with us". (Note to Retreat Master: Show the two spots, and then after a short pause conclude with the following prayer.)

LET US PRAY

Almighty and Everlasting God, by the cooperation of the Holy Spirit, You prepared the body and soul of Mary to be a worthy dwelling for Your Son. Grant that we who rejoice in her memory will be freed from present evil and eternal death through her intercession. We ask this through Christ, Mary's Son. Amen.

PRESENTATION VI—*This Saving Man Is God*

OPENING PRAYER

"In Christ's Love" by Francois Chagneau (Large Type Prayerbook—Peters & Young, Paulist Press, N.Y., 1972)

*"Nothing can separate us
From the love of Jesus Christ.
He brings us victory
Over the troubles of this life.*

*Even if life brings anguish to us
And the pangs of death,
Even if hunger destroys our body
And other men humiliate us,*

*Even if the cold pierces our flesh
And the heat sears it through,
Even if our hearts are tortured
And plunged down into death,*

*Even if men pursue and dog us
And put to death our brothers,
Even if we find only hate
And have to pass through fire,*

*All these sufferings are our glory,
We abide in Jesus Christ;
In him we find our strength
And in his love our life. Amen!"*

SHOW AND TELL

(Note to Retreat Master: If a cartoonist is available, have her draw in large squares a reproduction of the Peanuts cartoon reproduced here, and hang the drawings in a place where they will be seen by the retreatants before this presentation.)

Poor Sally Brown! Here she comes to school all eager to "Show and Tell". Trouble is she has something to show and tell that neither the teacher nor most of the pupils want to see or hear about. Dejectedly, Sally returns to her desk with her undisplayed box of stuff and laments, "All the life has gone out of Show and Tell". Many persons during Christ's lifetime did not want to see what he had to show, or listen to what he had to tell. The incidents of such rejection in the New Testament are almost too numerous to mention. St. John's entire gospel is built around several episodes of confrontation and rejection, leading irrevocably to the final rejection on Calvary. Our society today continues to turn its eyes away from looking at Jesus, the author of our salvation. Rather look to our own resources of material wealth, political acumen, massive power. Nor does it want to listen to what Jesus, through his Church, has to say to the needs of our civilization. Much better, they agree, to listen to those who promote material prosperity and luxurious living, than to the simple message of trust in God and peace to all men.

WHO IS THE SON OF MAN

The incidence of "Peter the Rock" in the sixteenth chapter of St. Matthew's gospel is so familiar to us that it does not need to be repeated here. Mainly we are interested in the question that Christ asked: "Who do people say that the Son of Man is?" When the answer to this was unsatisfactory, Jesus turned to the disciples near him and asked, "And you, who do you say that I am?" We know Peter's answer. "You are the Messiah, the Son of the living God." Down through the centuries the Church has advanced the meaning of these words to their significance after the resurrection, so that we accept them as defining Christ as truly the Son of God, the Second Person of the Blessed Trinity. Without getting into the arguments that prove Peter did not go, and could not have gone, beyond the characteristic of Messiahship, we can accept the traditional teaching of the Church that Jesus Christ, the saving man, is God. For the purposes of later meditating on what we know of the life of Christ, and to bring to life and color and sound images of Jesus given us by the gospel writers, let us look at some familiar scenes from his life. (Note to Retreat Master: Here show movie or slides or filmstrip on the life of Christ. There are so many available that it is not necessary to specify which to use.)

SON, THE ETERNAL WORD

An excellent summary of our belief about Jesus Christ is contained in the Dogmatic Constitution on Divine Revelation, a wonderful document from the Second Vatican Council. In the first chapter, number 4, we read: "Then, after speaking in many places and varied ways through the prophets, God 'last of all in these days has spoken to us by his son' (Heb. 1:1,2). For he sent His Son, the eternal Word, who enlightens all men, so that He might dwell among men and tell them the innermost realities about God (cf. Jn. 1:1-18). Jesus Christ, therefore, the Word made flesh, sent as a 'man to men,' 'speaks the words of God' (Jn. 3:34), and completes the work of salvation which His Father gave him to do (cf. Jn. 5:36, 17:4). To see Jesus is to see His Father (Jn. 14:9). For this reason Jesus perfected revelation by fulfilling through His whole work of making Himself present and manifesting Himself: through His words and deeds, His signs and wonders, but especially through His death and glorious resurrection from the dead and final sending of the Spirit of truth. Moreover, He confirmed with divine testimony what revelation proclaimed: that God is with us to free us from the darkness of sin and death and to raise us up to eternal life."

THE OBEDIENCE OF FAITH

The response to the question of who Jesus truly is cannot be given on a simple academic basis. Listen once again to the Fathers of Vatican Two speaking the words of response as found in the fifth section of Chapter One of the same Dogmatic Constitution on Revelation. "The obedience of faith (Rom. 16:26; cf. 1:5; 2 Cor. 10:5-6) must be given to God who reveals, an obedience by which man entrusts his whole self freely to God, offering "the full submission of intellect and will to God who reveals," and freely assenting "to the truth revealed by Him." A footnote on this section further amplifies the Council's position. "Note the general description of faith, 'by which a man commits his whole self': the Council desired to get away from a too intellectualist conception. Christian faith is not merely assent to a set of statements; it is a personal engagement, a continuing act of loyalty and self-commitment, offered by man to God." The Council Fathers conclude this fifth section of the document by further saying how faith proceeds. "If this faith is to be shown, the grace of God and the interior help of the Holy Spirit must precede and assist, moving the heart and turning it to God, opening the eyes of the mind, and giving 'joy and ease to everyone in assenting to the truth and believing it.' To bring about an ever deepening understanding of revelation, the same Holy Spirit constantly brings faith to completion by His gifts."

RELATIONSHIP OF FAITH

The relationship of a human being to God is that of creature to Creator. The relationship of a Christian to God is that of one redeemed to the Redeemer. Through our baptism we establish the bond of unity with our Saving God and with all those who, like ourselves, have been given the effects of Christ's life, sufferings, death, resurrection and ascension. Faith is a beautiful homage to pay to God. It is a choice made in his favor. Under the influence of grace, which is never refused to those who ask for it with a sincere heart, one prefers the word of Christ to one's own judgement, the will of Christ to one's own personal interests. This choice will be as much a work of love as an act of the mind. "I know him in whom I have believed." I know him in whom I have placed my trust; I know him to whom I am consecrated. There is a knowledge which proceeds from love, a knowledge which ends in a complete gift. The faith of a Christian should be so strong that he can say to Christ: "Your life will be my life, your death be my death." A Christian who does not have this burning faith would not know how to correspond with our Lord's demands.

THE WONDERFULNESS OF FAITH

In the Journal of the Ontario Association of Children's Aid Societies (32 Isabella St., Toronto 5, Ontario, Canada) some years ago there is a beautiful story of faith, the faith of one human being in another, which gradually grew into a mutual faith in each other and in God. The story is rather long, but let's try to condense it. It's about a priest who adopts a young lad into the boarding school of which he is principal. The boy had been rejected so many times that he now trusted no one. No wonder he always seemed to have a chip on his shoulder. However, slowly the priest was able to cut through the wall the boy had built around himself. Two years after Tommy had entered the school he and the priest had the beginnings of a fine relationship. After another two years the climax came when Tommy quietly remarked, "This has not been my best year, Father, in many ways. But I still want to be what I have always wanted to be, a priest." Of course, this put the priest on the top of the world; someday he would call his adopted son, "Father". Let me put the rest of the story in the priest's own words.

"Little did I know that within two weeks all my dreams would be ashes . . . It was midnight when the phone rang. "Father, the boys have had an accident!"

"How bad?"

"Tommy is dead!"

Tommy's funeral was truly beautiful. It was a perfect summer morning. The Church (where we offered Mass together just two weeks before) was not large, but it was filled with friends. There was no sadness, no sorrow, no stress on loss. After all, God had given us four happy years together and countless memories. I could see once more the shy, embarrassed 13-year-old; the eager guard on the basketball team; the blue-green waters of the Ottawa turning into spray behind Tommy's skis; and the blond head bowing for my blessing. Deep down inside I had a warm comfortable feeling, tinged with a touch of envy; my son had reversed our roles, now there would be someone waiting up there for me."

LIFE WITHOUT FAITH VERSUS LIFE WITH FAITH

(Note to Retreat Master: This section of this presentation is taken from "Before His Face" by Gaston Courtois, chapter two. Perhaps you would want to use the fuller treatment there, especially to present the examination of conscience—in a modified form—either thru a bulletin, or perhaps your own reading.)

Without faith life has no meaning. Our words, our gestures, our daily living mean nothing. If we have faith, everything becomes clear: the cross, the eucharistic host, suffering, sacrifice, death. The invisible becomes more real than the visible. The eternal has a greater value in our eyes than the transient. Our scale of values bases itself on that of God. It is through his eyes that we see everything, going beyond appearances to find in everything and in everyone the deepest reality, the only truth that counts. The more ardent faith is, the stronger it is for the hour of temptation. It is normal for us to have to struggle. An extreme and highly dramatic presentation of life is given in the book of Job, and rightly are these words put in the mouth of the chief character, Job: "The life of man upon earth is a warfare" (Job 7:1). Where would be the merit in conquering if we did not experience some attack? The devil is intent on conquering us. So St. Peter urges: "Stay sober and alert. Your opponent the devil is prowling like a roaring lion looking for someone to devour." Note, however, the victory will be sure if faith is unyielding. "Resist him, solid in your faith . . ." (I Pet. 5:9).

INCREASE IN FAITH   Cardinal Suenens wrote a dictum worth remembering: "Happy are they who dream dreams and are ready to pay the price to have them come true." Faith, in a certain sense, is a dream. And one that can evaporate on awakening, or which can be turned into the reality of eternal life. There is great encouragement in the final verses of the tenth chapter of the Epistle to the Hebrews. "Do not, then, surrender your confidence; it will have great reward. You need patience to do God's will and receive what he has promised. For, just a brief moment, and he who is to come will come; he will not delay. My just man will live by faith, and if he draws back I take no pleasure in him. We are not among those who draw back and perish, but among those who have faith and live." (verses 35-39). Faith is also likened to the roots of a tree reaching down into the soil. Faith, therefore, must plunge deeply into God to imbibe those graces which give vitality to our Christian lives. How else produce the one hundred fold fruit the Lord expects of us? The very graces of intimacy with God are a reward, even here, for growth in the life of faith. Our faith has led us first to the Christian life, and then a further impulse brought us into the relationship of a professed religious. It is in the full commitment of our daily lives to God and his love that our faith will grow and its rewards be ours. But we must leave the development of this to other presentations in the days to follow. Our increasingly secure belief in Christ as the saving man who is God is the touchstone for all the decisions of our lives. A beautiful summary of this relationship of the Christian to his Saving God is found in prophecy in the Book of Hosea (2:21-25). As I read these words let us think on them prayerfully, and offer them to God as a concluding petition to this presentation.

HOSEA'S PROPHESY
I will espouse you to me forever:
    I will espouse you in right and in justice,
        in love and in mercy;
I will espouse you in fidelity,
        and you shall know the Lord.
On that day I will respond, says the Lord;
    I will respond to the heavens,
        and they shall respond to the earth;
The earth shall respond to the grain,
    and wine, and oil,
        and these shall respond to Jezreel.
I will sow him for myself in the land,
        and I will have pity on Lo-ruhama.
I will say to Lo-anni, "You are my people"
        and he shall say, "My God!"

PRESENTATION VII—Our Salvation Is Accomplished through Redemption

OPENING PRAYER   *Let us pray to God through our mediator Jesus Christ. Let us say to him:*
R. *Pour out your love upon us, Lord.*
    We thank you, for from eternity you have chosen us for your people;
    —and you have called us to receive the glory of Jesus our Lord.
R. *Pour out your love upon us, Lord.*
    Unite all who bear the name of Christian;
    —may they all be of one mind in the word of truth, and one in heart by fervent charity.
R. *Pour out your love upon us, Lord.*
    Creator of the universe, whose incarnate Son undertook to work by the side of his fellow-men;
    —have mercy on all who earn their bread in the sweat of their brow.

R. *Pour out your love upon us, Lord.*
   Keep in mind also those who spend themselves in the service of their fellow-men.
   —Do not let them be discouraged by failures and misunderstanding.
R. *Pour out your love upon us, Lord.*
   Have mercy on those who have died;
   —let not the evil spirit have any hold over them.
R. *Pour out your love upon us, Lord.*
   O Lord, in your loving-kindness, hear the cry of your Church and grant her the forgiveness of sins. May your grace increase her dedication to your service, and your protection free her from fear and anxiety. We make our prayer through our Lord.
   May the Lord bless us, may he keep us from all evil, and lead us to life ever-lasting. Amen.
   Let us bless the Lord.
R. *Thanks be to God.*
(INTERIM ROMAN BREVIARY)

ANALOGY TO MARRIAGE

Frequently in the Old and New Testaments the relationship of God with his covenant people is expressed in the analogy of a marriage. Recall the number of wedding feasts alluded to. And the many stories about the bride and the bridegroom. It is true that this analogy of bride and bridegroom is also used in the Church to express the relationship of a professed religious with Christ. However, this does not occur in the scriptures, where God seeks to have us understand and appreciate what it is like to be commited to him. Although we are religious, nevertheless we should not shy away from a consideration of the marriage analogy simply because marriage is not for us. That God has used it for our instruction is sufficient motive for us to consider it. For a few minutes let us take a look at some slides depicting the pre-marital and marital situations. Please keep in mind that the analogy applies primarily to the relationship that exists between God and the one he has ingrafted into the society of his people through the sacrament of baptism. (Show slides of some good set on marriage.)

COMMUNICATION

The most important ability needed by those who are thinking about getting married is the ability to communicate with one another, an ability which hopefully will continue on through all the years of marriage. Communication means that you are willing to listen with your heart and mind so that you can truly understand and appreciate the other's ideas and feelings. This takes time and patience. Frequently, we are too eager to get our own ideas and feelings across, even to the extent of interrupting the other unnecessarily. But even when we seem physically to be listening, our minds may be on something far away from what our companion is saying. Are we more interested in ourselves than the other person? If so, it will be difficult to show the care and concern that should result when we know how the other person thinks and feels. Without care and concern there is not much opportunity for genuine love to develop. The concentration here is on listening as a major factor in the communication process, simply because most of us do not have any problem in talking. Do you listen to God?

SELFLESSNESS

This is not the place to concentrate on all the qualities that a person should have to go through a courtship successfully and then to pursue a happy course through all of married life. But selflessness is such a necessary ingredient that we cannot overlook it. Perhaps we are more familiar with the opposite, selfishness. Examples here would be redundant, since each of us could think of hundreds of cases of unhappiness caused by selfishness. Perhaps we can get at the elusive quality of truly thinking of others, especially in the love situation of marriage or that of the Christian's relationship with his God, by listening for a minute to a poem by Khalil Gibran in his book, "The Prophet" written in English after he had made his home here in the United States. The book was published in 1923, nine years before his death. In each poem a question is addressed to "The Prophet" (The Wise Man). This one is on love.

Then said Almitra, Speak to us of Love.
And he raised his head and looked upon
the people, and there fell a stillness upon
them. And with a great voice he said:
When love beckons to you, follow him,
Though his ways are hard and steep.
And when his wings enfold you yield to him,
Though the sword hidden among his pinions may wound you.
And when he speaks to you believe in him,
Though his voice may shatter your dreams
as the north wind lays waste the garden.

For even as love crowns you so shall he
crucify you. Even as he is for your growth
so is he for your pruning.
Even as he ascends to your height and
caresses your tenderest branches that quiver in the sun,
So shall he descend to your roots and
shake them in their clinging to the earth.

Like sheaves of corn he gathers you unto himself.
He threshes you to make you naked.
He sifts you to free you from your husks.
He grinds you to whiteness.
He kneads you until you are pliant;
And then he assigns you to his sacred fire,
that you may become sacred bread for God's sacred feast.

All these things shall love do unto you
that you may know the secrets of your heart,
and in that knowledge become a fragment of Life's heart.

But if in your fear you would seek
love's peace and love's pleasure,
Then it is better for you that you cover
your nakedness and pass out of love's
threshing floor,
Into the seasonless world where you
shall laugh, but not all of your laughter,
and weep, but not all of your tears.

Love gives naught but itself and takes
naught but from itself.
Love possesses not nor would it be possessed;
For love is sufficient unto love.

When you love you shall not say,
"God is in my heart," but rather, "I am
in the heart of God."
And think not you can direct the course of love,
for love, if it find you worthy,
directs your course.

Love has no other desire but to fulfill itself.
But if you love and must needs have
desires, let these be your desires:
To melt and be like a running brook
that sings its melody to the night.
To know the pain of too much tenderness.
To be wounded by your own understanding of love;

And to bleed willingly and joyfully.
To wake at dawn with a winged heart
and give thanks for another day of loving;

To rest at the noon hour and meditate love's ecstasy;
To return home at eventide with gratitude;
And then to sleep with a prayer for the
beloved in your heart and a song of praise
upon your lips.

GOD'S IDEAL SHATTERED

Kahlil Gibran's poem on love gives some idea of the ideal of love that God had in mind when he created Adam and Eve. So much care and concern, so much preparation on the part of God, the Creator, for the moment of relationship between himself and one created in his own image and likeness. The Book of Genesis in its early verses stresses so much the great love that God had for all of creation, but especially for man and woman. How wonderfully does the author of Genesis tell us in story form the love of friendship between Creator and creature. Along with his capacity for thinking, man received from God a tremendous capacity for loving. But this ideal was shattered when man turned on that love and destroyed its fruit, friendship. Unless God remedied the situation man would never be able to love again. Not to love anymore—this is hell. In the Diary of a Country Priest (Macmillan, 1937), Georges Bernanos has the curé trying to make Mme. la Comtesse understand that her hatred against God because of the death of her baby son, will cause her not only to lose God, but also to lose her little son for all eternity. The curé speaks:

Hell is judged by the standards of the world, and still less of this Christian society. An eternal expiation! The miracle is that we on earth were ever able to think of such a thing, when scarcely has our sin gone out of us and one look, a sign, a dump appeal suffices for grace and pardon to swoop down, as an eagle from topmost skies. It's because the lowest of human beings, even though he no longer thinks he can love, still has in him the power of loving. Our very hate is resplendent, and the least tormented of the fiends would warm himself in what we call our despair, as in a morning of glittering sunshine. Hell is not to love any more, madame. Not to love any more! That sounds quite ordinary to you . . . Alas, if God's own hand were to lead us to one of these unhappy things, even if once it had been the dearest of our friends, what could we say to it? The sorrow, the unutterable loss of those charred stones which once were men, is that they have nothing more to be shared.

PROMISE OF REDEMPTION

Such was the sad state to which she had reduced himself by sinning. Fortunately, the abundance of God's love is greater than any sin, since God's capacity for loving is infinite. And so the promise of redemption. Page after page in the Old Testament keeps alive God's will to save every person coming into the world. We know the history of redemption, so there is no need to repeat it here. We do need to meditate on these acts of God's mercy. More than that we need to celebrate God's abundant love in the Eucharist. This we do each day. Would that we brought more of ourselves to this communication of God in his revealing word, and in the sacrificial giving of his Son. The preface of each mass accentuates this tremendous act of love, God the Father giving us redemption through his Son, Jesus, in the love of the Spirit. It is difficult to pick the one preface that would express the common denominator of all of them. Perhaps the Preface for Sundays of the Year 1 would be a good choice. Listen. (If Retreat Master has a good voice, let him sing the Preface.)

Father, all-powerful and ever-living God
we do well always and everywhere to give you thanks
through Jesus Christ our Lord.
Through his cross and resurrection
he freed us from sin and death
and called us to the glory that has made us
a chosen race, a royal priesthood,
a holy nation, a people set apart.
Everywhere we proclaim your mighty works

for you have called us out of darkness
into your own wonderful light.
And so, with all the choirs of angels in heaven
we proclaim your glory and join in their unending hymn of praise:
    (Note: It would be very appropriate here to sing (or recite) the "Holy, Holy, Holy . . .")

Let me suggest to you that occasionally you meditate on one of the prefaces; they are marvelous acclamations of God's tremendous love for all mankind, but especially for those who have accepted his redemptive love in Baptism, and enhanced that acceptance by religious profession.

DO NOT ACCEPT SUBSTITUTES

One of the reasons why our society cannot heal its ills is that it seeks a cure outside the realm of God's mercy. It is somewhat like Cindy, a middle teen-ager. It was evident that when her boy friend came to see her he was more interested in free food than in her. One day Cindy in desperation said to her mother: "How can I get Bobby to pay attention to me?" Her mother replied: "Is there a perfume that smells like peanut butter?" Substitute for the real thing? Maybe this would work for Cindy. But substitute "redeemers" and "messiahs" for Christ do not work. The example of Christ and his teachings give us the principles we need for making decisions that merit eternal life. It's not bad to listen to commentators, statesmen, sociologists, philosophers, psychologists, and so forth, but we should be prudent enough to evaluate their cures for society in the light of Christ's teachings, especially as these teachings come down through the centuries to us through the Church. Page after page, hour after hour, video after video, tell us how to be happy here and hereafter. And many of the recommendations have merit. But do we really evaluate them in the light of Christ's Good News of salvation? Let me try to sum up the whole premise upon which the Christian approach to life here and hereafter is founded. It is found in the first part of the Dogmatic Constitution on Divine Revelation given to us by the Bishops of the Second Vatican Council (Chapter I, Number 2).

In His goodness and wisdom, God chose to reveal Himself and to make known to us the hidden purpose of His will (cf. Eph. 1:9) by which through Christ, the Word made flesh, man has access to the Father in the Holy Spirit and comes to share in the divine nature (cf. Eph. 2:18; 2 Pet. 1:4). Through this revelation, therefore, the invisible God (cf. Col. 1:15; 1 Tim. 1:17) out of the abundance of His love speaks to men as friends (cf. Ex. 33:11; Jn. 15:14-15) and lives among them (cf. Bar. 3:38), so that He may invite and take them into fellowship with Himself. This plan of revelation is realized by deeds and words having an inner unity: the deeds wrought by God in the history of salvation manifest and confirm the teaching and realities signified by the words, while the words proclaim the deeds and clarify the mystery contained in them. By this revelation then, the deepest truth about God and the salvation of man is made clear to us in Christ, who is the Mediator and at the same time the fullness of all revelation.

(For concluding prayer repeat the "Holy, Holy, Holy . . ." preferably sung.)

PRESENTATION VIII—Salvation Is Applied Through the Sacraments.

(Note to Retreat Master: If large posters of the Blessed Mother are available, hang them in conspicuous places of the retreat area. Juxtapose to them modern posters of women, lay and religious.)

OPENING PRAYER

AN ACT OF FAITH by James Young (*LARGE PRINT PRAYERBOOK,* Peters & Young, Paulist Press, N.Y., 1972).

O my God, I believe that you come close to us in your Son Jesus. I believe that he showed us how to live and that our only happiness comes in living as he did. I believe that it is in giving that we receive and in dying that we are born to new life. I believe that you sustain us each day. I believe that you have made us a "chosen race, a holy nation, a royal priesthood," and that we are all the Body of your Son and our brother Jesus. I believe that we represent him in this world when we love one another. I believe that you are ever with us and that all things work together unto the good of those who love God. I believe that you continue to speak to us in the community of believers which is your Church. I believe that you speak to me through the Spirit of Jesus dwelling within me. I believe that you are very close to me, Lord. Amen.

SALVATION THROUGH SACRAMENTS

We have all studied enough and taught enough to know that what Christ did for us in his life, death, resurrection, and ascension comes to us through the Church. The most sacred signs the Church uses to distribute these graces are the sacraments. It is not necessary for us to review the traditional seven sacraments, although they should form subjects for our meditations during the retreat. However, let us concentrate for a few minutes on the one that begins the whole process of our Christian relationship with God, Baptism. Because we are baptised we can say that we are "a chosen race, a holy nation, a royal priesthood." Through a series of slides and commentary let me review for you what the Almighty has done for you. (Note to Retreat Master: Show any good slides or movie on Baptism; there are plenty to choose from.)

SACRAMENT— SIGN OF GOD'S LOVE

Let us review very briefly what the Bishops at the Second Vatican Council reaffirmed about sacraments. "The purpose of the sacraments is to sanctify men, to build up the body of Christ, and finally, to give worship to God. Because they are signs they also instruct. They not only presuppose faith, but by words and objects they also nourish, strengthen and express it; that is why they are called 'sacraments of faith.' They do indeed impart grace, but, in addition, the very act of celebrating them disposes the faithful most effectively to receive this grace in a fruitful manner, to worship God duly, and to practice charity." (Constitution on the Sacred Liturgy, Ch. III, #59.) Rightly, therefore, do we consider the sacraments as special signs of God's love, evidenced most strongly and beautifully in the sacraments of the holy Eucharist and of Penance. What great care and concern God has for our need to be forgiven, and then to be ever so closely united with him in holy communion! Our appreciation for these signs of love is shown in the manner in which we use them. Hopefully our celebrations of these sacraments during this retreat are helping us to appreciate ever deeper and deeper the magnificence of God's love. Such appreciation leads us to return love for love, not out of obligation or constraint or fear, but out of the sheer abundance of the love that God has poured into our total being.

SACRAMENT— SPECIAL SIGNIFICANCE

Now listen for a moment to the Bishops in the Constitution on the Sacred Liturgy (Chapter I, #5) as they broaden the scope of the word sacrament. "The wonders wrought by God among the people of the Old Testament were but a prelude to the work of Christ the Lord in redeeming mankind and giving perfect glory to God. He achieved His task principally by the paschal mystery of His blessed passion, resurrection from the dead, and glorious ascension, whereby 'dying, he destroyed our death and, rising, he restored our life.' For it was from the side of Christ as He slept the sleep of death upon the cross that there came forth the wondrous sacrament which is the whole Church." These words, of course, put a special significance on the word, sacrament, but in no way contradict the meaning attached to these words by the seven sacraments designated by the Council of Trent. Rather the idea of a sacred sign, instituted by Christ, to give grace, is certainly found to be applicable to the Church. The result of engaging this statement "there came forth the wondrous sacrament which is the whole Church," ought to be increased love of the Church and all its members, and a renewal of our willingness to serve Christ in his members. St. Augustine writing about the kingdom of God says, "Two loves have built two cities: the love of self carried unto contempt of God has built the city of this earth; the love of God carried unto the contempt of self has built the heavenly city." (De Civitate Dei, XIV, 28). The Church, then, "the kingdom of God on earth," is the sign of God's love manifested in the world today.

MARY—THE IDEAL OF THIS SACRAMENT

Yet, I wish to go still further in this idea of sacrament. Unless we meditate deeply upon it, the notion of Church remains pretty much in the abstract. We need a concrete example of what it means when we say the Church is the sign of God's love. And it is more than an intellectual or even practical necessity that we be able to sort of visualize what that concept means. Someone has said, "No doubt about it—one of mankind's greatest discoveries has to be glass. While necessity produced the wheel, button and safety pin, it must have been man's innate desire to capture the beauty of the rainbow that created the art of glass-making." Remember the beautiful cut glass bowls, and cups, and candy dishes your mother or grandmother had? How they would sparkle and shine, especially when the light would reflect from them! Something of this nature there is in Our Blessed Mother. True, once God had decided to become man, and had deigned to do so through a human being, it was necessary for him to select some one person. But look how far he went beyond the ordinary necessity. Yes, it must have been something like an innate desire in God to capture the beauty of the rainbow that caused him to create the wonderful girl whom Gabriel addressed, "Full of grace". During one of his programs Art Linkletter asked a little girl: "Who is the most beautiful lady in the world?"

Her reply: "Mary."

"Mary who, honey?" quoth the emcee.

"Mary, the Mother of Jesus," the little girl said.

We are free to imagine the physical beauty of Mary as we wish. But the fact that she was a beautiful person is based on much more than appearances. Mary is revealed to us in the scriptures as a very happy, well-adjusted young girl, who knows her own mind. Not from self-sufficiency, but because she has prayed and sought for the will of God in her life. Mary's maturity of judgement, even at age fifteen or sixteen, causes her to face the realities of life as they are, not imagined or made fanciful. And so she questions what is really the will of God for her. Once her questions are answered satisfactorily, then she is dedicated for the rest of her life to the fulfillment of that will. It is in this characteristic, primarily, that Mary is the exemplar, par excellence, of what it means to be a member of the Church. Vatican Two has not depreciated devotion to Mary, but, on the contrary, has given it a more firm basis than ever.

MARY'S LIFE

In Chapter VIII of the document on the Church, the Fathers of the Council give a fine exposition of Mary's relationship with God, with Christ, and with the Holy Spirit, delineating her perogatives and privileges, of which we are well aware. In part II of this chapter, the Bishops show how Mary is foreshadowed in the prophecies of the Old Testament. Mary is the new Eve. "She gave to the world that very life which renews all things, and she was enriched by God with gifts befitting such a role." Then Mary's life as given in the New Testament is commented on, especially from the standpoint of the early Fathers of the Church. The reward of Mary's life of dedication to the will of God is summed up by the Council in this way: "She was exalted by the Lord as Queen of all, in order that she might be the more thoroughly conformed to her Son, the Lord of lords and the conqueror of sin and death."

MARY'S ROLE IN THE CHURCH

Now, then, the Bishops are ready to make their statements about Mary's role in the Church. These are found in part III of this eighth chapter. Let me read some of the statements.

"The maternal duties of Mary toward men in no way obscure this unique mediation of Christ, but rather shows its power. For all the saving influences of the Blessed Virgin on men originate, not from some inner necessity, but from the divine pleasure. They flow forth from the superabundance of the merits of Christ, rest on his mediation, depend entirely on it, and draw all their power from it. In no way do they impede the immediate union of the faithful with Christ. Rather, they foster this union."

"She (Mary) cooperated by her obedience, faith, hope, and burning charity in the Savior's work of restoring supernatural life to souls. For this reason she is a mother to us in the order of grace."

"For, taken up to heaven, she did not lay aside this saving role, but by her manifold acts of intercession continues to win for us gifts of eternal salvation."

"Through the gift and role of divine maternity, Mary is united with her Son, the Redeemer, and with His singular graces and offices. By these, the Blessed Virgin is also intimately united with the Church."

"The Son whom she (Mary) brought forth is He whom God placed as the firstborn among many brethren (cf. Rom. 8:29), namely, the faithful. In their birth and development she cooperates with a maternal love."

Having made these general statements, the Bishops next go on to state more completely Mary's role in the Church. We will come to this in just a minute.

THE CHURCH REACHES PERFECTION IN MARY

During the Italian campaign of World War II two New Zealand soldiers went to an Italian farmhouse. One was a Catholic. As the boys entered, the womenfolk were around the fire saying the rosary. They were terrified at the sight of the soldiers, until the Catholic boy took his rosary from around his neck and joined them. The rosary finished the womenfolk gave the soldiers bread, eggs, cheese and wine. On their way back to the camp, the non-Catholic soldier said to his companion: "That rosary of yours seems to be a universal language and the sight of those beads was more effective than a pistol." (Sentinel of the Blessed Sacrament, October 1943)

Because our devotion to Mary was based on what she could do for us, rather than on who and what she is, the Bishops of Vatican Two made clearer Mary's relationship with the rest of the Church. The next statement is rather long, but necessary for us, if we are to be renewed in our devotion to Mary, and if we are to fully understand how God works through the sacred signs of persons, as well as things, to accomplish our salvation.

"In the most Holy Virgin the Church has already reached that perfection whereby she exists without spot or wrinkle (cf. Eph. 5:27). Yet the followers of Christ will strive to increase in holiness by conquering sin. And so they raise their eyes to Mary who shines forth to the whole community of the elect as a model of the virtues. Devotedly meditating on her and contemplating her in the light of the Word made man, the Church with reverence enters more intimately into the supreme mystery of the Incarnation and becomes ever increasingly like her Spouse.

For Mary figured profoundly in the history of salvation and in a certain way unites and mirrors within herself the central truths of the faith. Hence when she is being preached and venerated, she summons the faithful to her Son and His sacrifice, and to love for the Father. Seeking after the glory of Christ, the Church becomes more like her exalted model, and continually progresses in faith, hope, and charity, searching out and doing the will of God in all things. Hence the Church in her apostolic work also rightly looks to her who brought forth Christ, conceived by the Holy Spirit and born of the Virgin, so that through the Church Christ may be born and grow in the hearts of the faithful also. The Virgin Mary in her own life lived an example of that maternal love by which all should be fittingly animated who cooperate in the apostolic mission of the Church on behalf of the rebirth of men."

RECOMMENDATIONS

We cannot conclude this conference, which requires much meditation on Mary as the preeminent sign of God's mercy to us, without taking note of the recommendations offered by the Bishops concerning devotion to Mary. So, it is urgent that we listen again to the Bishops of Vatican II.

"This most holy Synod . . . admonishes all the sons of the Church that the cult, especially the liturgical cult, of the Blessed Virgin, be generously fostered. It charges that practices and exercises of devotion toward her be treasured as recommended by the teaching authority of the Church in the course of centuries, and that those decrees issued in earlier times regarding the veneration of images of Christ, the Blessed Virgin, and the Saints, be religiously observed.

"But this Synod earnestly exhorts theologians and preachers of the divine word that in treating of the unique dignity of the Mother of God, they carefully and equally avoid the falsity of exaggeration on the one hand, and the excess of narrow-mindedness on the other. Pursuing the study of sacred Scripture, the holy

Fathers, the doctors, and liturgies of the Church, and under the guidance of the Church's teaching authority, let them rightly explain the offices and privileges of the Blessed Virgin which are always related to Christ, the Source of all truth, sanctity, and piety.

"Let them painstakingly guard against any word or deed which could lead separated brethren or anyone else into error regarding the true doctrine of the Church. Let the faithful remember moreover that true devotion consists neither in fruitless and passing emotion, nor in certain vain credulity. Rather, it proceeds from true faith, by which we are led to know the excellence of the Mother of God, and are moved to a filial love toward our mother and to the imitation of her virtues."

CO-REDEMPTRIX

As we begin to turn our thoughts to the next presentations which consider our relationship with God as Professed Religious, let us begin to take our clues as to just what this means by meditating on the Mary's role in redemption, and as a consequence the role of every Christian woman. In the Christian scheme of things, woman's cooperation with God for her role as a woman must be co-redemptive. This means that each woman, santified by baptism, is to perfect herself and lead others to perfection. It is a sobering thought that because of what you do, a human being or a whole world of human beings may come close to God or walk farther away from Him. Perfection of the Christian woman is to win God's life for others by being co-redemptrix like Mary.

CONCLUDING PRAYER

(The Singing of the "Salve Regina", perhaps by a special group, would be appropriate here.)

"Forgive me, if I have taken things too seriously, and forgotten fun and laughter.
Forgive me if I have allowed myself to be over-busy, with no time to stand and stare.
I pray now, for any who have lacked joy this day:
Any who have been without friendship;
Any who have missed the common decencies;
Any who have been without work;
Any blind, deaf, or crippled;
Any without strength of body;
Any wanting the mind's clear light;
Any without a sense of your presence;
Any who look into the future without expectancy.
We are your children amidst the immensities of time, and eternity.
Hold us in your keeping.
Amen. (From *A WOMAN'S BOOK OF PRAYERS* by
Rita Snowden. Collins, Fontana Books, c1968)

3. The Religious Dimension of our Relationship With God

PRESENTATION IX—Manifested in Prayer

(Note to Retreat Master: Suitable banners, posters, signs, etc. should be displayed in the retreat area. The last three TeleSPOTS on the film, "The Search" will be shown as the conclusion of this presentation.)

OPENING PRAYER

O God, bless this day every word, every service, every place which helps to bring us nearer to you.
Bless those who see you in circumstances that are outwardly discouraging.
Bless those who continue loyal in your service where there is none to see.
Bless those who witness to you in lands not their own, in a language not their own.
Bless those who prepare for the whole-time ministry of the Church in the world:

Give them unquestioning devotion and love;
Give them minds alert and flexible;
Give them bodies strong and practical.
Bless all whose gifts of speech and pen are devoted to healing the unhappy divi-
sions in the Church:
Save them from superiority;
Save them from shallow haste;
Save them from hindering discouragement.

(From *A WOMAN'S BOOK OF PRAYERS* by Rita Snowden, Collins, London c1968)

THE SIGN OF THE CROSS

After a severe attack of typhoid the small boy could neither swallow food nor speak. Nasal feeding was suggested. To test the tube that had been inserted through the boy's nose into his stomach, the doctor was about to pour a cup of water into the funnel end. "Stop, please," pleaded the boy's grandfather. "I forgot to make the sign of the cross over him. I have done that every time he has taken medicine." While he was making the sign of the cross another doctor, a relative of the boy, arrived. Just out of curiosity he examined the tube, and to his horror found that the tube had entered the lungs, rather than the stomach. Survival under those circumstances would have been extraordinary. The relative doctor said that, without knowing why, he had driven at top speed on his way to visit the family. (*Catholic Digest*, around 1944)

Not all of us have been so dramatically saved from a physical mishap. And, yet, it was "in the name of the Father, and of the Son, and of the Holy Spirit" that we were all baptised, and saved from a fate worse than physical death. Moreover, it was with the sign of the cross that our habits and ourselves were blessed on the day of our profession. Certainly we know the value of the prayer, the sign of the cross. Perhaps we need more frequent reflection on just what we are saying when we use this sacred sign. It is the motto for our relationship with God as Professed Religious. It is the summary, starting point, and conclusion of all other prayers that we engage in.

POWER OF PRAYER

"More things are wrought by prayer than this world dreams of." Our familiarity with these words makes them sound commonplace. Yet, we know they are true. And we believe in the efficacy of prayer. Listen to the entire poem by Lord Tennyson.

"If thou shouldst never see my face again,
Pray for my soul. More things are wrought by prayer
Than this world dreams of. Wherefore, let thy voice
Rise like a fountain for me, night and day.
For what are men better than sheep or goats
That nourish a blind life within the grain,
If, knowing God, they lift not hands of prayer
Both for themselves and those who call them friend?
For so the whole round earth is everywhere
Bound by golden chains about the feet of God."

No words, however, compare with those of Christ, when he speaks of the power of prayer. "Ask, and you will receive. Seek, and you will find. Knock, and it will be opened to you. For the one who asks, receives. The one who seeks, finds. The one who knocks, enters." (Mt. 7:7,8). And I am sure you recall the many other words that Christ spoke to convince his disciples of the power of prayer.

The "Pray Always" of both Christ and St. Paul has been turned into a greeting card poem by Helen Steiner Rice.

"Often during a busy day
I pause for a minute
to silently pray.
I mention the names
of those I love
And treasured friends

I am fondest of—
For it doesn't matter
where we pray
If we honestly mean
the words that we say,
For God is always listening to hear
The prayers that are
made by a heart
that's sincere."

PROBLEMS IN PRAYER

Certainly we believe in the power of prayer, even though on occasion we may doubt the efficacy of our own prayer. However, with religious, the problem with prayer is not that we quit praying because our prayers are not answered. Most of the time we let prayer go because we feel we are not getting anything out of them personally. The formats, the schedules, the times, the places all seem to become inimical to prayer. We get tired of the same words over and over again. We would like to feel more deeply the presence of God when we are praying. We would like to be able to adapt our mode and form of prayer to our own particular needs, and to select a time that is more suitable to us individually. All of these complaints are quite legitimate. Yet, solving them with no schedules, no places of prayer, no gathering of the community to pray, and such like remedies, would not improve the situation very much, if at all. It would seem that a look at the nature of prayer would point up much better the mode of praying that would be more satisfactory for the religious.

COMMUNICATION WITH GOD

Prayer is communication with God. It may be expressed silently, in words said to oneself, in words said or sung aloud, in gestures, postures, in all places and at all times. Almost everything can be a prayer. You are probably wearing a sacred medal, carrying your rosary beads, or showing devotion to a saint by having on your person a relic. Sometimes prayer is expressed in a call for help, or an exclamation of wonder at God's goodness, or an acclamation of his mercy. During World War II a young soldier wrote this unpublished letter to his sister.

"As I reached for my carbine, a shot struck me in the breast and blasted me down. Thinking I was dead, my pal jumped for me, grabbed my carbine as well as his own and blazed away with both guns . . . He was amazed when I rolled over and tried to get up. The force of the bullet had stunned me. Dazedly, I wondered why. I pulled that little Bible out of my pocket and in utter muteness looked at the ugly hole in the cover. The bullet had ripped through Genesis, Exodus, Leviticus, and through the other books, Samuel, Kings, and kept going. Where do you think it stopped? In the middle of Psalm 91, pointing like a finger at the verse: 'A thousand shall fall at thy side, and ten thousand at thy right hand; but it shall not come nigh thee. Only with thine eyes shalt thou behold and see the reward of the wicked." Sis, when I read that verse, it raised me three feet off the ground . . . In utter humility I said, 'Thank you, precious God.' "

The little Bible in his pocket was a prayer, his exhaltation on reading the verse was a prayer, and his words of humble thanks were a prayer. Thoughts, feelings, words, actions, things all communicate to God whatever we wish to say to him. This is prayer.

PROBLEMS IN COMMUNICATION

Prayer as a communication process suffers some of the problems of communication in other areas. The first barrier to good communication with God is language. Even in our private prayers we don't talk to God as if we were on familiar terms with him. We have to use archaic, formalized, and stale words, such as, "thou", "shouldst", "beseech". Surely God understands us in any language, or no language at all. But do we know what we are saying? Even in such a precious hymn as the "Magnificat", why do we have to say, "My soul doth magnify the Lord", instead of "My heart praises the Lord"? And even at that, what images are aroused by the language we use! Is your image of God enhanced by the term, "Lord"? Which image, created for you by these words, is better for you? "Covenant", "Agreement", "Contract", "Stipulation", "Compact", "Engagement", "Bargain", "Promise"—any one of these words expresses something of the relationship established with God by a profession of vows. At least in our private prayers let us communicate with God in language that is simple, straightforward, and yet humble.

When we add anxieties as barriers to the communication process, we have still more trouble with our prayers. We can be anxious about ourselves or about God or about our praying itself. In the "Deliver us . . ." prayer after the "Our Father" in the Communion Rite of the Mass, we have a most appropriate prayer for deliverance, especially so since it includes the motive of why we should be at peace and have confidence when we pray, or whatever else we do. "Deliver us, Lord, from every evil, and grant us peace in our day. In your mercy keep us free from sin and protect us from all anxiety as we wait in joyful hope for the coming of our Savior, Jesus Christ." Sometimes in community prayer we get anxious, call it up-tight, if you will, because someone says the wrong antiphon, or someone is dragging, or a thousand other things that distract us, especially in saying the office. Whenever we are more concerned about the formalities of our prayer (the right words, the right method, the right time, the right place) then our anxiety sets up a barrier to our communication with God. And when we worry about the outcome of our prayers, we concentrate on something that God has said that we leave to him. All we need to do is to pray with confidence. Schulz in one of his Peanuts cartoons touches on this urgency for prayer to produce excellent results immediately. Linus is shown sitting under a tree, apparently just relaxing. Next he has gone into the house and is confronted by Lucy.

"Where have you been?" demands Lucy.

"I've been meditating," responds Linus.

Lucy looks puzzled and affirms, "You don't look any different to me!"

So Linus explains, "Well, you see, I'm new at it."

Humbly putting ourselves in God's care, and then saying what's in our minds and hearts will do wonders for breaking down the barriers to the communication with God that we call "Prayer".

(Note: The material on this and the following pages is based on (1) "Prayer and Personal Religion" by John B. Coburn, and (2) the transcript of an interview with Thomas Merton shortly before his death.)

GOD BREAKS INTO OUR LIVES

(Note to Retreat Master: Some slides appropriate to the subject matter would be helpful during the following part of this presentation.)

Communication involves dialogue. And since prayer, as a function, is a communication process, it, too, involves dialogue. (Slide of someone praying.) It is God, however, who initiates the first step. He begins the relationship with us. Once God has begun the communication process then we can give our response, and we are praying. The very impulse to pray comes from God and this is his first step. (Slide of someone in an accident.) What is the first expression that comes to our lips when we witness a terrifying scene? "Oh, my God!" This is not blasphemy, but rather a cry from the depth of our souls inspired by our innately felt need for God's help. This is God touching our lives, entering into our being. And he enters differently into each person's life in this scene, but it is he who takes the first step. We can call this: "God breaking into our lives." (Slide of beautiful scene in nature.) Have you ever had the experience of being overwhelmed by the grandeur of God's creation? Such an experience, both exhalting and humbling you at the same time, is God's breaking into your life. (Slide of someone giving counsel.) Many times the vague, uneasy sense of something not just right with our lives is God touching us, and beginning the communication process of prayer. How we respond is important. Hopefully as we grow and mature in life our response will become more adequate to our prayerful relationship with God. (Slide of a saint.) We are inspired to become more than we normally are when we come face to face with saints. Again this is God breaking into our lives and asking us to respond in love—prayer.

SACRED SCRIPTURE— GOD BREAKING INTO OUR LIVES

(Slide of creation.) We live in the evidence of God's love. He first reached out to man in creation, making of man his friend, and giving him charge of all created things. The account of God breaking into the lives of those created in His own image and likeness fills the pages of both the Old and the New Testaments. (Slide of Christ.) But most of all God has entered our lives through His Son, Jesus Christ. In him God has given us the truth about Himself, ourselves, and others, and has shown us the way of response to His love. (Slide of medieval life.) In the middle ages Christ became the focal point of prayer and worship, and the structured life of the Church came to its peak. It is this period of the Church's history that has had the most profound effect on the prayer life of Christians. (Slide of European Cathedral.) Hand in hand with the development of society there developed the religious and social dimensions which, in effect, still rule and guide our lives today. Relationship with God and fellowman became catalogued in voluminous tomes, the dicta of which were visibly represented in stone, and glass, and precious jewels. Captions for these books, statues, pictures, stain glass windows were usually taken from the Bible to show when and how God had spoken to mankind. (End of slides.)

SOME OBSERVATIONS FROM THOMAS MERTON

Thomas Merton, about two weeks before his death, spoke with some acquaintances, who wanted to get his ideas on prayer. From a short pamphlet in which this conversation is reported, I have gathered the following remarks. The great thing about prayer is prayer itself. If you want a life of prayer, the way to get it is by praying. One recommendation is that we realize what we already have when we begin our prayer. Merton claims that everything has already been given to us by Christ. It is in prayer that we discover the abundance of this treasure. "The trouble is," says Merton, "we aren't taking time to do so. If we really want prayer, we'll have to give it time. We must slow down to a human tempo and we'll begin to have time to listen. As soon as we listen to what's going on, things will begin to take shape by themselves. We must approach the whole idea of time in a new way. We are free to love. And you must get free from all imaginary claims. We live in the fullness of time. Every moment is God's own good time. We don't have to rush after what we seek. It is there all the time, and if we give it time it will make itself known to us. This is what the Zen people do. They give a great deal of time to doing whatever they need to do. That's what we have to learn when it comes to prayer. We have to give it time."

THREE TeleSPOTS

As we conclude these remarks on the relationship with God established through the dimension of religious profession, let us experience in sight and sound some aspects of prayer: first, our attitude toward all men when we enter prayer; secondly, a reflection on Psalm 139; and thirdly, a hymn of praise. (Show the last three TeleSPOTS in the Franciscan film, "The Search".)

(Verses from Psalm 139)

CONCLUDING PRAYER

O Lord, you have probed me and you know me;
you know when I sit and when I stand;
you understand my thoughts from afar.
My journeys and my rest you scrutinize,
with all my ways you are familiar . . .
Where can I go from your spirit?
from your presence where can I flee?
If I got up to the heavens, you are there;
if I sink to the nether world, you are present there.
If I take the wings of the dawn,
if I settle at the farthest limits of the sea,
Even there your hand shall guide me,
and your right hand hold me fast.
If I say, "Surely the darkness shall hide me,
and night shall be my light"—
For you darkness itself is not dark,
and night shines as the day . . .
Probe me, O God, and know my heart;
try me, and know my thoughts;
See if my way is crooked,
and lead me in the way of old.

(Note to Retreat Master: If slides of the community making the retreat are available, they can be shown in the first part of this presentation.)

OPENING PRAYER

(Three prayers are presented here. Choose the one that most fits the group making the retreat. The prayers are from *A WOMAN'S BOOK OF PRAYERS* by Rita Snowden, already quoted from in this retreat material.)

A TEACHER'S PRAYER

O Lord of light and truth and love, I thank you for my place in your world family, for the training I have received; for the work I am allowed to do. I thank you for those from whom I have learned what I now know; for those around me continually probing and wondering and experimenting. I thank you for their glorious devotion to truth and beauty and service; for their great patience with growing minds. I remember with thankfulness my colleagues—especially (suggest they mention names silently)_____, and my friends _____, and my pupils_____. Inspire, inform, and support me this day. Amen.

A NURSE'S PRAYER

O God, my Father, I offer to you the love of my heart, the skills that reside in my hands and the strength of my body, this day.

Let the compassion of Jesus as he moved amongst the sick, ministering to the pain-wracked, the mentally distraught, and the frightened, be mine. When every bed in the ward is full and the bell keeps ringing and emergencies occur, keep me unflustered.

Grant me gentleness always, cheerfulness, and the power to match firmness with persuasion. So let me minister your gift of wholeness to those in my charge. Amen.

A SOCIAL WORKER'S PRAYER

O God, I am so glad that you have called me to work with people rather than with
*   things:*
They are your people, though they lay claims upon me;
They are your people, though they are often self-willed and foolish;
They are your people, though they bring suffering upon themselves, and upon
*   others.*
O God, I am grateful for my training, and for my colleagues who support me day
*   by day: but*
Every human situation presents new factors,
Every individual in trouble calls for a fresh concern.
O God, take my whole personality—body, mind and spirit, and work through
*   me:*
Deliver me from condemnation,
From arrogance, and intolerance,
From impatience.
O God, love these people, one by one, into new beginnings, and better life:
Meet them with sympathy always,
With gentleness when they need it,
With sternness when that can best serve.
For Christ's sake. Amen.

VOWS—A CONSIDERATION

Our consideration of the vows must begin with the thinking of the Church today as reflected in the documents of Vatican II. Chapter VI of the "Dogmatic Constitution on the Church" gives us the orientation to the life of the religious lived under vows. Since a retreat is not the time or the place to study these matters, it is hoped that opportunity has been provided, or will be offered, by the community to thoroughly investigate the nature of the vows and the consequent obligations assumed by each religious bound by them. Our purpose here is to put them in perspective to our whole lives, and to offer encouragement and inspiration in fulfilling them.

VATICAN II— CONSTITUTION ON THE CHURCH

Now then, the Bishops of Vatican II. "The evangelical counsels of chastity dedicated to God, poverty, and obedience are based upon the words and example of the Lord. They were further commended by the apostles and Fathers, and other teachers and shepherds of the Church. The counsels are a divine gift, which the Church has received from her Lord and which she ever preserves with the help of his grace." (#43) ". . . The teaching and example of the Divine Master laid the foundation for a pursuit of perfect charity through the exercise of the evangelical counsels, and [shows] how such a pursuit serves as a blazing emblem of the heavenly kingdom . . . From the very infancy of the Church, there have existed men and women who strove to follow Christ more freely and imitate Him more nearly by the practice of the evangelical counsels. Each in his own way, these souls have led a life dedicated to God . . . Hence the more ardently they unite themselves to Christ through a self-surrender involving their entire lives, the more vigorous becomes the life of the Church and the more abundantly her apostolate bears fruit." (#1)

VATICAN II— DECREE ON ADAPTATION AND RENEWAL

We have discussed the fact that we are members of the Mystical Body of Christ, living the life of religious. In our times renewal and adaptation of this life have become imperative. The thinking of the Church has been made manifest in the Decree on the Appropriate Renewal of the Religious Life from the documents of Vatican II. "The appropriate renewal of religious life involves two simultaneous processes: (1) a continuous return to the sources of all Christian life and to the original inspiration behind a given community and (2) an adjustment of the community to the changed conditions of the times." (#1 and 2) This statement forms the basis for all the considerations of renewal in the religious life in our times. A little different form of summary was given by one of the Fathers of the Council a few years ago. It was Cardinal Cushing of Boston who put it this way:

"If all the sleeping folks will wake up,
And all the lukewarm folks fire up,
And all the dishonest folks will confess up,
And all the disgruntled folks will sweeten up,
And all the discouraged folks will cheer up,
And all the depressed folks will look up,
And all the estranged folks will make up,
And all the gossipers will shut up,
And all the dry bones will shake up,
And all the true soldiers will stand up,
And all the members of the Church will pray up—
Then you can have the world's greatest renewal."

VOCATIONS—AN INDEX

The situation with vocations today is an index not only to the need for better recruitment, but more importantly, to the kind of service the younger generation wants to give to the Church through its dedications by the vows. (In this section suitable slides of the works of the proper community would be helpful.) (Slide of sister teaching.) If a young woman is thinking of a teaching congregation, it is obvious that what attracts her is not the idea of teaching geography or algebra or the domestic arts; what she wants is to become an apostle of Christ, to bring God to the world in and through the religious community. What decides her is the picture of a religious vowed to God and able to win souls for Him.

(Slide of sister nursing in a hospital.) It is the same if she is considering a hospital congregation. The young woman weighs the pros and cons of a lay nursing vocation and, if she then decides to enter religion, it is in order to be able to give the sick, and through them the world, not only nursing care but also the overflow of Christian life and happiness. She wants to be quite clear about the difference between being a lay nurse and being a nurse in religion.

(Slide of sister doing social work.) Many have found more opportunities to serve the disenfranchised in our society by not joining a religious community, or by leaving the community. So, there has to be another dimension to social service than the mere work involved, if one is to dedicate her life to this work. The one seeking this vocation desires it because in and through the religious congregation she can serve Christ better in his poor and suffering.

(Slide of sister taking vows.) The historical background of the religious life shows that the concept of the vows of religion being an extension and fulfillment of baptism has not been sufficiently underscored. This makes it understandable why the role of religious women as the moving spirits among women has not even been touched by the documents of Vatican II.

(Slide of sister at prayer.) Canon law has codified the religious life on the basis of the cloistered type of nun. This tends to inhibit rather than favor apostolic zeal. Only since Pius XII have we seen more supple adaptions appear. Those coming into religious life today want to see a much better balance between the life of prayer and that of active works. Both must improve.

(Slide of the community gathered together.) The ideal we are striving in these days of renewal and adaption is summed up in St. Paul's letter to the Colossians, the third chapter, verses twelve to seventeen. "Because you are God's chosen ones, holy and beloved, clothe yourselves with heartfelt mercy, with kindness, humility, meekness, and patience. Bear with one another; forgive whatever grievances you have against one another. Forgive as the Lord has forgiven you. Over all these virtues put on love, which binds the rest together and makes them perfect. Christ's peace must reign in your hearts, since as members of the one body you have been called to that peace. Dedicate yourselves to thankfulness. Let the word of Christ, rich as it is, dwell in you. In wisdom made perfect, instruct and admonish one another. Sing gratefully to God from your hearts in psalms, hymns, and inspired songs. Whatever you do, whether in speech or in action, do it in the name of the Lord Jesus. Give thanks to God the Father through him." St. Paul addresses these words to the lay Christians of his time. Do they not have all the more significance for those who have dedicated their lives to God in religion?

REFLECTION IN THE EYES OF THE LAITY

Many times we get a good idea of our needs when we see ourselves reflected in the eyes of others. It happened in a chapel of the Little Sisters of the Poor. Two old men inmates were sitting in the back of the chapel watching the renewal of profession by several of the nuns. "What are they doing?" one of the men asked the other. From years of dissipation and experience in reformation, the other whispered in a voice that carried all the way to the sanctuary, "They're going up to take the pledge."

Recently, on a serious note, I received the following reaction from a Catholic mother of five children who was doing some research work for me on retreats to Sisters. Let me read for you some of her reactions as she reported them to me.

"Perhaps I must admit that my views could be affected by the fact that I am a convert to the Church and any preconceived notions I have of what a sister is like came only from old Bing Crosby and Pat O'Brien movies. This image was a warm, outgoing creature with love radiating from her very being.

"My experiences, thus far, with few exceptions have caused my bubble, if not to pop, to droop exceedingly.

"My first experience was an invitation by a priest friend to attend some lectures he was giving at a local convent to take some notes. At first, I hesitated, as I, of course, had never been to a nun's home. After considering, I decided it would be a delightful opportunity. We were greeted at the door by a group of smiling sisters in today's modified garb. Father made brief introductions and then I found myself walking alone down long halls some feet behind Father who was surrounded by sisters. From then on I was on my own, as a guest in the home of strangers. In the back of the lecture room I found an inconspicuous place to sit. When Father began his lecture he made a brief mention of who I was and why I was there.

"At intermission there was chatting and dispersement for refreshments, and I found myself wondering if I should try to find anyone and the coffee pot, or just hide in the rest room until after the intermission. The second half of the lecture went as did the first.

"Mass was to follow the question and answer period, and so Father came to to show me the way to the Chapel. On the way to the Chapel small groups of sisters passed us, and they greeted Father in the usual way, with not a word or nod in my direction. After this occurred a couple of times, I got the funny feeling that perhaps by some strange miracle I had turned invisible. The cool, aloof propriety reminded me of my childhood visits to a home of relatives or friends where there was a lack of warmth and friendliness. It always left me with a feeling so heavy you could reach out and touch it. So different from going into the home of a stranger where a warm, glowing love made you feel welcome and the visit all too short. The feeling of coolness was accentuated at the time of the "Kiss of Peace". Since one or two rows separated me from an immediate partner to shake hands with, I looked around to see if there was anyone willing to receive an outsider's good wishes. I got no takers. All eyes were again cast down to pray, so I did likewise.

"This was my first experience as a guest in the convent. There were others in this same convent, and later in several others. My impressions have not always been as disappointing as my first, although subsequent visits to this first convent found the atmosphere as chilling as the first time. However, even at best, I still do not feel the overwhelming joy and love of Almighty God overflowing to place a mantle of welcome over the shoulders of the stranger in their midst."

DEDICATION

Whatever our life of vowed service says, it certainly must give evidence above all to the great love that God has shown us. In the discourse with his disciples at the Last Supper Jesus is recorded by St. John (17:22,23) putting the emphasis where it ought to be. "I have given them the glory you gave me that they may be one, as we are one—I living in them, you living in me—that their unity may be complete. So shall the world know that you sent me, and that you loved them as you loved me." In the renewal and adaption of our vows to the needs of the Church today, let us be careful not to be so caught up in the non-essentials that we do not have time or energy for that which is at the heart of the work of the Spirit in our times, namely the rededication of ourselves to the service of Christ under whatever circumstances we may find him. A little black boy was watching the balloon man at the county fair. There were all shapes and sizes and colors. Suddenly a red balloon broke loose, and soared high into the air until it could scarcely be seen. So many people were attracted by the sight that the vendor thought it might be a good idea to let another go. He let a bright yellow one slip free. Then he released a white one. The little black boy stood looking for a long time. Then he asked, "Mister, if you sent the black one up, would it go just as high as the others?" The balloon man, with an understanding smile, slipped the black one from its place and said, "Sonny, it isn't the color—it's the stuff inside that makes it rise."

ESCHATALOGICAL SIGN

Mixed emotions are always aroused when one refers to President John Kennedy. So be it. The following incident occurred when the premature baby born to the President and Mrs. Kennedy had taken a turn for the worse. The incident is recorded by two of the President's closest friends Kenneth P. O'Donnell and David F. Powers in an article in McCall's magazine for September 1972, entitled, "Johnny, We Hardly Knew You." "While they waited for an elevator to take them downstairs to the oxygen-chamber room, President Kennedy paced the hospital corridor restlessly and, looking into one of the rooms, noticed a baby girl who had been severely burned. He called the nurse and asked how the accident had happened. 'Does the child's mother visit her often?' he asked.

" 'Every day,' the nurse said.

"The President asked Dave for a pen and piece of paper. Holding the paper up against the glass of the room's corridor window, he wrote a note of sympathy to the mother, ending it, 'Keep up your courage—John F. Kennedy.'

"With his own baby dying downstairs,' Dave said, 'he had to stop and write a note to that poor woman.' "

Is it merely good humanitarian instinct that inspired that gesture of care and concern? I'd like to think that it goes beyond that. Because there is a belief in our ultimate union with God for all eternity, time and the things of time take on a new perspective. This is what our world desperately needs today. Call it a sense of values. But whatever, it needs to know that this is not the end of it; there is something magnificent to follow our brief span here. Whatever the dedication through the vows means, it must tell the world that we do believe in a hereafter, and that it is then our greatest fulfillment will come.

THE NUN IN THE WORLD TODAY

Let me conclude with some pertinent remarks by Cardinal Suenens in his book, *THE NUN IN THE WORLD* (The Newman Press, Westminster—Maryland, c1963).

"How does the religious appear in the world of today in the present state of woman's evolution? . . . One thing that strikes anyone who is at all observant is the immense place occupied by women in religion in the vast field of human suffering. 'Who suffers,' says St. Paul, 'and I do not suffer with him?' Women in religion live this phrase—at the bedside of the sick, with the handicapped and the bedridden, with the old people, lepers, deafmutes, and prisoners. They live it, day-long and year-long, with a devotion and disregard of self which compel our admiration. They are standing witnesses to the Church's maternal love, concerned about all our miseries, mindful always of the parable of the Good Samaritan and Our Lord's words about anything done 'for the least of these, my little ones'.

"Another striking feature is the considerable place they occupy at all levels in the world of education . . . People know that nuns have given up the possibility of a family of their own in order to be at the disposal of all families and be able to devote their whole care and attention to them . . . People admire the nuns of these teaching orders for their watchful devotion and the unstinted trouble they take.

"There are undoubtedly other ways in which religious are present in the world, for example in social assistance and parish work; but those we have mentioned are the most striking, and it is generally on them that the opinions and appreciation of the faithful are based."

CONCLUDING PRAYER

"O Mary, ever-blessed Virgin, Mother of God, Queen of the angels and the saints, I salute you with the most profound veneration and filial devotion. I renew the consecration of myself and all I have to you. I thank you for your maternal protection and for all the many blessings that I have received through your wondrous mercy and most powerful intercession . . . Protect me in life, guard and guide me in dangers, direct me in perplexities, lead me in the way of perfection, and assist me in the hour of my death, that I may come to Jesus, and with you enjoy Him, bless Him, and love Him eternally in heaven. Amen." (Adapted from PRAYER BOOK FOR RELIGIOUS by Father Lasance. Benzinger Bros., Inc. New York, c1934.)

PRESENTATION XI—Practiced Toward Christ

OPENING PRAYER

(Use one of the three prayers in Presentation X.)

ACCEPTANCE OF DEATH

"I don't see how you stand it. Don't you itch when you wear woolen drawers in May? I saw 40 pairs hanging on the nuns' clothesline this morning." This statement was made by a seven year old girl, just about ready to make her first holy communion. She had stumbled upon the room of a very ancient nun, Mere Supplice. The little girl noticed that the nun's face was yellow and cracked in a hundred places, the oldest person she had ever seen.

"Come closer," said Mere Supplice. The little girl felt the coldness of the bony hand. "My missal is on the table. Look there until you find a small blue card, a poem I learned when I was your age. Read it." The girl read.

"My soul, there is a country
Afar beyond the stars,
Where stands a winged sentry
All skillful in the wards . . .
If thou canst get but thither,
There grows the flower of Peace,
The Rose that cannot wither,

Thy fortress, and thy ease.
Leave then they foolish ranges—
For none can thee secure
But One who never changes—
Thy God, thy life, thy cure."

"Did you understand the poem?" Mere Supplice asked.

"Not at all; it says being dead's not so terrible."

"Will you do something for me?"

"Oh, yes, Mere Supplice!"

"Tomorrow when you go to the altar for the first time, give Him a message for me. Tell Him to please call me soon. I'm tired. I've waited so long."

When the girl returned to the main part of the convent she did not mention meeting Mere Supplice, or of learning Henry Vaughan's poem. But she did remember the message, and next morning after communion, she said, "Thank you, Lord, for the shoes. Please take care of Prince and Mother Gabrielle. Mere Supplice says please let her die—she's tired of waiting."

During the celebration after the mass, the portress whispered to the Mother Superior, who nodded her head.

"My dear Sisters in Christ, my dear children, Mere Supplice has gone from this life into eternity."

(This story is adapted from "Readers' of the Catholic Digest Choice".)

One thing the world needs is the acceptance of death. Your experiences, Sisters, have demonstrated to you, that perhaps except in old age and after long suffering, death is not looked upon with peace. This is one of the prime areas in which you can make Christ present in the world.

THE CHOICE OF DEATH

Because a woman's role is so intimately connected with life, she can accept death more knowingly than a man. And it's not because women live longer than men and after a long life find death a release. There is something unique in woman's connection with life and death. How else could the Blessed Mother have accepted the death of her Son, and not gone raving mad? There is mystery here. There is the revelation that when a woman gives life, she gives it not only for time, but for eternity. Since only a woman can fully experience and appreciate the process of birth that gives life, so it seems that she, more than man, can sense the giving of eternal life in the act of dying. Today everything that we see, or are encouraged to do, attempts to prolong life here, and to put off death until there is no further possibility of life. Our funerals are travesties of the real significance of death and its eternal meanings. Women, because they choose the possibility of death each time they give life, have a vocation to teach others how and why a deliberate choice of death is service to Christ. But, first you must make your own choice. While you are able make an act of acceptance of how and when you will die. Not because the manner of your death is clear to you, but because this greatest moment of life should be entered into freely and honorably. It does seem a little like suicide. But it is exactly the opposite. In suicide one takes death as a way out. In accepting the death God wills for us, we choose to be united with his Son in the redemption of the world and of ourselves, and thus enter upon the glorious climax of a temporary life now turned into life eternal. Once each of us has accepted death in union with that of Christ, then we can help others to make the choice of death that will be redemptive for them. Only by choosing wisely in the options that life brings to us will we be able to make that final option when the last moment comes. A woman is better able than a man to serve Christ at that moment as he dies once again in each of his members.

WOMAN'S ROLE

Let's look for a minute at the turmoil that comes to a couple when they try to reserve their roles from life-giving to, if not death-dealing, then life-denying. (Show TeleSPOT, "Signs of Love".)

Notice in the film how the resolving of the problem is brought about by their young daughter, a potential woman. Her instinct is for life. There are many things our world needs today. Perhaps that which we lack most is an enthusiasm for living. To promote this is the role of the Christian woman, and especially of one dedicated to the service of Christ. Pessimism, cynicism, bitterness can only be overcome by one who understands the love that Christ gave to the world. Can you think of the Blessed Mother as being on the verge of despair? Yet, many in our world are. It takes women who understand life and death to offer mankind the smile of hope. To fulfill your role as religious woman in the Church today, or in other words, to practice your relationship with God as a religious toward the Christ whom you serve, you have to know who and what you are in the Church today.

THE WORLD WE LIVE IN

Rather than discuss the modern history of woman, or go back to the problem of Eve, with which we are familiar enough, or even delve into St. Paul's masterful comparison of Eve and Mary, let us stay with our own times. The world we live in has been presented to us in hundreds of versions on television. The one where the contrast seems the greatest is in "All in the Family". The contrast is evident between Edith and her young married daughter, Gloria. However, there is even greater contrast between Edith Bunker, and the actress who portrays this lovable ding-bat, Jean Stapleton. In an article in McCall's magazine for September 1972, Mrs. William Putch (Jean Stapleton), makes some remarks that throw light on women in the world we live in, at least, as we know it in the American culture.

JEAN VERSUS EDITH

"I'm a liberated woman because I have a liberated husband," Jean says. Things work out smoothly in their family "because Bill is willing to do the jobs most people think only women should do. Archie might question his masculinity on this score. I don't."

Her Christian Science friends are among her greatest boosters. "Jean's successful, yes, but she doesn't forget the principles she's always stood for," says Mrs. James Hyatt of Chambersburg, who is Pamela's godmother (Pam is Jean's 13-year-old daughter). "She hasn't changed, except to get younger, happier and prettier."

Charles E. Perkins, a retired admiral from Carlisle, calls her a "whole, modern, Christian woman. Nothing will ever change her, she's so fundamentally sound."

One would hardly characterize Edith Bunker in such terms. "Edith is honest, warm and compassionate, which is why people like her," Jean says. "She is free of prejudice, intuitive and totally guileless, and she has a great capacity for enjoying people." The same words might be used to describe Jean, but Jean believes "I may not have the same compassion or be that unprejudiced. Edith is fearless in her honesty, and I don't think I can match her in that."

On the minus side, Jean sees Edith's life as "constricted." "She is apathetic about the world around her, ignorant, submissive, slow thinking. I always feel she thinks through a kind of haze.

"Edith and I are about the same age," she continues, "but her clothes and hair make her seem older. I also think her attitude ages her, it's so outdated."

THE LIBERATED WOMAN

"Outdated" is perhaps the best word to sum up the reasons for changes in women today. Jean Stapleton and Edith Bunker are pretty good examples of the "before" and "after" types of persons the world looks for in women today. Jean says she is a "liberated" woman, while her counterpart, Edith, is "constricted." Jean is a "whole, modern, Christian woman". This is the kind of woman the Church wants its Nuns and Sisters today to be, "whole, modern, Christian women". In paragraph 10 of the Decree on the Appropriate Renewal of the Religious Life from Vatican II we read: "The lay religious life, for both men and women, constitutes a state which of itself is one of total dedication to the profession of the evangelical counsels. This sacred Synod highly esteems such a life, since it serves the pastoral work of the Church so usefully by educating the young, caring for the sick, and discharging other services: The Council supports such religious in their vocation, and entreats them to adapt their life to modern needs". One adjustment of paramount importance is that of liberation. The liberated woman is not one who does whatever she pleases, when, where, however, with no regard for the laws of God or man, or the requirements of the neighbor. Rather her freedom is in the choices she makes to give her life for the needs of her fellowman. Again to use an old analogy: woman has the choice of being Eve or Mary. Either she ennobles her society by her presence, by creating a climate of beauty and human dignity, or she drags that society down to the level of inhumaness and lack of love. Even Lenin was able to write, "The experience of all movements of liberation proves that the success of a revolution depends upon the degree of participation by women." If the modern Christian woman must be a liberated woman if she is to fulfill her role, how much more so the religious woman! The place occupied by women in the world of today brings new dimensions to the apostolic work of the contemporary religious.

THE LIBERATED RELIGIOUS WOMAN

"Christianity is the greatest and most radical revolution for freedom in all history. The apostolate means nothing but the penetration of Christ through us to mankind and to society. The participation of women religious in the work of the apostolate can now be seen in high relief: their feminineness, with all that means today for their contribution, cannot be betrayed or stifled but must on the contrary be expanded and fortified by their vocation." (Cardinal Suenens, "The Nun in the World") The freedom of the woman religious today must be in her freedom of choice, the freedom to choose God's will. Much effort was expended by the community and herself to determine that this woman was entering religion of her own free will. Presumably, the professed religious remains in the religious life out of free choice. Hopefully, the structure of her community gives her the opportunities necessary to make free choices of the circumstances in which she will spend her life for Christ. Obviously, her choices will be made in the spirit of the founder of her community. John Henry Newman summed up quite well our approach here in the following analysis.

> "God has created me to do Him
> some definite service;
> He has committed some work to me
> which he has not committed to another.
> I have my mission . . .
> I am a link in a chain,
> a bond of connection between persons.
> He has not created me for naught.
> I shall do good. I shall do his work.
> I shall be an angel of peace,
> a preacher of truth in my own place
> while not intending it—
> if I do but keep His commandments.
> Therefore I will trust Him.
> Whatever, wherever I am,
> I can never be thrown away.
> If I am in sickness,
> my sickness may serve Him;
> in perplexity,
> my perplexity may serve Him;
> If I am in sorrow,
> my sorrow may serve Him.
> He does nothing in vain,
> He knows what He is about."
> (Christopher Notes, May 1971—No. 187.)

MARY, THE FREE WOMAN

In order to satisfy your minds on this business of freedom in religious life, let me ask you to meditate on the Annunciation account in St. Luke's gospel. Here you find Mary having the will of God announced to her. Even though it comes from an angel, Mary does not accept it blindly. No, she questions the angel carefully, especially as to the essential feature of what God is asking of her, namely, her virginity versus motherhood. Only when she is assured that God is aware of her own personal inclinations and desires, and that He will respect them, does she agree to become the Mother of God. Questioning God's will is not against humility, if it is done in Mary's way. In fact, to go blindly into any activity and say that it is the will of God, simply because someone has told us it is the will of God, is to act foolishly. We need to examine the facts of the case, pray over them, and then humbly make a decision we feel God will bless. The freedom Mary exercised in the Annunciation account was not the liberty to do anything she wanted, under any circumstances whatever. Rather, her freedom was to embrace with her total person what she had become convinced was the will of God for her. "Mary said: 'I am the servant of the Lord. Let it be done to me as you say.'" (Luke, 1:38) Because of this choice, Mary also accepted whatever would be its consequences. The joy of motherhood was hers, while still retaining the crown of virginity. The glory of having such a Son had to be shared with the ignominy of the crucifixion. The loneliness of separation was accepted before the magnificence of eternal union could be attained. We began this presentation with the story of a nun's acceptance of death. Because Mary was a free woman, freer than any other could ever be because of the special perogative of being immaculate, she was free to choose the death of her son, and her own union in that death for the redemption of mankind. This is the greatest choice offered to anyone. But it seems that, because of our intellectual preoccupation with a life lived to the full of it material possibilities, we need women who know what love must choose as the most important values in our society today. This is where the effective choices of women in religion can show us the way. Let us conclude by calling upon Mary to not only show the way, but also to obtain the graces needed to be truly liberated women, "free, with the freedom wherewith Christ has made us free."

CONCLUDING PRAYER   (Recite the "Angelus.")

PRESENTATION XII—In Service To the Neighbor

OPENING PRAYER   (Use one of the three at the beginning of Presentation X.)

WISHING   What would you wish men to do to you . . . ?
If you were totally alone, elderly and unable to care for yourself.
If you could not earn a living wage or secure the training needed to develop your basic skills.
If you were prevented from bettering yourself because of a physical or mental handicap.
If your children went to bed, night after night, hungry and undernourished.
If you were trapped into debt by inability to obtain banking services enjoyed by most people.
If you never had skilled, dedicated teachers to guide and inspire you to read and write properly.
If you were the victim of injustice created by political inefficiency or corruption.
If you and your family were forced to live in a one-room shack or a run-down tenement with little hope of ever getting out.
If you were unwittingly drifting into a life of drug addiction or crime.
If you were among the 80 percent of neglected children who have not seen a doctor or dentist for ten years.
If you were denied the God-given right to choose the neighborhood in which your family is qualified, both culturally and economically to live.
If you never received encouragement, a sense of personal worth or kindly discipline from a mother or a father—or anyone else who cared enough to teach you how to love.
What would I wish someone to do for me in such circumstances? I would like to feel that I would be one whom he would love and help. Then, the words of scripture come back to haunt me, "As you wish that men would do to you, do so to them" (Lk. 6:31). (Homiletic and Pastoral Review, Nov. 1969.)

UNIVERSAL YARDSTICK   Wise men in every age have recognized that there is but a single yardstick by which to measure our relationship with our fellow man. The world's great religions put it this way: (cf. Christopher Notes, June-July 1968—No. 167)

Buddhism: "Hurt not others in ways that you yourself would find hurtful." (Udanavarga 5:18)

Hinduism: "This is the sum of duty: do naught unto others which would cause you pain if done to you." (Mahabharata 5:1517)

Islam: "No one of you is a believer until he desires for his brother that which he desires for himself." (Sunan)

Judaism: "What is hateful to you, do not to your fellow man. That is the entire Law: all the rest is commentary." (Talmud, Shabbat 31a)

Christianity: "Whatsoever you wish that men would do to you, do so to them; for this is the law and the prophets." (Mt. 7:12)

So, the norm for charity is established. Christ did unto us what he wished we would do unto him. When he was on trial for his life the question came up as to what harm he had done others. Witnesses had to be bribed to lie so that something could be held against him. But Christ went beyond merely establishing a norm by his teaching and by his example. He added the reward of eternal life for practicing charity to others in his name, so that it would be the same as if we had done it for him personally.

BRINGING GOD TO OTHERS

As the world turns more and more away from God, it becomes more and more our responsibility to lead it back to him. Whatever else religious life accomplishes, its apostolate is to bring God to men and men to God. Theoretical knowledge will not accomplish the task. God can only be shown to others through love, manifested by our care and concern for them. Notice how this is highly dramatized in the one-minute TeleSPOT, entitled "The Puzzle". (Show the film.)

ARE YOU GOD?

This question is asked in many different ways: What is God like? What is the Church? Who is Jesus Christ? These are just a few of the forms the question takes. It is the human seeking the Divine to which it is related. Because we have been given the opportunity of experiencing our relationship with God on the three levels of our humanity, of Christianity, and of our religious profession, we are not only equipped to answer the question, but our lives must show the Way, and the Truth, and the Life. God can come to each individual in any way He chooses. However, we do know that His ordinary way is through nature, the Scriptures, through Christ and his Church. "For the One whom God has sent speaks the words of God; he does not ration his gift of the Spirit." (Jn. 3:34) Furthermore, we are the Church. So it is incumbent on each one of us to manifest God's saving mercy to all men. We know that this is the objective of our lives. But in this presentation let us try to particularize what special needs should be met, especially by those members of Christ who are women.

SURCEASE FROM TURMOIL

You step across the threshold as the doors close silently behind you. You feel the thrill of peace and quiet. From the stained glass windows Technicolored lights and shadows filter across the floor and onto the walls. In the quiet sanctuary a reddened candle light silently beckons you closer. As you move up the aisle of the nearly empty chapel, a feeling of awe and reverence wraps you in warmth and love. You genuflect and enter a pew near the front. Weariness and tensions drop away as if you were shedding a coat that has become too stiffling and heavy. The words of comfort seem to float from the tabernacle and come to rest within your restless heart. "Come to me, all you who are weary and find life burdensome, and I will refresh you." (Mt. 11:28) Before you go to others to offer them surcease from turmoil, gather to yourself the peace and inner contentment that comes from Christ. Women have a feeling for peace.

REVERENCE

Christ in the Blessed Sacrament also teaches us reverence. Reverence is so much needed in a world of violence. Where there is no reverence for things, and places, and events, and persons, then there is violence. And where there is violence there is no peace. One of the basic needs of our society, if it is going to achieve peace, is the restoration of the sense of reverence. Certainly it is the feminine instinct for life that causes woman to hold sacred the creative power God has given her. We must have reverence for God's creation of land and sky and ocean and lakes and valleys and rivers and rolling hills; reverence for atomic power and the blossoming of a flower; reverence for skyscrapers and the lowly hovel; reverence for the crowded city and the open countryside; reverence for culture and traditions of a nation; reverence for the sacredness of life, of marriage, of honesty, of the religious life, of downright goodness and love. We are a violent civilization because we have lost the sense of reverence for the holy in all of God's creation. When once again we have a feeling for the sacredness of human life in the womb, in our homes, on the highways, in our schools, in business, on our battlefields, in our prisons and concentration camps, and in all the things and events of life, then we will live in a world of peace, a world full of love and life, not of hatred and of death.

EXPERIENCING THE SACRED

Because you are women you experience more sensitively the sacredness in all things. Because you are women consecrated to God in religion this experience is accentuated in Christ. Lilies of the field, birds of the air, sheep in the pasture, lightning and thunder, seed being sown, wheat being harvested, all these captured Christ's attention. Nothing was trivial to him, since everything was created by His Father, and was to be redeemed by Himself. And, so, when he took bread in his hands, the reverence in which he held it caused him to look up to His heavenly Father and give Him thanks and praise. Likewise with the cup of wine. What awe the apostles must have felt as he gave them the loaf and the cup and told them to eat and drink for this was His Body and Blood! How precious that moment! A moment to be cherished, not only in memory for all ages, but in the actuality repeated by ourselves in every mass! No wonder there is a sense of respectful awe, and a feeling of peace, when we come before the priest and he gives us "The Body of Christ".

HUMAN DIGNITY

"The advancement of woman in our society has become a part of our customs. Never before has woman's influence been so noticeable. Never has her psychological ascendancy been more pronounced . . . Thanks to the development of her personality and culture, she takes part in her own characteristic manner in the social, economic and literary life of the world. She no longer acts through man by her influence on him, but in her own right and under her own colors . . . Woman holds the moral destiny of the world in her hand today more than at any other time in history." (Cardinal Suenens)

One area in which her moral influence must be felt is in the recognition of human dignity. There are two statements in the documents of Vatican II which women in religion can implement.

"For God has called man and still calls him so that with his entire being he might be joined to Him in an endless sharing of a divine life beyond all corruption. Christ won this victory when He rose to life, since by His death He freed man from death. Hence to every thoughtful man a solidly established faith provides the answer to his anxiety about what the future holds for him. At the same time faith gives him the power to be united in Christ with his loved ones who have already been snatched away by death. Faith arouses the hope that they have found true life with God." (Pastoral Constitution on the Church in the Modern World, #18)

"Drawn from the treasures of Church teaching, the proposals of this sacred Synod look to the assistance of every man of our time, whether he believes in God, or does not explicitly recognize Him. Their purpose is to help men gain a sharper insight into their full destiny, so that they can fashion the world more to man's surpassing dignity, search for a brotherhood which is universal and more deeply rooted, and meet the urgencies of our age with a gallant and unified effort born of love." (#91)

MORE THAN "DO-GOODERS"

Obviously, your call is to be more than "do-gooders" in the classroom, hospital, slum homes, wherever you minister to Christ. In the "Tumbleweeds" comic strip for October 22, 1972, the local town drunk is hauled into court once again. The judge reprimands him: "It's no wonder you're an habitual sot, Sopwell! All you ever think of are Bars, Taverns and Saloons. I'll let you off this time if you promise me you'll make a serious effort to improve your thought! To think of better, more important things!"

"Promish!" declares the drunk. Later the drunk and a companion are sitting on the steps of the Nugget Saloon.

"Penny for yer thoughts, Soppy," suggests the companion. Sopwell, the drunk replies in one word, "Distilleries."

How often have you found those who you were helping keeping the letter of your recommendations, but missing entirely the spirit. This is where the difference comes. And it does not come through words, and policies, and formularies. But it does have its impact when the human dignity of every man can be seen reflected in the lives of those who cherish what God has given to them. Therefore, in your dress, in your speech, in your actions, Sisters, you must be a person of humble, simple, cheerful human dignity. Most of all, those who are weighed down by the burdens and care of life must see a beautiful person—one who radiates by her enthusiasm for life the goodness and mercy of a God who loves all men. And don't be afraid to repeat your lesson over and over again. Even weight-watchers need the encouragement of a weekly meeting to inspire them to keep to their diet.

LISTEN CHRISTIAN! For the purposes of provoking serious meditation and firm resolutions in your apostolate, let me show a series of filmstrips entitled, "Listen Christian." (Show the filmstrip. Captions are printed on the filmstrip.)

(Note to Retreat Master: If there is still time, a very effective presentation can be made by showing the "Eucharist" film on one screen, and next to it on another screen slides of various activities and works of the community making the retreat.)

CONCLUSION As we conclude our presentations, Sisters, let me thank you for your cooperation during this retreat. I am especially grateful for your prayers, and ask you to continue to remember me in them, as I will remember you. Let us now end with part of a prayer to Our Blessed Mother composed by Pope Pius XII for the Marian Year, 1954.

"O well-beloved of God, hear the ardent cry which rises from every heart . . . dedicated to you. Bend tenderly over our aching wounds. Convert the wicked, dry the tears of the afflicted and oppressed, comfort the poor and humble, quench hatreds, sweeten harshness, safeguard the flower of purity in youth, protect the holy Church, make all men feel the attraction of Christian goodness. In your name, resounding harmoniously in heaven, may they recognize that they are brothers, and that the nations are members of one family, upon which may there shine forth the sun of a universal and sincere peace."

E. MATERIALS/RESOURCES

1. EXPECTATIONS

Sisters, your comments will help immeasurably. Write on back side of paper or add another sheet if you wish. Thank you.

1. In general, what do you hope for from this retreat?

2. What topics would you like treated in the conferences and discussions?

3. What topics would you like not to be treated?

4. Are you agreeable to engage in small group discussions? And small group prayer?

5. What is your opinion of the use of audio-visuals during retreat?

6. Please state your preferences in regard to the Liturgy of the Mass.

7. How do you feel about prayer in common: Morning Prayer, The Rosary, The Way of the Cross, Benediction?

8. May I count on your help for leadership in a) Discussions, b) Prayer Groups, c) Liturgy of the Mass, d) Recreation?

9. During meals, what is your preference: a) Music, b) Reading, c) Talking, d) Silence?

10. Each evening will be "free time". Let me know if you would like to organize something. Do you have any suggestions?

Please comment on any other aspects of the annual retreat that you think would be helpful to the other Sisters or myself.

2. RESULTS OF "EXPECTATIONS" QUESTIONNAIRE

In a recent retreat (Summer 1972) to forty-five Daughters of Charity, ranging in age from twenty-eight to seventy-five, and engaged in teaching, social work, nursing, and hospital administration, the expectations ran as follows, among the twenty-six who made their desires known.

1. In general, what do you hope for from this retreat?
Eighteen wanted better knowledge of self and relation to God.
Seventeen asked to be helped to a deeper spirit of prayer.
Fifteen felt they would like much time for solitude and relaxation.
Eight said that they needed revitalization.
New insights, appreciation of vocation in present times were mentioned by a few.

2. and 3. (Conference Topics) Over half of those answering wanted talks on Community Life in Today's World.
Ten wished "Acceptance of Each Other (as is—now)" treated.
Eight dealt with the problem of being oneself and doing God's Will within the structure of community life today.
Six thought that "Human Relations" was an important topic to be discussed.
Five wanted talks on Prayer.
Other topics mentioned were the following: Liturgy, Scripture, Personality of Christ, Appealing to Youth, New Approaches to the Sacrament of Penance, Healing Through One Another, Mary, Christian Joy, Creation, Vows, "New Morality", Discerning Spirit of God from the Spirit of the Devil, and "Need for Local Superior?" There were no strong indications against any topics, but the following one or two asked be avoided: Dogmatic Theology, Way-Out (Shocking Ideas), Defections from Religious Life, Frequent Referral to the Old Days, Things Dealing with Elementary Catechism, Hell, and Dialogue-Discussion Type Conferences.

4. Of the twenty-three who responded to the question on discussion groups, thirteen favored them, while ten did not. As it actually turned out during

the retreat, very few engaged in the general discussions, while about half of those making the retreat participated in small group discussions.

5. The majority were in favor of audio-visuals, but requested moderation in their use.

6. Not many preferences were stated in regard to the Liturgy of the Mass, except that it be well planned and celebrated with dignity and simplicity. Several asked that attention be focused on Christ, not on diversions.

7. Of the prayer forms mentioned in the questionnaire, except for the Divine Office, the majority preferred that prayers said in common be on a voluntary attendance basis. During this retreat the voluntary attendance exercises were well attended.

8. Five said they would give leadership in the areas requested, while twenty preferred not to act as leaders.

9. The majority preferred music during the meals, while only five said that they preferred the opportunity to talk.

10. The "free time" in the evening seemed to be preferred as just that, "free time", so that most of the retreatants used the time for private prayer, silence, rest, and other individual interests. Small groups did take the opportunity to view a couple of movies, to engage in group prayer, and to engage in small group discussions.

This retreat master found the "Expectations" questionnaire very helpful for his own information, and the use of it did focus the attention of the retreatants on the purpose of the retreat, better, he thinks, than a formal conference usually does.

3. EVALUATIONS

Sisters, your evaluations will help in estimating the results of this retreat. In addition, they will help in the planning of future retreats. Write on back side of paper or add another sheet if you wish. Thank you.

1. In general, were your expectations of this retreat realized?

2. What were you most pleased with?

3. What pleased you the least?

4. What are your reactions to the conferences?

5. Did you find the general and group discussions helpful?

6. Please comment on the Liturgy of the Mass.

7. Please comment on Morning Prayer.

8. Did you find the audio-visuals helpful?

9. Were you pleased with the use of the "free time" in the evenings?

10. What recommendations would you make for future retreats?

4. FEED-BACK

An extremely important feature of the retreat is obtaining the reactions of the retreatants, called "Feed-Back".

1. Questions and Answers. These can be obtained at the end of each presentation in a spontaneous way. A more formal way, which gives the retreat master a chance to prepare his answers, is the use of the question box, placed in a suitable spot for the Sisters.

2. The remarks made during the general discussions also give the retreat master some idea of how and what he is communicating.

3. During private interviews the retreat master can take the opportunity of sounding out the one he is interviewing.

4. Finally, at the end of the retreat make sure that the Evaluation sheet has been filled out. Some encouragement to have the Sisters do so is usually needed.

5. For the retreat master's future reference he ought to make tape recordings of the presentations, general discussions, and the homilies at the liturgy.

6. To fill in the background of the tape recordings the retreat master might ask one of the Sisters to take notes on reactions of the retreatants during the presentations, discussions and homilies.

5. Readings

1) Confession: Suggested Rite of Communal Celebration

INTRODUCTION

"They (the sacraments) are ecclesial acts of worship, in which the Church in communion of grace with its heavenly Head (i.e., together with Christ) pleads with the Father for the bestowal of grace on the recipient of the sacrament, and in which at the same time the Church itself, as saving community in holy union with Christ, performs a saving act."

Schillebeeckx, E. *CHRIST THE SACRAMENT OF THE ENCOUNTER WITH GOD*, p. 66. (New York, Sheed and Ward, 1963).

"That sin is socially pernicious and conversion socially constructive is very clearly expressed in the various penitential rites of the Church, particularly in the rite of the sacrament itself; the contrite sinner confesses not only before God, the source and goal of the entire sacred community, but also before the Church, militant and triumphant, and, above all, in the presence of the priest, visible representative of God and the Church. For sin has offended the Church, marred her harmony and unity; and conversion must lead the sinner back again to the community of love and life in the Church. Conversion—such is the clear meaning of the rites of the Church—is not the result of personal effort, but grace and gift from the sacred community of the kingdom of God, with which the sinner by his own free endeavor must cooperate toward reacceptance."

Häring, B. *THE LAW OF CHRIST*, Vol. 1, 415. (Westminster, Maryland, Newman Press, 1961).

This presentation consists of a brief explanation of the rite, the rite itself, and a suggested homily for the theme of mortification.

EXPLANATION

Without substantially changing the present ritual of confession, this community celebration seeks to emphasize the communal aspects of the sacrament of penance. It is suggested that this type of celebration works best with a group of from thirty to forty persons united together by some common bond, such as that of belonging to a society. For this number two confessors would suffice, one of whom would be the celebrant.

Approximately ten minutes before the celebration is to begin let the celebrant gather those who are going to participate outside the church proper, e.g., in the vestibule, or in the baptistry, for his explanation of the celebration and the procedures to be followed.

An explanation based on the above quotations from Fathers Schillebeeckx and Häring should emphasize the communal aspects of the rite. Full participation in the singing of the hymns and in the various responses should be encouraged. It is important to indicate that the telling of one's sins and the receiving of absolution is still done privately in the confessional. Because of the background of a particular group, the celebrant may find it necessary to review briefly the conditions necessary for a worthy confession, and then to point out how this rite meets all the requirements.

The celebrant should appoint and instruct those who will be active participants in the ceremonies: thurifer, cross bearer, acolytes to carry lighted candles, book bearer, music director, lector, commentator, and examiner.

Suitably the celebrant should be vested in cassock, surplice, violet stole and violet cope. Let him remove the cope while hearing the confessions, and then after all are heard, let him replace the violet stole with a white one and put on a white cope. The changing of the colors might be commented on as an external manifestation of the renewed Christian spirit through the reception of the sacrament.

When all are ready let the assembly line up two-by-two, and, preceded by the thurifer, cross bearer, acolytes, and book bearer, let them, singing the entrance hymn, proceed into the church and take their places in the front pews. It is important that they be grouped closely together. The celebrant follows the last pair, stands before the lectern where the book bearer has placed the open Bible, and, when the hymn is concluded, puts incense into the thurible and incenses the book. He then faces the assembly and proceeds with the opening greeting. The rest follows according to the suggested rite.

A suggested reading is that taken from the Gospel according to St. John, chapter 12, verses 23 to 36. A homily suitable for this theme of mortification follows the text of this rite. For the penance it seems useful to have all say a prayer together such as the 129th psalm ("Out of the Depths"), for which the celebrant should provide copies, and then give them the choice of doing one act of penance on their own sometime within the next couple of days, such as, giving an alms to the poor, not smoking for an hour, etc.

The rite presented here, including the explanation, homily, and the hearing of the confessions does not, normally, exceed one hour in length. Obviously, this rite can be adapted to other themes by changing accordingly the hymns, reading, homily, examination of conscience, petitions, and penance.

RITE

(The celebrant, vested in cassock, surplice, violet stole and cope, having incensed the Bible, faces the assembly and greets them. They stand.)

CELEBRANT: The Lord be with you.

ALL: And with your spirit.

CELEBRANT: Let us pray. Be pleased, we pray you Lord, to enlighten your servants with the light of your understanding. Cleanse them and make them holy that they may be able to renew the grace of their baptism. We ask you this through our Lord, Jesus Christ, who lives and reigns with you together with the Holy Spirit, God, forever and ever.

ALL: Amen.
(All are seated. The lector reads a passage from the Scriptures. After the reading the celebrant delivers the homily. Suggested reading: John 12:23-36.)

CELEBRANT: *(All kneel.)* Dearly beloved in Christ, what is your request?

ALL: We ask your blessing, Father, for we acknowledge that we are sinners; and we wish to renew our conversion to the Lord in his holy Church.

CELEBRANT: May the Lord be in your hearts and on your lips, that you may listen to the Good News of his salvation, take courage in his unspeakable love for all of us, and properly confess all your sins in the name ✚ of the Father, and of the Son, and of the Holy Spirit.

ALL: Amen.

CELEBRANT: Let us all pray the "I confess":

ALL: I confess to almighty God, to blessed Mary ever Virgin, to blessed Michael the Archangel, to blessed John the Baptist, to the holy Apostles Peter and Paul, to all the Saints, to you, Father, and to those of you here joined with me in this celebration of the sacrament of penance, that I have sinned exceedingly in thought, word and deed; through my fault, through my fault, through my most grievous fault.

CELEBRANT: Please be seated for the examination of conscience. The commentator will direct your thoughts to the words of Christ, and the examiner will suggest points for your examination.
(The commentator and the examiner come forward and face the assembly. The examiner should pause briefly after each question. After the examination is concluded they return to their places.)

Let us consider our attitudes toward penance and mortification. Our Lord has said: "I solemnly assure you, unless the grain of wheat falls into the earth and dies, it remains just a grain of wheat. But if it dies, it bears much fruit. The man who loves himself destroys himself; while the man who hates himself in this world, preserves himself for eternal life" (Jn. 12:24-25).

Am I convinced of the need for penance and mortification . . . to make reparation for past offenses . . . to develop self-control?
Do I neglect bodily mortification on the pretext that spiritual mortification is more important?
Have I understood that the spirit of mortification is part of my Christian heritage?
Have I not observed that self-mastery is one of the primary conditions of one's influence for good with family and friends?
Have I developed a sufficient appreciation of the meaning of reparation in the name of souls entrusted to me . . . an appreciation of the meaning of joining in the work of redeeming the world?
Should not the thought of souls to be saved be the best stimulus to generosity in my efforts at penance?

Let us now examine our practice of penance and mortification. Again the words of Christ: "If anyone is to be my servant; he must follow me; and where I am, my servant will also be" (Jn. 12:26). "If anyone wishes to come after me, let him deny himself, and take up his cross daily, and follow me" (Lk. 9:23).

Do I accept in joyous union with Christ the penance imposed upon me by the commandments, the precepts of the Church, and my state in life?
When I am suffering, do I try to conceal it, or do I tell everybody about it, seeking pity and consolation?
Am I willing to go out of my way in order to accommodate others? Do I mortify my natural tendency to apathy by trying to be alert and attentive during the liturgy . . . when conversing with others . . . when doing routine jobs?
Do I practice the mortification of being satisfied . . . of not seeking ease and comfort at all cost . . . of avoiding useless complaints?

We will pause for a few minutes for silent examination. (Pause.)
Let us now conclude the "I confess":

Therefore, I beseech blessed Mary ever Virgin, blessed Michael the Archangel, blessed John the Baptist, the holy Apostles Peter and Paul, all the Saints, you, Father, and those of you gathered here with me, to pray to the Lord our God for me.

May almighty God have mercy on you, forgive you your sins, and bring you to life everlasting.

Amen.

May the almighty and merciful Lord grant you ✤ pardon, absolution, and remission of your sins.

Amen.

We will now begin the confessional part of the sacrament.

Enter the confessional in the usual way. Begin immediately by saying how long it has been since your last confession. Accuse yourself according to what the examination of conscience has revealed to you. If you wish to confess sins not covered in the examination, feel free to do so. Then the priest will give you absolution and dismiss you. The other prayers will be said and the penance given when all have assembled here after all the confessions have been heard.

(At this time several verses of a suitable hymn may be sung. The celebrant removes the violet cope before going to the confessional. After all have been heard, he returns to the sanctuary, removes the violet stole, and puts on a white stole and white cope.)

Again we emphasize the communal aspects of this celebration by the communal penance. Let us remember that the liturgical penance of the sacrament of penance is a sign of the total reparation we owe to God's love for our own sins and those of the entire world. The penance for this celebration of the sacrament has two parts: a prayer part and a "do" part. Please kneel to receive your penance.

The prayer part is psalm 129, "Out of the Depths," which we will all now pray together.

The "do" part of your penance is to perform some act of mortification of your own choice within the next few days, such as giving an alms to the poor, or not smoking for a hour, etc.

Please stand for the following petitions and responses.
That we may have the spirit of Christian penance in our personal lives, we pray to the Lord.

Lord, grant us faith in your words telling us that we must do penance.

That by not being selfish in our family living we may make happier those with whom we live, we pray to the Lord.

Lord, grant us hope in your promises to reward those who take up their crosses and follow you.

That by being concerned more about others in our work and social activities than about ourselves, we may deny our selfish satisfactions, we pray to the Lord.

Lord, grant us love in fulfilling our obligations toward You and our fellowmen.

Let us pray. Almighty Father of our Lord Jesus Christ, who at our baptism gave us a new birth by means of water and the Holy Spirit, and have just renewed this glorious life by the forgiveness of our sins, may the sprinkling of this blessed water be for all of us here, and for all those for whom we pray, the pledge of everlasting life, of peace and joy, and of eternal refreshment, through Christ our Lord.

Amen.

Please kneel for the sprinkling of holy water.

(The celebrant sprinkles all with holy water, going down the aisle, if necessary. He returns to his place, gives the final blessing, and begins the recessional, which forms as did the processional, and all leave the church singing the recessional hymn.)

May the passion of our Lord Jesus Christ, the merits of the blessed Virgin Mary and of all the Saints, and also whatever good you do, and whatever evil you endure be for you the cause of the remission of your sins, the increase of grace, and the reward of everlasting life.

Amen.

May the blessing of almighty God ✚ the Father, and the Son, and the Holy Spirit descend upon you and remain with you forever.

Amen.

(Recessional)

Homily for Suggested Rite of Celebration on the Theme of Mortification

INTRODUCTION

One day the saintly Pope Pius X remarked to his secretary that because of his age the Lenten fare was hard on him. "But, Holy Father," said the secretary, "since you are the Pope, you can easily dispense yourself from the regulations of fast and abstinence." "I distinguish," replied His Holiness with some heart, "as Sovereign Pontiff, Yes; as a Christian, No."

GOD'S REVELATION AND OUR APPLICATION

I. We cannot dispense ourselves if we wish to be glorified. Christ refers to his passion and death as the "hour . . . for the Son of Man to be glorified." The passion and death itself is not the actual glorification, rather are they the means to resurrection, which is glorification. "Unless the grain of wheat falls into the earth and dies, it remains just a grain of wheat. But if it dies it bears much fruit" (Jn. 12:24). Christian mortification, or penance, is a dying. It is begun in our baptism and must continue on to the end of our lives. Otherwise, "it remains just a grain of wheat." St. Paul tells us that it is through our baptism that we die and are buried with Christ, so that we can rise with him (Cf. Rom. 6). Our lives are a continual dying. Yet because of our incorporation into Christ they are also a continual resurrection. It is by our free acceptance of death, by the act of obedience to the all-powerful will of God, by agreeing to be the grain of wheat dying in the earth, that we make the final and ultimate reparation for all infidelities and for all human rebelliousness. This we will never be prepared to do at the "most glorious moment of life" (Lacordaire), death, unless there is the daily dying that we call Christian penance or mortification.

II. We cannot dispense ourselves if we are to be servants. "If anyone is to be my servant, he must follow me; and where I am, my servant will also be" (Jn. 12:26). A servant is good and useful to his master, if he has disciplined himself to serve. His will is so controlled that he can be readily submissive to even the slightest wish of his master. This must not be thought of as degrading, but rather as the most ennobling type of service. We do not deprive our bodies of legitimate pleasures because they are our enemies. Rather they our partners. Mortification helps them be cooperative partners with us in our own personal development in holiness. But more than that, penance and mortification help our bodies be true partners with Christ in the redemption of the world. The real enemy of true personal fulfillment is *self*-will at all cost, not self-mastery, through prudent, purposeful, suitable use of mortification.

III. We cannot dispense ourselves if we are to "walk in the light." The light of Christ shining from where He has been lifted up is obscured when our minds are not controlled, our memories and imaginations cavort at random, our bodily senses are always surfeited. Those who seek to walk through life obtaining all and every pleasure that is available are walking in darkness and "he who walks in darkness does not know where he is going" (Jn. 12:35-36). Is not a lack of self-discipline accountable for so much darkness in our lives today? The darkness of insecurity, that of boredom, that of the need of infinite variety? The darkness in our understanding of suffering? Of the meaning of life and death?

CONCLUSION   More and more the determination of what kind and how much mortification we shall practice is being left up to the individual. Let us reflect that this is a choice of kinds and amounts, not the choice to exclude penance entirely from our lives.

(Oscar J. Miller, C.M. from *HOMILETIC AND PASTORAL REVIEW*)

2) Meditations on the Rosary

THE JOYFUL MYSTERIES   THE ANNUNCIATION: Lord, I pray that my whole life may announce your coming. May my little acts of kindness help others know you.

THE VISITATION: Lord, whenever I meet people may I visit them with your joyfulness. Help me, Lord, to go out of my way to visit those who are usually forgotten.

THE NATIVITY: Lord, you are born again each time we make another person feel loved. Help us give birth to your peace.

THE PRESENTATION: Lord, be present to us at every moment. May we make a present of you to others by sharing your presence with them.

THE FINDING IN THE TEMPLE: At times we seem lost, Lord, especially when we do not find you in one another. Help us love all men who are your temples.

THE SORROWFUL MYSTERIES   THE AGONY IN THE GARDEN: Lord, you prayed "not my will, but yours, Father." Help me know your will and follow it with joy.

THE SCOURGING: Lord, you must have experienced pain far beyond any of my little aches. Help me always to remember that my aches and pains should lead me to think of others who suffer so much more.

THE CROWNING WITH THORNS: A crown of glory awaits us if we are faithful to you, Lord. May our love and service of each other make us worthy of your rewards.

THE CARRYING OF THE CROSS: I know I must take up my cross each day, Lord, and follow you. Don't let me be a martyr who makes others suffer.

THE CRUCIFIXION: You laid down your life for your friends, Lord. Help me sacrifice myself for those in need, Lord, for you have made us friends with everyone.

THE GLORIOUS MYSTERIES   THE RESURRECTION: You live on, Lord, in all of us who believe in you. May our life in you be joyful, abundant, and full of fun.

THE ASCENSION: You left your disciples, Lord, so that they might grow in faith. Help me grow, Lord. Make me open to new people and new ideas.

THE DESCENT OF THE HOLY SPIRIT: Your Spirit, Lord, is a Spirit of Peace. May all my actions bring people together and help them see the best in one another.

THE ASSUMPTION: Your mother believed when no one seemed to, Lord. She was steadfast to the end. Keep me strong to the end too, Lord.

THE CORONATION OF THE BLESSED VIRGIN: May we all rejoice one day with all the saints, Lord, when all men will at last be at peace and there will be no more tears.

(*THE LARGE TYPE PRAYER BOOK* by Peters and Young, Paulist Press, 1972.)

He said to Moses
"I Am Who Am".
The flame is reflected
in our eyes
and we are who we are,
God's image.
But we are afraid
of our own faces
with burning eyes.
To be fully human—
to love
to laugh
to cry
to live like flame
in darkness
—is to be part
of who He is.
More than a man of clay,
more than a bush of flame,
we are who we are.
Once we know,
once we meet God's
face in a mirror,
on a street corner,
everywhere,
we are reborn.
The fire burns,
the bush grows,
the clay of our
being takes shape.
And we are who we are
who He is,
always.

Franciscan Communications Center

LAUDS   Begin as usual.

Psalms 2 (112), 3 (121), and 4 (126) with their antiphons taken from 2nd Vespers, Common of Feasts of the Blessed Virgin Mary.

Hymn: "Our Father" (Sung)

V.   *Let my prayer, O Lord,*
R.   *Come like incense before You.*

Ant. *Raise your eyes and look about: they all gather and come to you: your sons come from afar, and your daughters rise up at your side.*

Benedictus: (Sung)

Prayer: Celebrant.

MEDITATION   Theme: In reality, there is only one true prayer, only one substantial prayer: Christ himself. There is only one voice which rises above the face of the earth: the voice of Christ. This reunites and co-ordinates in itself all the voices raised in prayer.

Examination of Conscience:

1. Have I understood that Christ is the very essence of prayer, and that, outside him, there is no real prayer? As God made man, he achieves in his person the perpetual offering of creation to his Father.

2. Have I understood that, only inasmuch as I contemplate Christ, can I give him to the world by my life?

3. Am I sufficiently persuaded that time given to prayer is never time lost, if at that time the "I" disappears, to bury itself in the universal prayer of Christ who prays in me and at the same time takes upon himself the prayer of my sisters?

Resolutions:

1. To do everything in the spirit of prayer. Everything is a grace, and everything can serve to praise the Lord.

2. To unite myself with the incessant prayer of Christ and his continual offering.

Spiritual Bouquet: (Read the reverse side.)

4) *Dialogue Meditation (For Third Day—9 a.m.)*

> You see, the puzzle isn't puzzling at all
>   It's creation   The pieces of this
> puzzle Earth must come from us   In
> the beginning (even this morning) the
> face of the earth was a void, a puzzle
> without pieces   Then He came, and
> brought to the void the fullness of His
> being   And we created—a new day, a
> smile, a hot breakfast, a whole new uni-
> verse   Not puzzling, merely amazing
>   The pieces we give may not always
> fit: creation is that risk, well worth it
> "In Christ, a new Creation;" in all of us
> the care that makes the puzzle come to life

Franciscan Communications Center

5) *Morning Prayer (For Fifth Day—9 a.m.)*

> This is the wilderness:
> our world.
> We are so thirsty
> —for hope, for mornings,
> for one green tree left standing
> on a downtown street.
> Rain and snow and the taste of tears
> are not enough;
> we need water in the wilderness,
> and He brings it,
> striking, like Moses,
> our stone hearts and setting love free.
> "I am doing a new thing,
> and I will give drink to my people".
> We drink,
> and we are new.
> Our love for each other makes
> the wilderness bloom.

In our hearts, one flower:
the flower of peace, of tomorrow,
of creation.
It looks like all of us.
It looks like the face of God,
reflected in the water
in what was once a wilderness.

Franciscan Communications Center

6) *Morning Prayer (For Sixth Day—9 a.m.)*

"Behold I am with you always"
a candle in an empty room,
a traffic light turning green,
sunrise over grey buildings
where pigeons live.
His life in us
glows around dark corners,
finds its way into kitchen cupboards,
passes from hand to hand like sparks.
This is what resurrection means:
passing out of darkness
without looking back,
the warmth of life amid life.
"I am with you,"
and His presence grows
to fill earth,
to spill over the horizon like sunrise,
to shoot skyward like a candle flame.
This is what miracle means:
Christ with us,
and we with each other,
living in the light.

Franciscan Communications Center

F. LITURGIES/HOMILIES

1. MORNING PRAYER   (Outline)

First Day—Creative Lauds according to the Bulletin "I Am Who Am", which is appended.

Second Day—Rosary, the Joyful Mysteries, meditations for which are appended.

Third Day—Dialogue Meditation, suggestions for which are appended.

Fourth Day—Way of the Cross based on Michael Quoist's "Prayers".

Fifth Day—Meditation on the Sacrament of Penance.

Sixth Day—Candle and Salt Service, suggestions for which are appended.

2. LITURGY   (Outline)

First Day—Mass of the Eucharist (#904 Lectionary)
    Homily—The Sacrament of Life

Second Day—Mass in honor of the Holy Trinity #165-167 Lectionary)
    Homily—The Image of God in Each of Us

Third Day—Mass for the Sick (#871 Lectionary)
    Homily—The Christian Dignity of Suffering

Fourth Day—Mass in Honor of the Baptism of Our Lord (#21 Lectionary)
    Homily—Commitment to Faith

Fifth Day—Mass for Forgiveness of Sins (#886 ff. Lectionary)
    Homily—The Loving Mercy of God .

Sixth Day—Mass of Religious Profession (#784 Lectionary)
    Homily—Dedication to Loving Service

3. *First Day—Mass of the Eucharist (Lectionary #904-909)*
Homily—The Sacrament of Life

READINGS

I—Acts 2,42-47 (#905,1).
    Responsorial Psalm—Ps. 147,12-13,14-15,19-20. (#906,7)
    Alleluia—Jn. 6,51,52. (#908,1)
II—Jn. 6,51-58 (#909,7)

(Note to Retreat Master: If the retreatants are agreeable, it would be well to show the film, "The Eucharist". If this is done, then this homily is omitted, except for some brief comments about "Life" as evidenced in the film.)

EXPERIENCE OF REVERENCE

Who of us has not experienced the feeling of peace in the presence of the Eucharistic Lord? During mass or during the other hours of the day when the chapel is quiet and we are alone in His presence? Clare Booth Luce attributes her conversion to Catholicism to what she felt the day she entered a quiet Catholic church to pray. And here is life in fullest measure. Since our innermost and most persistent desire is for life, no wonder we experience a sense of awe and reverence when we are in the presence of him who declared, "I came that they might have life and have it to the full." (Jn. 10,10) Because Christ looked upon all created things with a feeling of reverence for the sacredness of the life created by His Father, he was able to look upon every human being with that same feeling of reverence. Note his courtesy to the rabbi teachers in the temple when he was twelve years old. Note his concern at the insistence of his mother for the young newly married couple at the wedding feast of Cana. Compare his treatment of the woman taken in adultery with the disdain and snobbery we would have manifested. Is our reverence for the sacredness of the person able to stand up under denial and betrayal? How would we have treated Peter and Judas? Reverence for the sacredness of the Person, Jesus Christ, truly present in the Blessed Sacrament, must be reflected in our reverence for every person who comes into the circle of our lives.

FELLOWSHIP WITH THE APOSTLES

The first reading gives us a picture of the apostles and first disciples in their communal life. They devoted themselves to instruction, the communal life, the breaking of bread, and prayers. Sounds like a retreat, doesn't it? Hopefully, during these days, we, too, will have a reverent fear overtake us as God works His will in us. The accounts of those early days of Christianity all have an undercurrent of enthusiasm, a verve for living to the full the life that springs from the Risen Savior. In their number were men and women who had witnessed personally the very things that now made life worth living, and death worth desiring. God had kept his promise to send the Messiah, and Jesus had proven himself to be the Christ. Fellowship with the apostles caused them to go about their daily lives "with exultant and sincere hearts". Let us pray that our fellowship together during this retreat will be the inspiration we need to go about these days "with exultant and sincere hearts." It is true that each retreat should prepare us for death, but, still more, it should give us new motivation to live our lives with a relish for the vocation that God has given to us. When others see this liveliness in our mode of life, then they will be motivated to follow Christ, and day by day the Lord will add to our numbers those whom He calls.

PROMISE FULFILLED

The promise of Christ ("I came that they might have life and have it to the full.") is one that he fulfills every day. Not merely in the good life of a consecrated religious, but in the special ways of his friendship. The analogy to food that we have in the gospel is carefully chosen. In the scriptures the taking of food with another is a special sign of intimate friendship. So, the many parables of bride and bridegroom, of wedding feasts, of breaking bread together. Nourishment and sustenance for life is thus intimately linked up with the very process of living itself. And so the providing of spiritual nourishment in the eucharistic banquet is, first of all, the fulfillment of the promise we just heard from the sixth chapter of John's gospel. Second of all, the giving of himself as our food is Christ's pledge to fulfill the promise for life, here and hereafter. No wonder, then, the reverence with which Jesus fulfilled his promise to give Himself. How marvelous that we can find in the eucharistic promise the assurance that through Christ, with Christ, and in Christ, we can live a full life here and for all eternity. "Just as the Father who has life sent me, and I have life because of the Father, so the man who feeds on me will have life because of me."

ENTER INTO LIFE

Let us then, Sisters, enter wholeheartedly into these saving mysteries. For we feed on the flesh of Christ, and drink his blood. Let us enliven our belief that we will have life eternal, and we will be raised up on the last day.

4. Second Day—Mass in Honor of the Holy Trinity (Lectionary #165-167)
Homily—The Image of God in Each of Us

READINGS

I—Prv. 8,22,31 (#167, Reading I).
Responsorial Psalm—Ps. 8,4-5,6-7,8-9 (#167).
Alleluia—Jn. 16, 12-15 (#167).
II—Jn. 3, 16-18 (#165, Gospel).

GIFT OF LIFE

" 'Slain' girl turns up alive!" This headline in the newspapers reported the climax in a bazaar situation in which two girls were murdered. The parents had identified one of the bodies as that of their missing daughter. Actually, the girl was at a friend's home, although this was not known to her parents. When she heard the news that she was dead, the girl reported to the police. "Listen", she said, "all I wanted to say is I'm not dead, please. I'm here breathing." It must be quite a shock to read that you are dead, and then to realize that you're not. The gift of life is such a precious thing! Yesterday we saw that the Eucharist is our source of living to the full. Because we are created in the image and likeness of God, the life given us is eternal. The scriptures attempt to unfold this mystery.

READING FROM PROVERBS

In its effort to give us some idea of what life truly is, the Church applies to us what the sacred writer originally said of the gift of Wisdom, in reality of God Himself. Before the foundations of the earth were established, God had each of us in mind. My life is not an arbitrary thing, dependent on the whim of a impersonal force. Listen once again to the beauty of the poetry in which God reveals His intense love for each human being. (Read again.)

COMMUNICATING LIFE

Because we are created in the image and likeness of God, there can be a relationship between Creator and creature. How reveal this mystery? The pages of the Bible tell us in many different ways what it means to have this relationship with the Creator. But notice that it is usually in the form of an intimate communication, the type of thing that happens between intimate friends. In fact, the intimacy is described in many places as that of the lover for the beloved. So, the gospel promises that the intimate secrets of the Father will be revealed by the Spirit because He will have received them from the Son. Perhaps, if we understand something of friendship, we are able to fathom something of the wonderful relationship we have with God because we are created in His image and likeness. God does not merely communicate to us the power to be alive. No, He communicates life in its fullness.

FRIENDSHIP

Kahlil Gibran in his book, "the Prophet" (Alfred A. Knopf, New York, c1923) has the wise man speak of friendship.

And a youth said, Speak to us of Friendship.
And he answered saying:
Your friend is your needs answered.
He is your field which you sow with love
and reap with thanksgiving.
And he is your board and your fireside.
For you come to him with your hunger,
and you seek him for peace.

When your friend speaks his mind you
fear not the "nay" in your own mind, nor
do you withhold the "ay."
And when he is silent your heart ceases
not to listen to his heart;
For without words, in friendship, all
thoughts, all desires, all expectations are born
and shared, with joy that is unacclaimed.
When you part from your friend, you
grieve not;
For that which you love most in him may
be clearer in his absence, as the mountain
to the climber is clearer from the plain.
And let there be no purpose in friendship
save the deepening of the spirit.
For love that seeks aught but the disclosure
of its own mystery is not love but
a net cast forth: and only the unprofitable
is caught.

And let your best be for your friend.
If he must know the ebb of your tide,
let him know its flood also.
For what is your friend that you should
seek him with hours to kill?
Seek him always with hours to live.
For it is his to fill your need, but not
your emptiness.
And in the sweetness of friendship let
there be laughter, and sharing of pleasures.
For in the dew of little things the heart
finds its morning and is refreshed.

SHARES HIMSELF

In the Eucharist we are invited to share life with him of whom the scriptures say: "I found delight in the sons of men." (First reading) His invitation comes to us daily to join him in the banquet of love, banquet that gives life here and for eternity. He recognizes us as his friends because we are created in the image and likeness of his Father, and he himself is the firstborn of all creation. At the inauguration of the eucharistic meal before his death, Jesus revealed to his disciples, and through them to all of us, the intimacy of his relationship with us. "As the Father has loved me, so have I loved you. Live on in my love . . . This is my commandment: love one another as I have loved you. There is no greater love than this: to lay down one's life for one's friends. You are my friends if you do what I command you. I no longer speak of you as slaves, for a slave does not know what his master is about. Instead, I call you friends, since I have made known to you all that I heard from my Father." (Jn. 15:9-15)

5. Third Day—Mass for the Sick (Lectionary #871-875)
Homily—The Christian Dignity of Suffering

READINGS

I—2 Cor. 4, 10-18 (#872, 2)
    Responsorial Psalm—Ps. 102, 2-3, 24-25, 19-21 (#873, 2)
    Alleluia—Col. 1,24 (#874, 3)
II—Jn. 15, 1-8 (#875, 4) Gospel.

SUFFERING IN ALL FORMS

We are all familiar with the sufferings that Charlie Brown of the "Peanuts" cartoon goes through. And Lucy always seems able to add to his mental anguish and his feelings of inferiority. In one strip Lucy proclaims to poor Charlie. "You're probably the most wishy-washy person I've ever known! You're really not much use to anyone, Charlie Brown! You're weak, and dumb, and boring, and hopeless!" After a slight pause to let all this sink in, Lucy then questions, "Incidentally, how come I never hear you sing anymore?"

A little boy at school for the first time was sobbing bitterly. "What's the matter, Billy?" asked the teacher.

"I don't like school, and I have to stay here until I'm 18," he cried.

"Don't let that worry you," said the teacher. "I have to stay here until I'm 65."

And in the Wizard of Id cartoon the king visits one of his more derilect subjects whose house and yard are a model of pollution. The king asks, "How's the world treating you?"

"Rotten!" replies the subject.

The king looks at him, and the house, and the yard and replies, "Maybe it's just trying to get even."

Yes, there are many forms of suffering, and some of them are our own fault. However, most of them we find it difficult to account for, and certainly very hard to accept. In a little booklet published by the Franciscan Mission Associates the title indicates some of the forms of suffering. "Meditations and Prayers for the Sick, Aging, and Homebound." And inside the booklet the listing goes on:

For those taken sick,
For the disabled, convalescents, and shut-ins,
For those confined to bed,
For those who cannot eat,
For those unable to sleep,
For the aged and infirm,
For the mentally afflicted,
For those in great pain.

I mention this litany so that it will remind us of those whom we wish to remember in this mass for the sick, and perhaps add them to the Prayers of the Faithful.

SUFFERING NOT USEFUL IN ITSELF

You have to be some kind of a nut to want suffering or to enjoy it for its own sake. There is no value in suffering in itself. And it is a shame that so much suffering in the world right now is not having any value attached to it. And it would be doubly tragic if our suffering was to no avail. Let me illustrate from another cartoon, Berry's World. The drawing shows an extremely old man lying in bed. At his bedside the doctor is speaking to the old man's elderly daughter. "I think he'll live for years. What keeps him going is the possibility that he may be a winner in the Reader's Digest contest." Silly, isn't it? And yet many suffer with less value to their pain. Pope Paul VI, attempting to counteract the meaninglessness of suffering declared: "Here is something big and new; suffering is no longer useless. If united to Christ's pains, our pain takes on something of His expiatory power, of His redemptive power, of His saving power."

REDEMPTIVE SUFFERING

Pope Paul gets his message from St. Paul in the epistle that was just read in this mass. "Continually we carry about in our bodies the dying of Christ." Our union with Christ, expressed in the gospel, is the source of the value our suffering can have. We believe in the redemptive value of Christ's suffering, for he chose the agony of the cross to redeem mankind. We must also believe in the value of our suffering, since he suffers again through us. Therefore, once again Christ redeems, but now through us. It is our union with Christ that can make our suffering a vocation to redeem the world. Our motto must be that of the alleluia verse: "I will make up in my own body what is lacking in the suffering of Christ, for the sake of his body, the Church."

LEARN THIS LESSON AND TEACH IT

Our special dedication to the service of Christ should have a two-fold apostolate in regard to suffering. First, we must learn the value of our own suffering, and be willing to accept it in a redemptive fashion. And very excellent to do this when we are well. The acceptance of suffering should include its final climax, death. But it must not end there. In the epistle St. Paul declares, "We believe and so we speak, knowing that he who raised up the Lord Jesus will raise us up along with Jesus and place us and you in his presence." The second part of our apostolate is to teach our belief to others, especially those who are sick. In a world of instant medicine and a health syndrome, let us make sure that the eternal value of pain and its necessary companions are recognized by the sufferer and all those who are responsible for his life and his death.

THE ETERNAL VALUE

"I am the true vine and my Father is the vinegrower," declares Christ. He prunes away every branch, but the fruitful ones he trims clean to increase their yield." St. Paul in the epistle, puts the same lesson in a little different way. "The present burden of our trials is light enough, and earns for us an eternal weight of glory beyond all comparison. We do not fix our gaze on what is seen but on what is unseen. What is seen is transitory; what is not seen lasts forever." An unknown author has said:

"In some future time,
maybe a thousand years,
maybe tomorrow,
we will know a life sublime,
no more tears,
no more sorrow.
We will stand on some high hill
and see a world
made beautiful by God,
Who came to kill
all hatred—sword and rod.
And we will live accordingly.

6. *Fourth Day—Mass in Honor of the Baptism of Our Lord (Lectionary #21)*
   Homily—Commitment to Faith

READINGS

I—Is. 42, 1-4, 6-7. (#21,A,B,C.)
    Responsorial Psalm—Ps. 29, 1-2, 3-4, 3,9-10 (#21)
II—Acts 10, 34-38. (#21)
    Alleluia—Mk. 9,6 (#21)
III—Lk. 3, 15-16.21-22 (#21, C.)

(Note to Retreat Master: If the retreatants are agreeable, it would be well to show the film: "Story Line—Afraid of the Storm". If the film is used, then begin the homily with the paragraph below entitled "The Father Is Pleased.")

KINSHIP WITH LARGER THINGS

William Saroyan, writer and philosopher of our times, has observed that the creation of anything really worthwhile demands isolation—that and an essential intensity of concentration for so long a time period as to produce an antisocial state in the artist. The loneliness is not of a desperate or abject quality but has a kind of majesty to it—"a kinship with larger things". In spite of isolation, the artist is not alone.

For over thirty years Saroyan has commented on the American way of life in his short stories, plays and novels. His term, "kinship with larger things," is most expressive of what faith is. For what deals with the larger things of life here and hereafter? And it is through faith that we establish a kinship with these things and with God. The isolation demanded for the growth and development of faith is more difficult to come by today than perhaps ever before in the history of mankind. For man seeks to isolate himself not only from his surroundings but also from God. And in doing so he loses the pivotal point of his life, becomes disastrously disoriented from eternal values. He loses "his kinship with larger things".

WILL TO BE COMPLETELY FREE

Cardinal Danielou, in a Sunday Visitor article, "Christian Faith and Today's Man" explains the difficulty this way. "There is a difficulty with which the religious man of today must deal, a difficulty that is no longer derived from scientific thought but from the will to be completely free. The fundamental temptation of modern man is not atheism so much as the close connection he establishes between his own development—that is, emancipation with regard to systems of slavery to which he was subjected in the past—and emancipation from God." In looking at this problem, Cardinal Danielou makes a distinction that we should consider. "One manifestation of this error (to emancipate man from God) . . . has been to confuse recognition of higher values, to which one submits spontaneously, with submission to exterior compulsion . . . This identification is scandalous, since it means confusing two things that are poles apart. Man's greatness lies in subjecting his own freedom to the imperative of higher values; on the contrary, it is degrading for him to surrender to compelling forces in his environment."

VITAL FAITH NEEDED

This is, then, a serious problem facing us today. Cardinal Danielou rejects a defeatist attitude, however. "A defeatist attitude . . . is the real termite inside the Church. Today, on the contrary, it is necessary to have a vital and dynamic faith, able to overcome those difficulties that we encounter today."

"For this reason," continues the Cardinal, "I believe we will have to struggle within the Church itself—and it will not always be an easy task—to keep the place we wish to give God in our personal life and in the life of society, having the courage to take a stand when these fundamental attitudes are wrongly attacked."

THE FATHER IS PLEASED

The readings for this mass tell us that the Father is well pleased with his Son. And since the Father is so pleased, He gives us His Son as our way, our truth, and our life. We celebrate the Baptism of Our Lord. It is a sign of his commitment to the vocation of Messiah-Redeemer. At age approximately thirty, Jesus had had opportunity to observe the signs of his time. He had come to know the temperament of relatives and friends, and realized they inherited the vacillation of a people who were loyal to God when they needed him, but then turned away from him in time of prosperity. Furthermore, Jesus was well aware of the thinking of those established in positions of religious and civil authority. In short, he knew by now that anyone opposing the present regimes, either of the Romans or of the Jews, would be doomed to death. Knowing all this, and being sensitive to the call of His Father to be Messiah-Redeemer, Jesus nevertheless wholeheartedly embraces his vocation. No wonder the voice from heaven proclaims, "You are my beloved Son. On you my favor rests."

IS THE FATHER PLEASED?

The ritual of Baptism implies that when this sacrament is received God looks with favor on this new child of His. This child, or adult, has, through the godparents, or personally, commited himself totally to the Christian life. The vocation of each one is different, God, through the Church, asking each one of us to respond to the needs of our time and place. If we are to imitate Christ, then we need, especially during the time of retreat, to ask ourselves some questions. Is the Father pleased with us today? Do I try to make each day's decisions in the light of the teachings of faith? Am I courageous in the decisions that faith demands of me? Do I trust God to bring me through the difficulties that faith sometimes seems to create? Have I the habit of looking beyond faces at souls and beyond souls at Christ, who wishes to live and grow in those souls?

RENEWAL OF PROMISES

At the end of the retreat you will be renewing your religious vows. Now, in this mass, as we consider the commitment Jesus made to His Father for our salvation, and as we recall the commitment of our Baptism, let us renew the pledges made in that sacrament. During this renewal we will say the two prayers that express our filial relationship to the Father, in whose image we are created, to the Son, our brother, who has redeemed us, and to the Spirit, our lover, who sanctifies us. The "Our Father" is a plea that our Father will continue to be pleased with us. The "Creed" expresses the affirmation we make in our Christian vocation.

(Note to Retreat Master: Use one of the formulas for the renewal of the baptismal vows. The one for Holy Saturday is easily adapted to this occasion.)

7. Fifth Day—Mass for the Forgiveness of Sins (#886 ff. Lectionary)
Homily—The Loving Mercy of God

(Note to Retreat Master: This mass is celebrated in conjunction with the Communal Celebration of the Sacrament of Penance, which replaces the usual Penitential Rite. A format for the Communal Celebration of the Sacrament of Penance is appended.)

READINGS

I—1 Jn. 1,5-2,2 (#887, 2.)
　Responsorial Psalm—Ps. 103, 1-2, 3-4, 8-9, 11-12 (#888, 2.)
　Alleluia—Rv. 1,5 (#889, 3.)
II—Lk. 24, 46-48 (#890, 5.)

CELEBRATING GOD'S MERCY

In every mass we celebrate God's infinite mercy. We are the descendants of a people who realized that Yahweh looked with kindness on their sinfulness and forgave them at the first hint of sorrow. Bulls, sheep, goats, doves, flour cakes, and oil sacrificed in an exuberant moment of joyous acclamation of a saving God. But the forgiveness was only in prospect of that one sacrifice of God's own Son, offered once on the cross, but repeated daily on our altars. "Do this in memory of me." The best statement of this mercy of God is found in the fourth eucharistic prayer. We need to hear it repeated now, in that segment that precedes the consecration.

"Father, we acknowledge your greatness:
all your actions show your wisdom and love.
You formed man in your own likeness
and set him over the whole world
to serve you, his creator,
and to rule over all creatures.
Even when he disobeyed you and lost your friendship
you did not abandon him to the power of death,
but helped all men to seek and find you.
Again and again you offered a covenant to man,
and through the prophets taught him to hope for salvation.
Father, you so loved the world
that in the fullness of time you sent your only Son to be our Savior.
He was conceived through the power of the Holy Spirit,
and born of the Virgin Mary,
a man like us in all things but sin.

To the poor he proclaimed the good news of salvation,
to prisoners, freedom,
and to those in sorrow, joy.
In fulfillment of your will
he gave himself up to death;
but by rising from the dead,
he destroyed death and restored life.
And that we might live no longer for ourselves but for him,
he sent the Holy Spirit from you, Father,
as his first gift to those who believe,
to complete his work on earth
and bring us the fullness of grace."

COMPLETE HIS WORK ON EARTH

It is a great sign of love to associate another with your favorite project, especially where there is really nothing selfish to be gained by you. Added to all the signs of God's love is the giving of the Spirit so that we might complete his work on earth. The Spirit of God given to us in our Baptism so unites us to Christ that what we do he does. Even more, since the time of his ascension into glory, he no longer acted on earth as he did during the thirty-odd years of his life. From that day on, or at least from the day of the first Pentecost, Christ acts through his Church. The redemptive merits obtained by Jesus on Calvary's cross are applied to each person through the Church. It is especially in the sacraments that salvation comes to mankind. Once we have been initiated into these sacred signs through our baptism, we, too, become instruments of God's mercy. God wishes the salvation of all men. Our prayers, sacrifices, good works, participating in the mass, receiving holy communion, going to confession, everything that we do can be Christ completing the work of redemption. What a wonderful association! How joyfully we should celebrate this mysterious action! Such a beautiful expression of God's love for us—to call us to be redeemers with his Son!

COMMUNAL PENITENTIAL RITE

To heighten our realization of this unique privilege, we have entered into a communal celebration of the sacrament of penance, and have joined it to the sacred rite of the mass. From the confessional, just as from this altar of sacrifice, flow the saving merits of Jesus Christ, our Lord. But if we do not enter into these mysteries, Christ's work of redemption cannot be completed. Not only is it a privilege to be called to be redeemers of the world with Christ, but there is a responsibility upon us to use these means of grace, to "bring us the fullness of grace." What we do individually and privately for the salvation of souls is greatly treasured by God. But He looks with infinite satisfaction on the liturgical actions we perform in common. For then we are in communion with the Trinity in and through the Mystical Body of Christ, which is the Church, which we are. Long may Christ reign in and through us.

8. Sixth Day—Mass of Religious Profession (#784-788 Lectionary)
Homily—Dedication to Loving Service

READINGS

I—Sg. 2,8-14 (#784,5.)
Responsorial Psalm—Ps. 84,3,4,5-6,8,11,12. (#786,8)
I—Eph. 1,3-14 (#785,7.)
Alleluia—Jn. 15,5 (#787,4.)
III—Jn. 15,9-17 (#788,13.)

THREE FACTORS

These readings point out the three factors involved in any dedication to the religious life: God, yourself, and service. The relationship is beautifully expressed in the first reading depicting the call of the lover to his beloved. The theology of the union with Christ through religious dedication is illuminated by St. Paul in the second reading from the Ephesians. The source of the energy necessary for such a dedication is clearly indicated by the beautiful disclosure by Christ that we are his friends. During these six days we have been re-created for ourselves the awesomeness of our relationship with God as human beings, created in His image, united with his Son in the mystical body, and dedicated to his service. Let us briefly review and summarize our views of God, ourselves, and our service.

GOD

Since the sacred scriptures revealed God to us in figures of speech, let us look at some modern similies expressed by a grade school boy.

"God is like Ford—He has a better idea.
God is like Coke—He's the real thing.
God is like Bayer aspirin—He works wonders.
God is like Hallmark cards—He cared enough to send the very best.
God is like Standard—You expect more from him and you get it.
God is like Sears—He has everything.
God is like Alka Seltzer—Try him. You'll like him!"

Of course, the young boy's grammatical expression is turned around. It's not God who reflects the various attributes of Ford, Hallmark, Sears, etc., but rather these companies that reflect something of God. And so it is with all of us. Each one of us reflects something of the goodness of God. The joyous personality gives us a slight hint of the eternal blessedness. The careful, concerned, sympathetic ones among us let us know just a small aspect of the loving concern God has for all mankind. The truly sorrowful (not the morose, guilt-ridden, selfish sorrow) help us to appreciate God's sorrow for the evils one man inflicts on another. Yes, the wonderful attributes of God are reflected in everyone and everything around us. It is by examining these reflections that we increase our relationship with Almighty God on the threefold bases of our humanity, our Christianity, and our religious dedication.

OURSELVES

The second of the three factors involved in our religious profession is ourselves, God and our service being the other two. For the sake of brevity, let us get to specifics immediately. Because we are human beings we have the power to know. Only you can appreciate a sunset (a dog can see it and feel the warmth). Only you can appreciate a sonata (a cat can hear it). Because we are human beings we have the power to love. You can know what is good and hence you can love this good. You can love selflessly. You can love so perfectly that there is nothing more to give. And yet your love is free. You can give it or withhold it.

Yet, this is not the full picture. For we are human beings who have been raised to the level of Christians. Because of this we have a supernatural resemblance to God and a consequent relationship with Him. You are destined to see God as He is, with a knowledge that is called vision. This knowledge is foreshadowed in the reading from the Ephesians. ". . . he . . . predestined us through Christ Jesus to be his adopted sons—such was his will and pleasure—that all might praise the divine favor he has bestowed on us in his beloved." Then, Paul repeats the promise made in the Garden. "He (Christ) is the pledge of our inheritance, the first payment against the full redemption of a people God has made his own, to praise his glory."

Secondly, through grace we possess a gift called charity. The reading from John's gospel which we heard a few minutes ago amply illustrates this gift of love. The words of Christ are a plea, as well as a command. "Live on in my love."

SERVICE

The highest ideal of service to which you can strive to show your love for God, for yourself, and for your neighbor, is found in imitation of the Blessed Virgin Mary. She is the ideal between the lines of all three readings today. The beloved who seeks her lover first and above all. She was the first to hear the good tidings of salvation and to respond to them. She is the perfect example of those who live on in His love. Your service of God is like the rosary, with its joyful, sorrowful, and glorious mysteries. There is joy in giving of yourself. There is sorrow in giving up many legitimate pleasures for the sake of the kingdom. But there will be the glory that will come to you, both here and hereafter, for the love you have lavished on others, because you loved God so much. And at no time during the day do you render better service than you do in this very act of sacrificial love.

II. MODERN

By The Rev. Denis Lynch

and Sister Sandra Sutterlund, S.S.J.

A. THEME/PARTICIPANTS

This is a four day retreat, having as its theme *Womanhood*, and is directed toward religious women. It is intended to be conducted within an individual parish setting or within a city with the combination of several parishes. The proximity of places of work and prayer has a dual provision: 1) it provides an opportunity for the people of the parish to share some of the talks and discussion periods; and 2) the parish liturgy becomes the public forum in which to celebrate a renewal of vowed commitment by the religious women. The daily schedule includes presentations, discussions, communal prayer, and ample time for relaxation and reflection.

Because of the proximity of places of work and prayer, the retreat is to be conducted when the daily work distractions are minimized—e.g., for teachers at semester break, or at the end of the school year. With some slight modifications—e.g., the exclusion of the vow renewal ceremony or the condensation of the full day schedule—this experience could be applicable to lay women of a parish.

The retreat opens with a night session providing the participants with an atmosphere of relaxation and reflection so as to be better acclamated to the exercises of the subsequent days. This procedure was selected because retreats have traditionally begun with a full day's schedule and its corresponding intensity. The participants do not have sufficient time to adequately prepare themselves and therefore they are unable to participate at an optimum level the first full day. It is hoped that this brief initial evening session offers an adequate setting for the following days.

B. OUTLINE/SCHEDULE

OPENING SESSION

1. The first evening opens with an informal supper for all the participants.
2. The first session includes: a) general description of the retreat; b) communication questionnaire; and c) discussion; d) the Compline service; e) spontaneous recreation.

FIRST DAY

Theme: Being Woman
1. Informal breakfast.
2. Private morning prayer.
3. 10:00 a.m.—Presentation and discussion: "The Dignity of Woman in Sacred Scripture".
4. 12:00 noon—Lunch.
5. Afternoon free for reading and reflection.
6. Eucharistic Celebration before supper.
7. 5:30 p.m.—Supper.
8. 7:30 p.m.—Presentation and discussion: "Reflection on Being Woman".
9. Compline Service.

SECOND DAY

Theme: Woman and Prayer
1. Morning prayer. This prayer service, as well as those which follow, are to be the creative response from the participants.
2. 10:00 a.m.—Presentation and discussion: "Reflections on the Spirit".
3. Brief and informal lunch.
4. The afternoon is spent emphasizing the physical conditions which are necessary for prayer, initiated by the presentation: "The Prayer of Jesus".
5. Picnic supper.
6. Eucharistic Celebration before evening presentation.
7. Evening presentation and discussion including the parishioners. "Prayer".
8. Compline Service.

THIRD DAY

Theme: Woman—with Man
1. Informal breakfast.
2. Metanoia Service, including presentation and discussion: "Metanoia—Returning to Jesus".
3. 12:00—Lunch.
4. Afternoon free for reading and reflection.
5. Eucharistic Celebration before supper.
6. Evening presentation and discussion, including the parishioners: "Woman—with Man".
7. Compline Service.

LAST MORNING

1. The culminating activity is the renewal of vows which takes place during the parish liturgy.

FIRST EVENING

The following is a suggested opening procedure:
1. Informal supper for which every person can share the responsibility of preparing and cleaning up.
2. General description of the retreat given after supper; the description indicating the topical matter of each day and presenting the library of pertinent books, articles, etc., that are available.
3. Open discussion of plans which includes ideas and suggestions from the participants, thus attuning individuals to each other.

4. Distribution of a communication questionnaire with this explanation: Any group of people that comes together, does so for a purpose. But even when that purpose is clear, we often do not take enough time to develop an awareness of what every individual brings to the group and to the situation. Each of us has come with certain ideas, experiences, expectations and prejudices. Some expect much, others expect very little. Some will participate often, others will participate less often. Therefore, these ten incomplete sentences provide an opportunity to discover our present attitudinal position and also offer a means of evaluating the success or failure of this time shared. Therefore, every person should complete the question form individually. These are not to be collected but are yours to be personally reserved or to be shared with each other. Please respond honestly. At the conclusion of this retreat an evaluation will be possible by comparing what really happened and what the ten sentences indicated as expectations.

THE TEN QUESTIONS

a. In a group, I find it easiest to:
b. My feelings about being a member of this group are:
c. My present feeling about speaking before a group is:
d. In this group I expect the leaders to:
e. I expect this group to be able to:
f. The group can expect me to:
g. I certainly hope that this group does not:
h. The reason that most groups fail to reach their objective is:
i. Objectives of any group are best reached if the members of that group will only:
j. In this group I certainly expect to:

5. Reflective discussion during which time the following two questions are considered:
a. As religious women, in the past year what has been your most frustrating experience?
b. What has been the most fulfilling experience?
6. Prayer: Compline service.
7. Games and singing.

C. GUIDELINES

1. DIRECTIONS ON HOW TO USE THE MODEL

—the optimum conditions for implementing this retreat schema are:
a) participation is by choice;
b) prior knowledge of all participants;
c) comfortable parish setting.
—retreat directors should consist of a team of a man and woman.
—including leaders, the group should not exceed 15 in number.
—discussions should be initiated by the individual presentations; discussions are to be conducted informally, with the leaders acting as catalysts and directors. (The objective of the discussion is to stimulate participant sharing without the leaders assuming a dominant role.)
—during the evening sessions in which the parishioners are included, it is well to divide into smaller discussion groups, each group including some of the retreatants.

2. EVALUATION OF THIS MODEL

The effect of this retreat was very favorable. This is shown most clearly by the unanimous desire of the participants to continue to make further retreats together. In addition, the parishioners who participated were grateful and positively affected by their inclusion in the retreat. Finally, the highest compliment was expressed in gratitude for presenting a subject that is very important but was seldom treated explicitly in former retreat experiences.

3. ADDITIONAL REMARKS AND SUGGESTIONS

—It is impossible to condense this retreat experience into one evening or one day session; however, it is felt that individual subjects can be meaningfully and effectively presented of themselves.
—Flexible scheduling has been a decided preference by the participants. Any further tightening of the schedule was strongly discouraged.
—"Creative prayer service" does not mean spontaneous prayer; rather, it means prepared prayer services by the participants. This active participation is to further encourage the participants' involvement.
—The Agape meal is a celebration of reconciliation and of at-one-ment with the Lord and with each other. It is important to provide a conducive setting in the dining room, one which fosters a community, or family, spirit.

D. TALKS/EXERCISES

1. FIRST DAY—Theme: Being Woman

Private Morning Prayer:

Other morning and evening prayer services were creative responses from the participants.

Presentation and Discussion:

THE DIGNITY OF WOMAN IN SACRED SCRIPTURE (Rev. Dennis Lynch)

Gal. 3:23-29.

What are the insights, if any, that Sacred Scripture offers us about woman that any other book or discipline cannot? Let me begin by suggesting a general perspective.

The history of the Church's attitude toward woman is paradoxical. That is to say, the Church teaches and encourages the value and dignity of the human person but, by not enabling the woman to have a more active and official role in the Church, it minimalizes the woman as a human person. I am not saying that the Church is the only institution which is responsible for minimalizing the role of women, nor can we expect the Church to be totally unaffected by the prejudices which exist in its cultural context. But the problem that seems to have arisen is that this inequality between man and woman appears as having divine approval, as if God had intended it that way. For example, 1 Tim. 2:11-14; 1 Cor. 11:3,8,9.

It is interesting that the Industrial Revolution, not Christianity, has been credited with freeing woman. The Church did not actively work against this emancipation nor did she champion it. The Church continued to reflect the paradoxical frame of mind toward woman as human being made in the image of God, and the idea, part of societal tradition, that woman is inferior. But regardless of what was a part of the past, there is an increasing desire within both the society and the Church to erase anti-feminine attitudes and structures.

Let me try to suggest a way of understanding the problem. First of all, woman is stereotyped. She is categorized as having a vocation to be surrendering and to be hidden—cf., the symbols of veils and habits. She is expected to be self-less and therefore does not achieve individual realization, but merely a generic fulfillment in motherhood, whether it is physical or spiritual. She is said to be timeless and conservative by nature. Secondly, the added problem is that many women are insensitive to, or see no need in changing their stereotype. Let me suggest why this might be so.

In psychoanalysis there are the theories of repression, projection and introjection. There are some feelings and attitudes that are not permitted expression in society. These are often projected on weaker or disadvantaged people: the Jews in Germany and Russia, the blacks in South Africa and the whites in Appalachia. What happens is that the repressed problems of society are projected on a certain group of people and that people accepts the role that it has been given—e.g., the "lazy nigger" in fact becomes one. This creates a vicious circle—viz., the members of the oppressed group do in fact become inferior in the way society imposes. The prejudice is reinforced and the stereotype becomes grounded in nature. In a parallel fashion, the role of woman as inferior has been projected on her to such a degree that all of society has come to believe that her inferiority is grounded in nature; that it is the divine plan. This is the problem in a general sort of way. How do we try to rectify it without becoming bra-burning radicals! What we don't need is a "theology of woman," because this categorization implies an assumption that woman can be best understood apart from man. There seems to be no need for ever formulating a "theology of man" basically because man seems to have reached the fullness of human nature. A "theology of woman" 1) validates an inferior position; 2) emphasizes sexual differentiation above personhood; and 3) presumes that woman or man can be best understood alone rather than in relationship.

We *do* need a theological anthropology which will envisage the dynamics of being a human being. Therefore, to consider woman in Sacred Scripture is not to consider a theology of woman, but rather to investigate the ingredients of being human that are revealed in God's actions toward the people, and specifically to investigate the elements of the plan of salvation that are revealed in the heroines of Sacred Scripture. In other words, we can't expect Sacred Scripture to come out with ideas that would be identifiable with the ideals of contemporary women's liberation because Sacred Scripture doesn't contradict its cultural context. Therefore, the question is not what does Sacred Scripture tell us about woman, but rather what does woman in Sacred Scripture tell us about the God-human being relationship.

The three elements of this relationship that are reflected in woman's description in Sacred Scripture are mystery, relationship, and openness.

a) One of the reasons that woman acquired an inferior position in society was that she threatened man. Birth, menstruation, her ritualistic position in pagan worship (and its corresponding characterization of temptress and sorceress), all combined to portray woman as mysterious. As a consequence, man became distrustful of her. In addition, the growth of man's world dominance cautioned him about relinquishing his power to anyone, especially to such a mysterious figure as woman.

The portrayal of woman as mystery is reflected in Scripture—for example Eve the mysterious temptress; the ritualistic purifications of woman as delineated in the Pentateuch, the unpredictable Gomer; the charm and wit of Judith; the beauty and sensitivity of Esther.

It is true that the human person cannot be totally fathomed. This mysterious dimension seems to be especially applicable to woman.

The mysterious nature of God's plan of salvation is intensified and personified in the heroines of the Bible. The reference to and mention of woman in Scripture is usually associated with mystery and unpredictability—similarly is the plan of salvation characterized.

b) Notwithstanding the subservient position of woman vis-a-vis man in the Scriptures, the man-woman relationship is extensively utilized to portray the God-human relationship. Throughout Scripture (e.g., Hosea, Song of Songs, Psalms, Pauline analogies) God and his people are described as intimate lovers whose relationship is characterized by the dynamics and elements of the man-woman relationship. Therefore God and his people are portrayed as faithful and also faithless; the relationship is broken but again covenanted after repentence and forgiveness. The freedom of the participants in the relationship is maintained as is their interdependence. In other words, using the analogy of the man-woman relationship, God is portrayed in personal terms and as one who is in a relationship of love and fidelity but who is also totally other.

c) Many people consider what happened to Mary as being unique. Indeed it is when we appreciate the fact that Mary is the Mother of God. But there is an interesting parallel, if not a precedent, in the figures of Sara and Elizabeth, who also bore sons as the result of mysterious divine intervention. Conception occurred when both women were far beyond the age of child-bearing. All three women reflect the anawim spirit in their response—i.e., a total openness to and dependence upon God. They reflected the receptive and open stance of man vis-a-vis God.

In conclusion we look to Sacred Scripture for assistance in deepening our knowledge about the God-human relationship. Our relationship with God is as multi-faceted as the portrayal of women in Sacred Scripture. Some of the elements of the God-human relationship reflected in the Scriptural description are mystery, relationship and openness. Ultimately it is in the Person of Jesus that the God-man-woman mystery is brought to its wholeness. In Jesus there is no distinction "There is neither Jew nor Greek; there is neither slave nor freeman; there is neither male nor female. For you are all one in Christ Jesus." (Gal. 3:28)

OUTLINE

—The Church reflects society's paradoxical attitude toward women.

—Scripture offers no "theology of woman", but rather the epic-turning event of redemption.

—Therefore, the heroines of Scripture offer insights into the mystery of the God-human being relationship.

Suggested reading and resource: *THE ADVANCING DIGNITY OF WOMAN IN THE BIBLE*, Rev. Thierry Maertens, St. Norbert Abbey Press, 1969.

12:00 noon—Lunch.
Afternoon free for reading and reflection.
Eucharistic Celebration before supper. (Homily: "Co-operation," p. 44)
5:30 p.m.—Supper.
7:30 p.m.—Presentation and Discussion (to the exclusion of men) "Reflections on Being Woman", (Sr. Sandra Setterlund, SSJ)

In the Book of Genesis is written: "It is not good for man to be alone; let us make him a helper like unto himself." Here is suggested the equality between man and woman: ". . . . like unto himself," woman was created.

Reflecting upon Scripture's positive references to woman, we can refer to the Book of Proverbs in which woman is brought forth as a personification of wisdom and understanding.

Woman is also steadfast and faithful, dedicated; as exemplified in the persons of Esther and Judith, truly great leaders of the Old Testament. Woman is simple and receptive as Elizabeth and Sara. As they, woman has the power to introduce the sacred, the holy, into everyday life. Woman is co-redemptrix as Mary. That is, she shares in the plan of new creation, of redeeming and healing all that is weak within man. Through her presence is extended the power of healing.

To elaborate on these spontaneous reflections on woman, it is necessary to begin with what I believe is basic to the nature of woman: i.e., woman needs to exist in relationship to others. Her nature is that of being other-orientated.

As women, we have the power, the mystery, the wonder-gift of procreation—whether the form of that procreation is physical or spiritual. At this point, I am reminded of a well-known phrase from Sartre, often referred to in existential philosophy. In his play, *No Exit*, Sartre writes: ". . . . hell is other people." I would say that in woman's life, hell is NOT having other people. Cannot each of us say that the essence of joy in our lives is that of giving of ourselves and receiving in mutuality; of loving and being loved? Isn't woman's greatest desire that of "pouring herself out", making of her whole person a gift to another? And isn't her greatest frustration that of being denied this privilege of self-donation?

In this self-donation to others, woman essentially maintains a distance from others . . . which could be another definition for reverence. In woman's desire to be and to give of herself, she respects the fact of necessity that others have the same desire and need. Therefore, a distance must be maintained, one in which every person discovers, develops, and sustains his and her own uniqueness and mystery. Separation is a necessary factor in human relationships and realization of this prohibits woman from becoming domineering, possessive and suffocating in her relationships with others. Friendship and love thrive on otherness! When we can truly respect and revere one another as "other" and yet risk the revelation of ourselves, deepest communication in and of trust and confidence becomes possible, almost inevitable. Within this self-revelation rests woman's capacity and need for surrender. (Hold this term "surrender" as distinct from "submission.")

Because woman's call is to be Love Incarnate, we can attribute to her the qualities of love: respect and reverence, simple, free, unique, gentle, liberative and tender. Woman must be happy—i.e., delightful, in wonder, awesome. She can, and should be, delighted with life, its joys, its wonders, its elements of surprise and unpredictability, as well as its awkwardness. In this "life of delight" woman has the need to be nurtured in and through tenderness. Tenderness isn't softness but rather it is the quality of being a woman: a person of integrity, patient with a spirit of undisturbed acceptance and understanding of the growth process in another's life, being "mother." Tenderness is allowing life to amuse us in a delicate and perceptive way.

Woman also needs to be dependent: i.e., 1) knowing *where* and *that* she belongs, and 2) sometimes allowing another to be strong for her. Woman is simple, a continued manifestation of the simplicity of Mary. She is a gentle person, someone pleasant to be with, sensitive, perceptive, willing to become pregnant and to procreate new life in whatever way is contributive to her state in life. Woman is in touch with ALL of life—*all* that breathes: creation, persons, the Lord. She is the valiant woman.

Discussion Questions

1. In my own life, what does it mean to me to be a woman?

2. What qualities or characteristics which are operative in my own life would I especially associate with the fact that I am a woman?

—How do I feel about these qualities within myself?

—Do I like them? tolerate them? reject them?

—Why is it that I feel this way about these qualities?

3. Do I have an image or picture in my mind of the "woman I would like to be?"

—What are the qualities which I admire in this "woman I would like to be?"

—Why do I find these particular qualities to be characteristics of my "ideal woman?" Why are they important to me?

If the following is used for discussion, it is suggested that all participants read *FLIGHT FROM WOMAN* by Karl Stern.

"The meaning of an individual woman's femininity, the role of the feminine principle in the social fabric of the world: these have never been as important and as pressing as they are today. The reason is simple: technocracy has never been as pervasive and corrosive as it is presently in 20th. century Western culture. Technocracy (as distinct from technology) is the triumph of the isolated rationalistic, pragmatic, functional, work-oriented stance toward the world. It is associated with what philosophers and psychologists generally speak of as the masculine way of being-in-the-world. What is needed to preserve the human quality of life on this earth is a balance of the intuitive, caring, preservative attitude which is characterized as feminine." (*FLIGHT FROM WOMAN* by Karl Stern)

4. The author Stern says that the "flight from the feminine" is characteristic of the age in which we live. What does this phrase mean to you?

5. What part do the following play in a "flight from the feminine?"

    a. strong work orientation

    b. denial of the feeling or affective level of the personality

    c. fear of tenderness, love

    d. fear of dependence, passivity

    e. undue activism

    f. undue intellectualism

    g. the militaristic and/or competitive atmosphere of intra-national and inter-national relationships.

6. How do I in my own life "flee from the feminine?"

7. What particular dangers do I find within religious community life which foster a flight from the feminine in myself or in others with whom I live?

8. What does this mean to you: "the polarity of the sexes corresponds to a polarity in human intelligence—that of discursive reason versus intuition"?

    a. What are the two ways of knowing? How do you think they are related to the masculine and feminine ways of being in the world?

    b. Discuss the complimentarity, rather than the superiority-inferiority of both ways of knowing.

c. What is the connection between the following sets:
feminine—artistic—poetic—mystic
masculine—scientist—builder—progress

9. If I were asked to state my personal stand on the question of women's rights in the country, in the Church, in religious communities, what would be my position? This seems vital today especially in the light of:
   a. recent national strikes and demonstrations
   b. "legislations" and exhortations for women regarding their role in the Church, especially in connection with the liturgy
   c. recent Curial pressure on American sisterhoods.

OUTLINE

—Woman needs to exist in relationship to. . . . her whole life is other-orientated, making of herself a gift to others.

—The vocation to genuine womanhood is the vocation to surrender. . . . to love and to bring new life wherever woman is called.

—Woman is in touch with ALL of life; she is delightful, gentle, simple. . . . a person of integrity.

Compline service—creative response from the group.

2. SECOND DAY—Theme: Woman and Prayer

Morning Prayer

"Reflections on the Spirit" (Rev. Dennis Lynch)

Presentation and Discussion

Reflections on the Holy Spirit open the consideration of prayer. From the Scriptures we know that only in the Spirit do we proclaim Jesus as Lord and God as Father. It is only in a relationship of constant openness and receptivity to the Spirit that a genuine prayer life is nurtured. But how do we fathom the mystery that is Spirit! The Old Testament metaphor of the Spirit of God being as a wind is apropos for a point of comparison. Reflection on personal experiences with the wind offers an insight into the presence and meaning of the Spirit.

What is the wind if not an unexpected, a surprising, and an unpredictable phenomenon! The when, the how, the where of its movement is beyond the control of any human force. Its force is mysterious and invisible; it can be as gentle as it can be cruel. The wind disturbs and yet knows how to caress.

Physically, the wind offers the comfort of refreshing coolness in the heat of summer and becomes an unwanted intrusion in the chill of winter. Spiritually, the movement of the Spirit is likened to the personality of the wind. The pains of inner growth are occasioned by His disturbing presence and are balanced by His grace of deep serenity. The Spirit moves one beyond stagnation and complacency with the certainty that there is definite purpose in His movement.

When we consider people like Abraham, Moses and the prophets we discover the radical effect that God's Spirit had in their lives and beliefs. The "anawim", the "poor in spirit" were those who were not only poor in fact, but who also lived their lives in total openness to God's Spirit. With this Presence they were able to endure even the most intolerable living conditions.

The Spirit of God is the source of sustaining joy and peace. (Gal. 5) The truly free person is Spirit-filled; the truly free person lives joy and enjoys flexibility. Life is a mystery and a wonder, surrounding one with the beautiful.

Life's fulfillment is offered to us as gift from Jesus through His Spirit. We grow and we become whole in the uniting reality of Father, Son and Spirit. We begin to celebrate being alive—we begin to pray.

OUTLINE

—A most appropriate symbol for the Spirit is the Old Testament imagery of the wind.

—The best way to understand the symbol is to experience the wind itself.

—Therefore, the Spirit, like the wind, is mysterious, unpredictable, indescribable, and dialectically comforting and chilling.

Lunch	Brief and informal.
Afternoon Experience	It is suggested that in preparation for the evening session the afternoon be spent alone. Each person should seek out a physical situation (e.g., a hill, a field, a lake, or a lake shore) which will provide an expansiveness of vision. The purpose is to create the space in which the mind and spirit can experience total freedom. (For example, this group drove *together* to a near-by hill and then "climbed the mountain" and prayed *alone*.)
Presentation and Discussion	"The Prayer of Jesus" (Rev. Dennis Lynch)

The phrase "Jesus prayer" has become synonymous with the contemporary movement known as the Jesus People. But, this is not my concern. What I would like to do is share some random reflections on how the prayer life of Jesus may provide some insight into our individual prayer life.

—When Jesus was asked to show the apostles to pray, He prayed the "Our Father." Within this prayer are the two great themes or ingredients of all prayer: simple praise and petition.

—Petition has unfortunately taken on a "give me" emphasis. Prayer has become merely a list of wants that God is expected to satisfy. A prayer of petition should take on a personal admission of limitations and one's need to be dependent upon God. Petition is the expression of the person of hope who looks to the future with a sense of joyful expectation.

—The Psalms were the prayer of the Old and New Testaments. In its varied manner, the Psalms express a simple and profound belief: viz., You are God and may you always be God. You are my God and you will always be my God.

—An interesting aspect of Jesus' life is that He taught in the temple but He never prayed there. The world became the temple of prayer for Jesus. That is to say, Jesus was very fond of solitude. Except for the Our Father and the Last Supper, Jesus "went off alone to pray." His favorite places were the desert and the mountains, both providing the physical setting which encouraged a vision and expansiveness of spirit.

—Prayer is communion in the mystery and in the will of God. Prayer consists of being receptive to God so that He might be God, not only in Himself but also in man and in all of creation.

—Prayer needs to become more a listening experience, rather than an on-going, never-ending dialogue. In prayer, one needs to become comfortable in "doing nothing." A good prayer life necessitates growth for which a sensitive awareness is needed.

—Prayer is a response to God who initiates, who is the first to call forth.

—Prayer needs the discipline of the body; i.e., fasting and body posture. Both offer a deepening awareness of self, a self-consciousness of standing in relationship to Another.

No books were taken for the "mountain experience", only these thoughts were shared before the participants entered the solitude of the hills.

OUTLINE	—A not insignificant element in prayer is the physical setting. —Jesus taught us how to pray not only in words but most especially in terms of where and in what spirit we should pray. —Therefore, a good pray-er is one who consistently and constantly recognizes that he is a beginner.
Supper	A picnic before returning home.
Evening	Presentations and discussions included the parishioners.
Eucharistic Celebration	Including the parishioners, took place before the evening session. (Homily "Accomplishing Salvation," p. 45)

Presentation and Discussion   "Prayer" (Sr. Sandra Setterlund, SSJ)

By way of simple definition, prayer is a conversation between two persons who love each other. Two main dimensions come into focus with this definition: 1) that which we commonly refer to as "vertical prayer" is our love-communion with the Lord (as the prayer of solitude of Jesus on the mountain), while 2) that which we refer to as "horizontal prayer" is love-communion between one person and another (as the prayer of involvement of Jesus among the people). Neither can be treated, or considered, solely of itself, as both deepen and bring to fruition each other. That is, our love for God deepens our love for others, as human love extends itself into our relationship with Christ, thus making Him more comprehensible as man and God. Our relationship with Him as Lord intensifies in its personal dimension.

Prayer is a dialogue, a simple dialogue. We come to a deeper knowledge of another through sharing ideas, fears, needs, etc. We lose the fear of trying to impress another. So, too, we come into a fuller realization of who the Lord is, and our relationship with Him deepens through open dialogue. He takes us as we are. In both dimensions though, the human and the divine, silence is just as much a necessity as is speaking. We listen to what a loved one is saying to us, and perceiving what he cannot, or is not, saying to us. The same with God—we need the silence of listening to Him, to His Word. We need the tranquility and the serenity of allowing His Spirit to mold Himself into our lives. Perhaps His only "demand" is to accept Him when we are ready. There may be times in which our silence seems empty and somewhat discomforting, but it was St. Paul who said: "The Spirit pleads with unutterable groaning." In whatever situation we find ourselves, in whatever disposition we are the Spirit remains faithful within us. (The Lord is patient.) Sometimes the Spirit groans and pleads within us in expressions that we ourselves cannot understand. (The Lord is faithful—are we?) Much depends upon our own receptivity and willingness to allow the Spirit to have His way in our lives. God never forces Himself upon us—rather He waits indefinitely for us to let Him in, to receive and accept His presence in our lives. Prayer then becomes our human heart in conversation with God; thus, we have the human-divine relationship. Prayer takes time; it is slow development, as is love, friendship, deepening knowledge of another person.

It is important for us to think of God as Person, not as a concept, an idea, or a principle. Because we are human by nature, we need the fullness of relating to Him humanly. It doesn't really matter by what name we address God. What is important is that that name has personal meaning for us. God's love is not dependent upon the phraseology we use in addressing Him—the important thing is that we DO come to Him in trust, in surrender, in faith and anticipation of His love-filled wonders and in the desire to grow more deeply in love with Him. God is like unto us. In Hebrews, the reference to Jesus reads: "He had to become like his brothers in every way. . . . (Hebrews 2:17).

Nothing in life makes sense unless we can honestly and simply come to Jesus and make Him intimately a part of our lives. We must feel a need for Him, and then as we begin to respond to Him, that response converts itself into a constant awareness of the Lord. His presence is real to us—as real as our presence is to each other.

Questions for reflection and discussion:
1. Is my prayer alive?
2. When my prayer becomes arid, what is my reaction?
3. When it is difficult to pray, do I continue to try, or do I become passive in my efforts?
4. What is my personal contact with the Lord at the present?
5. Who is the Lord to me?

OUTLINE

—Prayer is a conversation between two persons who love each other.

—In prayer, silence is as essential a dimension as dialogue; prayer is a slow development, our human heart in relationship to God.

—Prayer is a living awareness of the Lord; His presence is as real as our presence to one another.

Compline service—creative response from the group.

3. *THIRD DAY—Theme: Woman with Man*

Morning Prayer

Metanoia Service.

This should be timed so that the celebration of the sacrament of penance will culminate in an Agape meal at noon.

Presentation and Discussion

"Metanoia—Returning to Jesus" (Sr. Sandra Setterlund, SSJ)

"Yet even now," says the Lord, "return to me with all your heart, with fasting and with mourning, and rend your hearts and not your garments." (Joel 2:12)

Metanoia begins with a change of heart, with a turning toward the Lord. Being the inner renewal of a person, metanoia is an ongoing process because of itself human nature needs reconciliation. For the Christian, reconciliation and forgiveness become a state of being, one person for another. Human imperfections demand a constant return of person to person with the need to be forgiven.

Scripture has the Lord's call as ". . . return to me with *all* your heart," and response to this call implies an inner emptiness, an utterance of "Here I am, Lord!" It is a response that allows us to never be pleased with our weaknesses and failures yet always believing in the healing power of Jesus. By nature every person is good and is intended to be integrated—to be a whole person in the grace of the Lord. Sin, or failure, is a transgression against one's integrity while metanoia is a return to that integrity through relationships that heal and reconcile.

Metanoia is the secret of those who are empowered by the Spirit. Recognition of the need and petition for forgiveness is the fertile soil in which the gifts of the Spirit remain dynamic. One develops an awareness of her individual charisms and learns to delight in presenting her unique "I am" to the Lord. Life then formulates the question—how do I remain faithful to being the person HE wants me to be unless I constantly return to Him with *all* my heart. Metanoia becomes a *way of life.* Once one experiences intimacy with the Lord, as with another person, that experience remains an integral part of life. Meeting Jesus is a communion of love, a touching of the heart that is never forgotten.

As necessary as it is to experience the height of this love, it is also as necessary to be humiliated by failing in that love. Failure occasions a deeper awareness of and sensitivity toward the beloved. If love is genuine it is more painful to fail than to be failed by the beloved. It is concluded, then, that the deeper the love relationship, the greater is the need for forgiveness and reconciliation.

At this point, it is well to consider the revolutionary metanoia-person of the New Testament: Paul. The extraordinary account of Paul's conversion is familiar but it is well to note that this metanoia experience became a state of being for him. Paul lived in constant "returning to the Lord." His penitent heart was a lifelong attitude from his moment of conversion. In his later writings Paul still considers himself "the foremost of sinners," (Tim. 1:16) and acknowledges his need for reconciliation with the Lord and forgiveness from fellow Christians.

While metanoia depends upon an individual's disposition of heart, it is also a communal action of acceptance. In his letter to the Thessalonians, (2 Thess. 3:14-15) Paul exhorts the Christian community not to treat the repentant person as an enemy but to welcome him as a brother. Members within the community of believers are invited to become vulnerable, to recognize the limitations of human nature, and to forgive one another. Metanoia also demands a spirit of honesty with self so as to grow more deeply conscious of the relationship of responsibility to the community. Greater honesty intensifies one's presence to the Lord, developing within oneself the grace of fidelity to love and the capacity to forgive. Jesus is the personification of fidelity and forgiveness. Often being disappointed by loved ones He never tallied their faults but remained constant in His love-commitment to them, a commitment that hoped and believed in reconciliation. Permeated with the Spirit of Jesus, then, we have the power to be reconcilors, to gift creation with wholeness, to be metanoia-persons who return to the Lord with all our heart.

Meditative response: sing "Keep in Mind."
Readings: Luke 7:36-50.
Communal examen.
Celebration of the Sacrament of Penance. While the group shares spontaneous prayer, silence, or music, the opportunity for private confession is available in a separate room.
General Absolution. After a communal prayer of absolution, the group proceeds to the dining room table for the Agape meal and the Eucharistic Prayer.
Afternoon is free.

OUTLINE

—Metanoia is an inner renewal which becomes an ongoing process because of itself human nature needs continued reconciliation.

—Sin is a transgression against one's integrity while metanoia is a return to that integrity through relationships that heal and reconcile.

—Metanoia depends upon one's inner disposition of heart as well as the community's spirit of forgiveness and acceptance.

Eucharistic Celebration before supper. (Homily: "Tread Softly," p. 46)

Evening Presentation and Discussion

"Woman—with Man" (Sr. Sandra Setterlund, SSJ)

Speaking in context, whether married or celibate, none of us are exempt from the need for heterosexual relationships. In the Old Testament it is recorded that God created woman so that man would not be alone. Life itself pivots on the relationship of woman with man. Creativity—of one's self and of each other—is brought to its fullness; i.e., man needs woman to realize the fullness of his manhood and woman needs man for the same fullness of personhood. Heterosexual fulfillment is not only discovered in love-making, although the body does have an important role in communication between woman and man. The physical, psychological and sexual differences between man and woman are differences that give vitality to life. It is true that life could well become stagnant if we did not have the challenge, the reciprocity, and the complementarity of the sexes. With each other, woman and man develop their ability to create life in all its dimensions. Within this creativity there remains the elements of surprise and mystery, the wonder of the unpredictable.

It is only in the meeting of an authentic man and an authentic woman, and in the relationship they share, that the strength of each is revealed and developed. The real and the deepest powers of our human nature are stirred whenever man and woman encounter each other and bring about a fuller realization of their unique identities. For any sustaining relationship between a woman and man, the ingredients of trust and love are necessary. It is in the depths of self-revelation between themselves that the individuals remain separate and often times baffling to each other. Because of the basic differences in their human nature, conflict is inevitable between man and woman, but in the spirit of love and trust this conflict is healthy. It gives a foundation to the relationship and does not become a destructive force. It is also with genuine love and trust that sex does not become a weapon, a threat or a fear. Commitment to one another overrules conquest of one another.

Mature sexuality is a celebration of love! It is a celebration of individuality, a sincere rejoicing that the other IS different. Love, then, is the liberating force through which man and woman can reach beyond each other to extend the joy, freshness, and depth of their love to others. Trusting love never contains itself but takes on the characteristic of endless giving . . . it *needs* to be extended.

Because each person possesses the inherent quality of transcendence, love is the means by which man and woman are able to reach beyond themselves and surrender to each other not for the sake of their own pleasure, but for the sake of each other's happiness. The body becomes a means through which affection and love are expressed, but remains as only a single means. Deep communion of souls, of minds, of hearts is, and can be, just as intimate an expression of love as sexual intercourse.

To love someone is to become vulnerable and to be vulnerable is frightening! There exists a silent pain that can never really be explained to and understood by the loved one. Vulnerability is an openness to the pain of never being enough for the beloved and risking the possibility of being used, being forgotten, or being rejected. Persons who love chance the pain of being broken or the ecstasy of being fulfilled. In this surrendering, love celebrates life.

OUTLINE

—No one is exempt from the need for heterosexual relationships as life itself pivots on the relationship of woman with man.

—Through the basic elements of trust and love, man and woman develop a relationship of commitment rather than one of conquest.

—In a mutual surrendering and vulnerability, man and woman share a love that celebrates life.

Compline service—creative response from the group.

E. MATERIALS/RESOURCES

The following books were and should be available to the group.

THE ADVANCING DIGNITY OF WOMAN IN THE BIBLE, Rev. Thierry Maertens,
 St. Norbert Abbey Press, 1969.
THE FASCINATING FEMALE, Dorothy Dohen, Deus Books, Paulist Press, 1964.
THE FEMININE MYSTIQUE, Betty Friedan, Dell Book, 1970.
THE ILLUSION OF EVE, Sidney Callahan, Sheed & Ward, Inc., 1965.
THE QUITE POSSIBLE SHE, Janet Golden, Abbey Press, 1966.
OUR MANY SELVES, Elizabeth O'Connor, Harper & Row Publishers, 1971.
WOMAN—A CONTEMPORARY VIEW, F.J.J. Buytendijk, Newman Press & Association Press, 1968.

Periodicals on the theme of Womanhood:

ST. ANTHONY MESSENGER, March 1971.
SISTERS TODAY, March 1971.
THE CHICAGO THEOLOGICAL SEMINARY REGISTER, March 1970.

The following material was used and is recommended for the creation of prayer services.

THE PRAYER OF CHRISTIANS.
GOD IS HERE, LET'S CELEBRATE, Leslie F. Brandt, Concordia Publishing House, 1970.
GREAT GOD, HERE I AM, Leslie F. Brandt, Concordia Publishing House, 1969.
FIFTY PSALMS, Huub Oosterhuis, et al., Herder and Herder, 1967.
THE PSALMS FOR MODERN MAN, American Bible Society, New York, 1970.
YOUR WORD IS NEAR, Huub Oosterhuis, Newman Press, 1968.

F. LITURGIES/HOMILIES

1. SUMMARIES

1) *Subject:*   Being Woman
    Talks: The Dignity of Woman in Sacred Scripture
                      Reflections on Being Woman
    Services: Homily based on— Cor. 4; John 17
                      Closing prayer service—creative response from the group.

2) *Subject:*   Prayer
    Talks: Reflections on the Spirit
                      The Prayer of Jesus
                      Prayer
    Services: Morning prayer service—creative response from the group
                      Homily based on—Rom. 3: 19-30
                                    Luke 18: 9-14.
                      Closing prayer service—creative response from the group

3) *Subject:*   Metanoia
    Talk: Metanoia—Returning to Jesus
    Services: Communal Sacrament of Penance.

4) *Subject:*   Woman—with Man
    Talk: Woman—with Man
    Services: Homily based on—1 Kings 3:5, 7-12
                                        Matthew 13: 44-52
                      Closing prayer service—creative response from the group

5) *Subject:*   The Evangelical Counsels
    Talks: 2 homilies on—1 John 3; Matthew 5
    Services: Liturgy in the parish, public renewal of vows

COMPLINE SERVICE

Theme: The Lord is with us!

Call to worship: Luke 1:31
                    Do not be afraid; God loves you dearly. The
                    Holy Spirit will come upon you, the power of
                    the Most High will overshadow you.

Response: I belong to the Lord, body and soul. Let it happen as you say.

Leader: Our help is in the Name of the Lord.

Response: Who made heaven and earth.

Leader: Genuine love is neither diminished nor threatened by the inclusiveness of many persons. Its power grows as persons readily share the presence of the Spirit of Love in their lives. But, in this sharing we sometimes fall short. Conscious of our need for forgiveness and reconciliation, we now ask these two gifts of God and of each other.

Examen:

Confiteor: In our love we stand before God, our Father, Mary the Christ-bearer, John the Baptist, the Christ-proclaimer, all the saints who see God face to face, and each other, and pledge our sorrow for being unworthy servants of the Word. It is through our own choice that we have fallen short of being truly what we were called to be. We ask to be made clean and refreshed so that we may begin again to love more fully.

Leader: Christ, our Brother, come dwell in our hearts.

Response: Come quickly to answer our prayer. Glory be to the Father of mankind, and to Love-Incarnate, and to the Spirit of peace. As it was in the beginning, is now, and ever shall be world without end. Amen.

Recite: (alternating sides—taken from *God is Here, Let's Celebrate!*) Psalm 145:

1. God is here—let's celebrate. Let us enlist our lives in perpetual celebration over God's goodness and greatness. Let us announce to the world God's presence and proclaim His loving concern for all men.

2. How compassionate He is over all that He has created, how tender and loving toward His failure-fraught creatures! He will not cop out on His promises to us. His blessings are not reserved only for those who fit obediently into His design for them.

1. He is just—and He is forgiving. He gently picks up those who have fallen and restores them to sonship and servanthood. He sustains those who are wavering in weakness and grants them His grace and strength.

2. He reaches into the void of empty lives and enriches and fulfills their hungry hearts. He is near enough to hear our every cry, to sense our every need, to grant us whatever is necessary to make us happy and productive as we seek to follow and to serve Him.

1. How incomparably glorious is our great God! May our mouths articulate and our lives demonstrate His ever-present love for all the creatures of our world.

All: Let us celebrate the eternal mercy and goodness of our God. Alleluia.

Sing: SPIRIT OF GOD

Reading: (Magnificat)
My life praises the Lord and everything that is truly me is glad because I know God. He makes me happy in my lowliness and from this time on all people shall see God's holiness through the things He has done for me. He makes the proud humble and to the poor He gives wealth. The hungry taste of His goodness, the rich He empties. Failing not to keep His promises, He fulfills His words to Abraham and all His people.

Leader: I entrust to you, Yahweh, my love for this world.

Response: At last, Lord, you can dismiss your servant in peace, as you promised. For with my own eyes I have seen your salvation, which you have made ready for every people—a light to show truth to the Gentiles and bring glory to your people Israel. Glory be. . . .

Leader: Lord have mercy.

All: Christ have mercy.

Leader: Let us pray together:
God, our Father, in all that is most living and incarnate in you, you are not far away from us, altogether apart from the world we see, touch, hear, smell, and taste about us. Rather you await us every instant in our action, in the work of the moment. There is a sense in which you are at the tip of my pen, my spade, my brush, my needle—of my heart and of my thought. By pressing the stroke, the line or the stitch, on which I am engaged, to its ultimate natural finish, I shall lay hold of that last end towards which my innermost will tends. This we ask of you through Christ our Lord. Amen. (Chardin's *THE DIVINE MILIEU*)

Closing Hymn: (to be chosen by the group)

3. CEREMONY

Liturgy For The Public Renewal Of Vows
The renewal of vow ceremony takes place during a parish liturgy. The blank spaces are relative to the Community celebrating this occasion.

Our Community _____ began its renewal program _____ ago. We searched, and we continue to search, for the best way in which we can live out the Gospel values as we understand them. In our personal lives, which are lives of service to you, the People of God, we seek to live and speak the message of the living Christ. Today we wish to renew our profession of vows in your presence, asking you to act as witnesses for the whole Church. The truth and goodness and beauty of the past has brought us to this day. We are grateful. Our continued honest search will lead us into tomorrow. We approach that tomorrow with confidence in you, and in the Lord, knowing that the Spirit of Christ goes before us in our search.

Opening song:

After the Epistle: If the Community has an Apostolic Creed it is professed at this time. Otherwise some other form of a faith-statement can be written and proclaimed for this celebration.

(Commentary) As a Community we are yet exploring more creative and relevant means of serving you and working with you in building a better world. Our goals are expressed in this our Apostolic Creed.

Homily: cf. material in Presentation IV, pp. 46-50.

Offertory procession: With these Offertory gifts we remember the words of Jesus to His Apostles:

I am the Light of the World—and so we proceed with the Paschal Candle, believing that Christ is the Light of our lives;

He said, *I am the Bread of Life*—and we bring forth the fruits of the earth: water, wine and bread;

He said, *I am the Truth*—and for us, the Sisters of _____ the truth is contained in the words of our Constitution _____;

We ask God, our Father, to receive these gifts in the name of His Son, Jesus.

Offertory song:

Renewal of Vows: (before Communion) At this time we wish to pronounce publicly our vows of poverty, chastity, and obedience as we often renew them within our own Community. It is in our _____ tradition of vowing ourselves to the Gospel life that we understand this commitment to be our way of following the Lord Jesus.

(The vow formula is either the Community form or one written personally by each Sister.)

Communion song:

Closing song:

It is suggested: 1) that the readings and songs chosen reflect the theme of commitment, and
2) that the Sisters participate in the Liturgy to the fullest extent possible—i.e., office of lector and homilist, Offertory procession, distribute the Eucharist, extend the Kiss of Peace to the entire congregation.

Suggested readings: 1 John 3; Matthew 5.
Suggested songs: W.F. Jabusch: What Can We Offer?
Ray Repp: Till All My People Are One; To Be Alive
Sebastian Temple: All That I Am; Follow Christ; Happy the Man; Magnificat; Prayer of St. Francis; Take My Hands
Joe Wise: Regina's Song; To Be Your Body; We Are Your Bread; Yes To You, My Lord

4. HOMILY

Theme: The Dignity of Woman
Suggested readings for the Liturgy: 1 Cor. 4; John 17.

There have been many stereotyped images of woman throughout the history of man, and one of the most popular, and thereby the most offensive to women, is the image of woman as one who submits. This image highlights woman's secondary position and replaces her prerogatives and preferences with those of man.

Fortunately, this negative attitude is being eliminated today, but we must not throw out the baby with the bath water. That is to say, we must not lose the positive dimensions of submission. I would like to suggest that surrender reflects this positive dimension and is the essence of the Gospel.

In his book, *INTRODUCTION TO CHRISTIANITY*, Joseph Ratzinger states that: "Man is redeemed by the cross; the crucified Christ, as the completely opened being, is the true redemption of man. . . . If we look at it now, not from the point of view of content but from that of structure, we see that, in the last analysis of man, it expresses the primacy of acceptance over action, over one's own achievement." (p. 183) For an outside observer this is the stumbling block associated with Christianity—viz., the folly of the cross is wisdom, while the wisdom of the world is foolishness. That is to say, maturity and meaning are not based on what man does or possesses or achieves, but on his capacity to receive.

Life and love are neither burdens to be endured, nor unattainable ideals carroted before man by God, nor responsibilities to be stoically exercised; they are gifts to be celebrated. Happiness results from affirming what we are graced with, and relaxing actively in the presence of the Giftor.

5. HOMILY

Theme: Prayer
Suggested readings for the Liturgy: Rom. 3:19-30; Luke 18:9-14.

Even though a woman-bishop is still a long way off, there has been a decided change in attitude and atmosphere in the Church relative to the role of woman as minister. I don't want to get into any deep theological discussion because the Word of God within the Liturgy is to be proclaimed rather than debated. Therefore, what I wish to suggest is a reflection on redemption which has some meaning relative to man-woman equality.

St. Paul's teaching of salvation can be capsulized in one word—"boasting." What is meant by this is the self-assertiveness of man vis-a-vis God. For Paul this self-assertiveness was reflected in the Jewish adherence to the Law, or in the delicate reasonings of Greek philosophy, or in the esoteric knowledge claimed by some of the enthusiasts of his time. Today, this same kind of boasting can be reflected in several attitudes toward spirituality: if I say a certain type or number of prayers—I am holy; or, if I do not change anything in my religion—I am faithful; or, if I consider those who are outside my mentality or interest group as lost—I am saved. On the other hand, for Paul ALL men are ungodly; ALL men are in need of salvation. NO ONE has any claim on God's salvation.

But there are subtle ways of "boasting"—e.g., automatically excluding people because of sex; immediate and prejudiced classification of people based on what has been; the suspicion of others because of color or reputation. Each of these actions, however innocent it may seem, goes against the fabric of Christianity. That is to say, the Gospel reminds us that we have *nothing* about which to boast; that we are to stand in openness to the gratuity of God's salvation.

As the Church reflects on its attitude to the question of equality between man and woman, it must reflect across the board about itself and acknowledge that its only boast is in the Lord.

6. HOMILY

Theme: Woman—with Man
Suggested readings for the Liturgy: 1 Kings 3:5, 7-12 and Matthew 13:44-52

American society has been described as a very narcissistic society because of its insatiable consumer appetite. Despite its great gestures of generosity in foreign aid and responses to disasters, it becomes more apparent that these actions were and are performed for less than mere loving reasons. In addition, our environment is being buried in manufactured junk which the average person doesn't need but feels advertised to consume. A further reflection of this mentality is the consumer attitude toward education. Here, too, more and more is automatically better and better. To be educated is automatically equated with going-to-school for "x" number of years; and wisdom is the result of degrees earned. Ironically, we live in an educated society but have few men of wisdom; (wisdom being understood in its purest denotation).

I would like to suggest another understanding of wisdom, based on the Word that has been proclaimed. That is to say, wisdom finds its foundation as well as its application, in a concern for the *other*. Solomon's wisdom was the ability to discern the good for others. Both the reign of Solomon and the Kingdom that Jesus preached involve the emphasis on the *other*.

Secondly, wisdom is the result of God's gracious gift to man. Man is the requester and the searcher for wisdom—when it comes, it comes, as a gift received, as a surprise of discovery.

If wisdom is other-centered, then ignorance is self-centeredness, an ignoring of the *other*. Hence, many years of study and/or degrees in education don't guarantee wisdom; nor do many years of life assure it. Both young and old can be wise if they are genuinely open to others which is God's gracious and personal gift of love.

7. HOMILY

Theme: Public Renewal of Vows

Suggested readings for the Liturgy: 1 John 3; Matthew 5.

As we experience the renewal of vows, we have to ask the question about religious life and vows. We do so not for apologetic reasons, but for commitment purposes. Up to the Second Vatican Council there was a peculiar kind of thinking which said that those who did not follow the evangelical counsels, (poverty, chastity, and obedience*) were not following the way to perfection. But with *The Constitution on the Church*, and its placing of "religious life" (Chapter VI) within the perspective of the *universal* call of all Christians in the Church to holiness (Chapter V), we have a change in the former understanding. The paradox that must be retained is: *all* Christians are called to live a full Christian life; and a life governed by the evangelical counsels has a special value and a special function. Because of the complexity of the entire subject, and the particular significance of today, I would like to limit my remarks to the "special" value and function of a life governed by the evangelical counsels.

First of all, those who have publicly opted for a life according to the evangelical counsels can be considered the elect. This "election" reflects the characteristics of Israel's election—viz., not a position of preference; not a necessary prerogative of moral authority; but a life of service, responsibility and severe accountability.

Secondly, a life according to the evangelical counsels realizes and points to the essential dimension of faith. This faith can be understood in two ways. In the first place, a person can genuinely understand what is involved in the renunciation demanded by the evangelical counsels only if he is one who loves the beauty of life, one for whom marriage is a valid occasion for fulfillment, one who can love deeply and personally. If these are absent, then one wonders about the health of the person's choice. In other words, an act of renunciation which knows *all* the positive and negative factors involved, and has thought them out *completely*, ceases to be such. For the choice of a life of the evangelical counsels or the renunciation of other life styles, is an act of faith (a kind of a leap) in God's guiding and saving presence within one's individual life.

In the second place, the life of the evangelical counsels points to a specific meaning of the visible Church. Whereas the Word and the Sacraments are God's grace as tangibly *offered* in the Church, the *full* and *genuine* living out of the life according to the evangelical counsels points to the grace of God as *accepted* and *operative*. But this "already" of God's salvation, needs to be balanced by the "not yet" of the Eschaton.

Therefore, those of you who are today publicly recommitting yourselves to a life of the evangelical counsels come as those with responsibilities; you come not in honor but in humility. You present to this community as well as to the world, a concrete incarnation of faith in God's fulfilling and sustaining presence —therefore, again you come not in honor but in humbleness. We all thank and praise God with you, offer our support and criticism, and challenge you to live this life enthusiastically.

(*It is to be noted that this is the traditional distinction. Other terms can be substituted: e.g., poverty, celibacy, and cooperation.)

8. HOMILY

Theme: Public Renewal of Vows (Alternate)
Suggested readings for the Liturgy: 1 John 3; Matthew 5.

The time of vow renewal always, as it should, occasions a time of reflection on the vows of poverty, chastity, and obedience. Needless to say, there has been limitless writing, preaching and discussion on these evangelical counsels. But today I would like to be specific and share some thoughts on the virtue of poverty. I chose this area because its meaning has been keenly examined due to the exodus of people from priestly and religious life. That is to say, it was only *after* leaving the religious life that many *first* experienced a poor life.

Theologian Karl Rahner, himself an order priest, has made the statement that a rich order cannot have poor members. That is to say, it is very difficult to accept someone as living a life of poverty when in reality all individual needs (in the material realm) are provided by the religious community. Therefore, evangelical poverty cannot be synonymous with dependence. It demands an element which distinguishes it from the poverty of those people who depend on someone else for their existence and meaning in life—e.g., even though people on welfare depend on others for their livelihood, they hardly are living evangelical poverty.

In addition, we live in an economic and technical atmosphere which makes us approach the Gospel admonition with discerning spirits. In other words, poverty is relative reality. What is considered poverty level wages in the United States is a king's ransom in many underdeveloped countries. Jesus traveled on foot and preached in the marketplace. This is still valid, but modern means of transportation and communication can enhance the preaching of the Gospel—of course the latter is not free of expense.

I don't want to pursue or attempt to formulate an absolute description of poverty. I do this for two reasons: 1) this presupposes a more thorough treatment of the Gospel narratives as well as the historical expression of poverty which would be a whole course of study and 2) an absolute description doesn't emphasize enough the specific expressions which each situation demands—i.e., poverty for someone in Appalachia would be different than for a college campus minister.

I would like to suggest that any consideration of poverty must begin with a basic faith perspective. That is to say, fulfillment in the life of the believer is the result of God's gracious gift of salvation, a totally other-worldly reality. *Total* fulfillment is only anticipated, but the actual now-manifestation of that presence is made real in Jesus. This already-but not yet dialectic means that the believer is one who travels lightly and is wary of any reality that will distract him from the Lord.

Therefore the person of poverty is foremost the person who is faithful to the Lord; who acknowledges that the last days have begun; who wants to be found waiting when the Lord comes again. If this is the heart-conviction with which the believer begins, the actual reflection of this in his life will not be a contradiction.

III. COMMUNITY BUILDING, SPIRITUAL RENEWAL WORK SHOP

By Maury Smith, O.F.M.

and Charles Bloss, O.F.M.

A. THEME/PARTICIPANTS

1. INTRODUCTION

The designers of this community building, spiritual renewal program want to emphasize from the beginning that this spiritual workshop was designed for a particular group of sisters. This is an example of what can be done, and is not intended as a blanket design for every group. The design includes inputs from the social sciences in the areas of group dynamics, value clarification, and exercises from an organizational development viewpoint.

The designers met with a committee of the community three months before the scheduled time for the spiritual renewal. The purpose was to get to know the sisters, what their situation was, what their needs were, what their expectations for the spiritual renewal were, the spirit of their community, the ages of the sisters, the kind of spiritual needs they felt they had, what they were hoping to accomplish by this renewal, and the problems of community that they faced at this particular time. We explored what kind of approach would best suit their needs. Alternating topics and group dynamics were considered.

On the basis of the first meeting, the designers then made a tentative design they felt would meet the needs and expectations of the sisters. A second meeting was held with the sisters one month before the workshop in order to allow them to respond to the tentative design and make changes in it. We wanted to get all the sisters involved in the creation of the spiritual renewal. All the sisters were divided into teams. One team discussed the liturgy, another team morning and evening prayers, another team was in charge of physical decorating of the meeting rooms and dining room. They also prepared meal prayers. Another team acted as a guest committee and planned the party Sunday evening.

The goal of the design was to help the sisters of this particular apostolate gain a better sense of community among themselves. There were two themes that permeated the designing of the weekend. One focus was on the individual sister as a sister and person. The other was on community and personal relationships. Saturday was devoted to considering the sister as a person. Sunday was spent on the theme of a person and the community. Follow-up was desirable with a carry over into the participants' everyday lives, and so the last day's session (Monday) was devoted to "back home application."

To build community, maximum interaction between and among the groups of sisters was designed. Since the sisters came from various cities we initially promoted interaction in the whole group, asking that they form groups by mixing them liberally and freely as we broke them up into small groups. The fourth and fifth session we broke them up according to cities they had come from to help build their spirit within that city. The final two sessions, we broke the sisters up into the actual convents in which they lived. We hoped by this to create a total community spirit and at the same time to improve the community spirit of each city and each convent.

2. DESCRIPTION OF THE AUDIENCE

(The names of the cities have been changed in order to avoid identifying the particular sisters for whom this workshop was designed.)

The following outline gives an indication of their general settings and of their age range.

    I. Rockford
       A. St. Theresa—4 younger sisters
   II. Rockford
       A. St. Georges—4 older sisters
  III. Joliet
       A. St. Patrick—2 younger and 2 older
  IV. Decatur
       A. St. Philomena—4 older sisters

V. Chicago
   A. St. Mary—10 older sisters
   B. St. Elizabeth—5 older sisters living at school and 3 younger sisters living in an apartment
VI. Peoria
   A. St. James—3 older sisters working in grade school and 2 younger sisters working in the high school.

3. AGE BREAKDOWN

20 in their sixties.
10 in their fifties.
 5 in their forties.
10 in their thirties.
 5 in their twenties.

Most all of the sisters were teachers, and most taught in a high school setting. Their religious community had been going through changes common to sisters' communities in the last five years. There had been a transition from the older traditional hierarchial government to a more modern democratic leadership in their convents. They had also experienced the loss of a number of sisters, as most congregations have. There was some gap between the older and younger sisters, but in most instances no strong animosity. In the Chicago group, at St. Elizabeth, there were some hurt feelings because three of the younger sisters had moved away from the school and established their own apartment, leaving the five older sisters to themselves. In one of the other communities, there was some friction between the older and younger sisters about the life style.

There was a newly elected regional superior who wanted to help the sisters develop a sense of community and common cause. The committee of sisters agreed their greatest need was to feel a bond of community, of working together. They also felt that there was an identity problem for some of the sisters in relation to the many changes in the church today. This committee of sisters estimated approximately 2/3 of their sisters felt dislocated and hurt by some of the changes. Older sisters were especially hurt when younger sisters moved away from them.

Another area of concern was the sisters' need to grow in a sense of personal value and worth. The committee of sisters felt that a minority of about 10 sisters felt worthless, not seeing the value of the work to which they were assigned or the community in which they lived. Another area of concern felt to be very important by the committee was the older sisters' feeling left out by some of the changes in the order. Some of the older sisters had complained of loneliness. This was felt when the younger sisters mixed with people and families. The older sisters were stuck at home, not knowing how to drive.

It was on the basis of this information that the tentative design was formed. One month before the meeting, the designers met with the committee once more, to go over their tentative plans and to allow the sisters to evaluate and to make changes they felt would help them achieve the goals established for the retreat. To be explicit, the main goal of the retreat was to build a community spirit among the sisters. There were several sub-themes: through the workshop they hoped to improve communication between the younger and older sisters, they hoped to help the sisters explore their identity and build up feelings of self worth.

B. OUTLINE/SCHEDULE

1. OUTLINE OF CONTENT:

SESSION I. Expectations
    Introduce: Personal Journal
               Dyadic Encounter
SESSION II. Personal Commitment to Religious Life
    Introduction to Value Clarification
SESSION III. Identity Search in Religious Life
SUNDAY THEME: Community and Interpersonal Relationships
SESSION IV. Person and Community
SESSION V. Conflict/Change in Religious Life
SESSION VI. Growth in Community
    Love Seat Experience
    Party for the Community
MONDAY THEME: Back-home Application
SESSION VII. Back-home Application.
    Closing of journal and dyadic time.
    Evaluation of the Spiritual Renewal.

2. SCHEDULE

Friday: Time to get settled and renew acquaintances.
Saturday and Sunday:
8 AM to 8:45 Rise and breakfast
9 AM to 11:30 First Session
12 Noon, Lunch
2 PM Celebration of Eucharist
3 to 5:30 Second Session
6 PM Supper
7 to 9:30 Third Session
Monday:
8 AM to 8:45 Rise and breakfast
9 AM to 11 Last Session
11 AM Eucharist
12 Noon, Lunch

On Saturday we will consider the individual as a sister and as a person.
Sunday we will examine community and interpersonal relationships.
On Monday we will attempt to make application to your home situation.

In a workshop of this kind you are responsible for your own learning. Any time you have ideas, suggestions, materials, criticisms, etc., please inform the staff.

During the sessions feel free to get up and move around, get coffee, take care of personal needs, or simply leave for awhile to relax. Most of the work of this workshop will be done by you through your individual contributions. Think of yourself as a resource person. You have talents, gifts, skills, and experience to share with your fellow sisters. Look at the staff as additional resource people for you. Make use of us. Call us for consultation at any time during the sessions.

3. LEADER'S OUTLINE

Meet three months ahead of time with a committee of sisters to determine their expectations and needs.

Meet one month ahead of time with tentative design and content. Get all the sisters involved in planning for this spiritual renewal.

Friday Evening:
9:00 P.M.   Brief Introduction
               Informal social recreation

Saturday—Theme: The Individual as Sister and Person

8:00 A.M.	Rise and continental breakfast
9:00 A.M.	Morning Prayer
9:15 A.M.	I. Session: Expectations
	Getting Better Acquainted: "Who Am I?"
9:35 A.M.	Three hopes/three fears about workshop
9:40 A.M.	Break into six mixed groups to collate their individual lists.
10:10 A.M.	General Session: Report from each group on newsprint; discussions.
10:40 A.M.	Introduce: Personal Journal (10 minutes)
	Dyadic Encounter (30 minutes)
12 Noon	Lunch
2:00 P.M.	Celebration of Eucharist
	II. Session: Personal Commitment to Religious Life
3:00 P.M.	Introduction to Value Clarification
3:10 P.M.	Value Clarification Strategies:
	Word Associations
	Love list
	I Urge You Telegram
	Hope to Accomplish
3:55 P.M.	Break into another set of mixed groups for small group discussions.
4:25 P.M.	Value Clarification Strategy: Coat of arms
4:40 P.M.	Small group discussion
5:20 P.M.	Journal Time
5:30 P.M.	Optional Dyadic Time
6:00 P.M.	Supper
7:00 P.M.	III. Session: Identity Search
9:30 P.M.	Optional Evening Prayer.

Sunday—Theme: Community and Interpersonal Relationships.

8:00 A.M.	Rise and Continental Breakfast
9:00 A.M.	Morning Prayers
9:15 A.M.	IV. Session: Person and Community
9:20 A.M.	Ten areas involved in being a Woman Religious
10:00 A.M.	Small group discussions in city groups
11:00 A.M.	Small group discussion
11:30 A.M.	Journal & Dyadic Time
12:00 Noon	Lunch
2:00 P.M.	Celebration of the Eucharist
	V. Session: Conflict/Change in Religious Life
3:00 P.M.	Film: "Is it always right to be right?"
3:15 P.M.	Broken Square (in city groups)
4:15 P.M.	Value Sheet on Religious Life Today
4:30 P.M.	Small Group Discussion in City Groups
5:20 P.M.	Show Film again
5:30 P.M.	Journal and Dyadic Time
6:00 P.M.	Supper
	VI. Growth in Community
7:00 P.M.	Introduction: Love Seat
7:15 P.M.	Each individual makes list of at least ten good personal qualities she has.
7:30 P.M.	Small group sharing in convent home group.
8:30 P.M.	Evening Prayers
8:45 P.M.	Party

Monday: VII. Session Back home Application

8:00 A.M.	Rising and breakfast
9:00 A.M.	Morning Prayers
9:15 A.M.	Dyadic Partner Closing Time

9:45 A.M.	Make a list of what you have learned during workshop, using your journal.
10:00 A.M.	Small group discussion with convent home group: What you have learned and how you can continue learning at home.
10:30 A.M.	Evaluation of the Renewal
10:45 A.M.	Journal Time
11:00 A.M.	Closing Celebration of Eucharist. Place journals on altar at offertory. Re-dedication to Christ after Communion.

C. GUIDELINES

In order for this model to be successfully implemented, it is necessary that the leaders have some knowledge of group dynamics and value clarification. We would suggest that you refer to the bibliography and do some reading in this area, and if possible, work with someone experienced in group dynamics and value clarification. Again the designers of this model wish to remind you that this particular spiritual renewal was designed for this unique group to focus on their needs and expectations. We think this model would work with a group similar to the group it was designed for. However, we wish to point out that in a group process and experiential learning approach to spiritual renewal, a constant effort is made to get the sisters involved in their own learning process. Designing the spiritual renewal to include sessions to help them evaluate their own situation and choose the areas on which they wish to concentrate is, therefore, extremely important.

The full length schedule for the leaders and the full explanations of how each of the sessions was conducted, have sufficient information that a person should be able to use them. However, a few general comments about this approach would be helpful.

Notice that this spiritual renewal actually began with the formation of a committee of sisters who worked with the leaders to design the process. They had a great deal of information and input about what it was they felt they needed and what they hoped to accomplish through the spiritual renewal. The committee of sisters were met with three months ahead of time, and on the basis of a long discussion with them, the tentative model was designed and brought back to them one month before the actual conducting of the spiritual renewal. At that time the committee of sisters helped the leaders to particularize and to decide on various details of the conducting of the workshop, in order to make the workshop fit the needs of this unique group of sisters, and to help accomplish the goals that the committee of sisters had asked of the leaders.

One of the features of this design was to accomplish a maximum of interaction and interchange between all of the sisters attending the workshop. In the first three sessions, the sisters were mixed into small groups without reference to the city they came from or the convent they came from. In the middle two sessions, they were broken up into groups which were representative of the cities in which they lived. For example, all the Chicago people were put together, and then the Rockford people were put together in a group, and the other three small cities were put together in a group to encourage community building in the cities in which the sisters resided. Finally, in the last two sessions the sisters were asked to move into their actual convent settings, and work together in the community in which they lived. This was especially important for the last session, in which the task was to set goals and make decisions as to how they themselves could follow up and could in their own community continue the community spirit developed during the workshop.

Another feature of this design was to encourage the sisters to keep a personal journal of what happened and how they felt about what happened during the workshop. This is a crystallization process by which all individuals are encouraged to reflect on their experiences and gather the learning value for themselves from the experience and how they are reacting to what they are experiencing. As described in the text, they use a notebook and on the back of the first page, write "events," list the objective events of each particular session. On the facing page, they write "subjective" and describe their feelings and their reactions to what is happening. This becomes very helpful for them, especially at the end of the workshop, when they are given the task of listing the learnings acquired from the workshop, in order to make decisions on how they might continue the community spirit they have built during the workshop. Some people refer back to their journals six months, a year, or even several years later as a source of growing.

Another feature of this design is the alternation between time spent in groups, individual time, structured time for two people to get together. The goal of the two people getting together was that they might learn some skills in interpersonal relationships in a dyadic framework. This gave the opportunity to grow in one-to-one relationships. We used the little booklet by John E. Jones and Johanna Jones, called THE DYADIC ENCOUNTER. This booklet helps two people to get to know one another in a relatively short time, and gives some listening skills, indicating how feelings might be shared. Generally speaking, we asked that the participants choose as their partner someone whom they did not know, but would like to get to know.

A very important issue in this design was to get all of the sisters as involved in the creating of the spiritual renewal as possible. We had already begun to do this by having a committee of sisters who were totally involved in the planning of the spiritual renewal. The other sisters were involved by being put into committees to take care of the liturgy, design morning and evening prayers, decorate the retreat center and create meal prayers for the group. One committee was in charge of the party Sunday evening.

The designers of this spiritual renewal felt it would be a crime to bring in ready made liturgies and scripture services. There is a great deal of talent and resources within a group of sisters of this size, and it was important to tap those resources and give them an opportunity to express their talents and creativity.

The homilies during the Eucharistic celebrations should be based on the themes the sisters chose in their planning of the liturgical celebration. The priest leaders should meet with the liturgical committee, so that he can design his homily to fit into their theme. The priest leader should offer himself as a resource person to meet with all of the committees. This is another opportunity to be in contact with the sisters and to get to know them and be of service to them.

D. TALKS/EXERCISES

1. STAGE ONE: **Introductions**

Friday evening: Brief Introduction

The sister who is chairwoman of the committee for the sisters introduces the three priests who will be leaders of this spiritual renewal. The priest chairman of the team talks very briefly welcoming the sisters to the retreat center. He encourages them to spend the evening in renewing acquaintances and in getting to know one another. (It was decided by the planning committee that there would be no activities Friday evening, because many of the sisters were coming from quite a distance and had been teaching all week. Another option for a group which would not be under this strain would be to begin with Saturday morning's session #1 at this Friday evening time. Another project or session could be added Saturday morning.)

Saturday Theme: The Individual as Sister And Person

Rise and continental breakfast
Morning prayers (created by the prayer committee of sisters.)
First Session: Expectations.

THEME: The goal of this session is to double check the expectations of the sisters for the workshop, and to introduce the practice of the personal journal and Dyadic Encounter time.

MATERIALS NEEDED   Pencils, paper and pins.
The Dyadic Encounter booklets: John E. Jones and Johanna Jones. *DYADIC ENCOUNTER*, Iowa City: University Press, 1969. The address is Box 615, Iowa City, Iowa 52240.

1) Exercise One: Who Am I?

THEME: The goal of this exercise is ice-breaking and beginning interaction among all the participants.

MATERIALS NEEDED   Pencil, paper, and pins.

DIRECTIONS: Give the sisters five minutes to list at least ten sentences to complete the phrase, "I am _____." This is very general; they can write whatever they wish as a completion to the sentence, "I am _____." Once the sisters have completed at least 10 sentences of "I am _____," they are to pin the sheet to their chest so that others can easily read what they have written. It is good to tell them to write in large letters and use felt pens, in order that they may be easily read by others.
Ask the sisters to mill around in silence and read one another's lists.
After they have read one another's lists, ask the sisters to choose a partner with whom they would be interested in talking for approximately six minutes.

PROCESS: This is a very easy introductory exercise. It exchanges a lot of information about one another, giving individuals an opportunity to see what others think of themselves, as well as an opportunity to talk to one person in the group more intensively. An option to this exercise rather than completing the sentence, I am, would be to use the same exercise, asking them to list what their hopes and expectations for the workshop would be, and to then discuss these briefly when they get into the dyad.

2) Exercise Two: Three Hopes & Three Fears about the Workshop

THEME: The goal of this exercise is to have the participants reflect on what their expectations are for the workshop.

MATERIALS NEEDED: Pencil and paper
Blackboard or newsprint for the total group to be able to see what they are doing.
Masking tape.

DIRECTIONS: First have each individual take three minutes to write out three hopes she has for the workshop and three fears she has for the workshop. This can be explained as what they hope will happen in the four days that they are together, and three things they would like not to happen during the workshop.

      Next break the sisters up into six mixed groups to collate their individual lists. Ask them to appoint a secretary. Instruct the secretary to write their hopes and desires in summary on newsprint so that it can be read by the whole group later. Give them approximately ½ hour to collate their materials. They may be able to do this in a shorter time; move with the group.

GENERAL SESSION: After the groups have had time to discuss and collate their individual lists into a group list, ask the secretary of each group to present their list. Use newsprint hung with masking tape. It is important for the leader to listen carefully and to acknowledge the expectations of the total group; what they are hoping to accomplish this weekend. Hopefully, the work of the committee has been on target, so that the group is in accord with the plans of the planning committee. However, it may well be that some need or some expectation in the group has newly emerged, or the leaders may have to drop a particular session for which there seems to be no interest, replacing it with a session which seems to be of more importance to the sisters at that time. The leader must be sure he understands where the group is and how they see their needs and what they would like to accomplish, checking that his pre-planning has been on target. This period also gives him an opportunity to present an over view of the workshop and to allay any fears, especially any of the fears about sensitivity training. As he goes over the list of fears, it would be well for the leader in an honest way to allay any fears or anxieties that the group might have, by explaining to them exactly what the leaders will be trying to do. This procedure also is an opportunity to make the group aware that they are responsible for the workshop.

PROCESS: This kind of opening usually creates an interest and a sense of ownership in what is happening during the workshop. The participants are made aware of the fact that from the very beginning they are responsible for their own learning, and have a say about what is to happen during the workshop. This helps to build trust and confidence between the leaders and participants and also gives the participants a sense of security; that they are in charge of what is happening to them. Some may feel that to have this expectation session after already doing so much pre-planning is unnecessary. However, I have found on occasion, that committees take care of their own needs and do not adequately reflect the needs of the total group. In this particular workshop the committee happened to have been on target fairly well, but in other groups I have worked with the committees have been off target. Generally speaking, to have the expectation session in not redundant in the least, but is very helpful to getting the workshop started off in a good spirit. It shows that the leaders are concerned about the participants' unique needs and that they are not running the group through a stereotyped mechanical program.

3) Exercise Three: Personal Journal

THEME: The goal of the journal is to help the participants to reflect on the events and their reaction to the events as they experience the workshop. It is a crystallization process in which they are gathering together their responses and their learnings from the workshop.

MATERIALS NEEDED: Small notebook and pencil

DIRECTIONS: Encourage the participants to keep a personal journal of the workshop. Do not demand that they keep one, but ask them to keep it. They will find them of use during the workshop and also later when they may wish to review what they have learned during the workshop. Tell them: On the backside of the first sheet of notebook write the label: Objective events. On this page they will write out what is actually happening, the exercises, projects and how they occur. On the second page facing the back of the first page write: Subjective reaction. On this page they are to write in diary fashion their reactions and responses, their feelings about what is happening. Tell them that they will be given some time at the end of each session to write and also they could each night before going to bed take an opportunity to keep their personal journal up to date. Emphasize that the journal is for their private use and they will not be asked to share it.

PROCESS: The journal aids reflections and self discovery.

Individuals find it a lot easier to write out their feelings first, before they voice them. This is also true of ideas as well as feelings. It is also an instrument which helps the individual to crystallize her learning experience. Many people refer back to their personal journals months and years later, and find them of benefit to their growth.

4) Exercise Four: Dyadic Encounter

THEME: The goal of the dyadic encounter is to give the individuals an experience of relating to one person and thus complete the many experiences that they have during the workshop in relating to the large group and small groups. The booklet gives practice in listening and sharing feelings.

MATERIALS NEEDED: The Dyadic Encounter Booklet for each participant.

DIRECTIONS: The participants are told that one of the features of the workshop is that they grow in their interpersonal relationships in order to be able to build community. One phase of growing in community is the one to one relationship as well as the one to group relationship. They are asked to read the instructions in the booklet very carefully. Emphasize that they are not to read ahead. They have the freedom not to answer any of the questions if they do not wish to. They are then asked to stand up and to mill around and to choose someone on whatever basis you think will help them for a particular workshop. We usually ask them to choose someone whom they know very little or someone they would like to get to know better. If it had been thought desirable since the group was about half young people and half older people, we might have asked them to choose so that there is an older person and a younger person in each dyad. Another option in this particular group would have been to ask them to choose someone from the same city, so that perhaps they could continue their dyadic encounter even after the workshop. However, our particular purpose was to build toward a total spirit of community throughout the entire group. We chose to ask that they choose someone they did not know. In a workshop where you felt the participants could handle it and your goal was to break through prejudice and stereotyping, you might bluntly ask that they choose someone that they think they will not like. Almost inevitably they end up liking the person once they are past "just impressions."

Encourage the participants to use the instrument and not let the instrument use them. They may well want to share at length one of the questions in the booklet, and not talk at all about some of the others. Encourage them to take as much time as they wish during their free time to be together, and leave it up to them to decide how much time they wish to use on this project.

PROCESS: Generally speaking, participants respond very favorably to this opportunity to have a one to one relationship during their group experience. Most participants find it easier to relate one to one than one to group. The booklet is designed in such a way that it helps the dyad to grow in ability to listen and to express feelings. The booklet begins with light, superficial questions and gradually deepens to important personal questions. On occasion, there are some individuals who are threatened by a close one to one relationship. In those instances, it is best that they not be forced but allowed to choose not to participate in this exercise.

2. STAGE TWO: Personal Commitment to Religious Life

1) Introduction to Value Clarification

It is important in the world we live in with its many changes and complexities that we learn how to choose the values we live by. In this afternoon's session, we'd like to explore and give an appreciation and understanding of what a value is and what the criteria of a value are. This is only a very brief introduction to value clarification. We think you will find this very interesting and very stimulating. A value is something that is freely chosen from alternatives, and is acted repeatedly upon and which the individual celebrates and affirms publicly as being part of his development as a person. In order to be a full value it has to fulfill all seven criteria: that is, freely chosen, from alternatives, and is actually acted out repeatedly in one's life. Not only this, but a value is also something that once we act upon it we celebrate, that we rejoice in it and we are willing to affirm it publicly.

In this description of what a value is, there are contained seven criteria. These may be divided into three primary aspects: 1.) choosing; 2.) prizing; and 3.) acting. In the area of choice, a value must be chosen freely. There can be no coercion. The person is totally accountable for the choice he makes. Secondly the choice must be made from alternatives. If there weren't any alternatives, then there would be no free choice in the first place. One would be able to accept only what he was faced with. A third aspect of choice is the thoughtful consideration of the consequences of each of the alternatives. And, therefore, choices that were made without thought of the consequences are really not value choices.

The second broad category is prizing. A value that has been chosen freely from alternatives, with realization of the consequences of the alternatives, should be prized and cherished. In other words, the person is happy with the value he has chosen and holds it as something dear to him. So much so, that the second characteristic of his prizing is his willingness to affirm the value publicly and to let other people know he lives by it.

The third broad area of value is acting upon the choice. One way in which we can check the validity of what we say is to simply ask the question: have I acted on it or am I still thinking about it? Is it a value I hold in my hand but do not act upon? There must be some commitment to action shown in behaviour and attitude. The value must be repeated; it must become something that you live by, a pattern of behaviour for you. These are the seven criteria that we look to when we try to explore and find whether something is a value for us.

OUTLINE: The area of choosing:
1. To choose freely.
2. To choose from alternatives.
3. To choose from alternatives after considering the consequences of each alternative.
Prizing:
4. Cherishing and being happy with the choice.
5. Being willing to affirm the choice publicly.
Acting:
6. Actually doing something with the choice.

7. Acting repeatedly in some pattern of life.

What is important here in this definition of value is the process; how we arrive at a value. We have all kinds of values. People have a tendency to interject values from their parents, from authorities, from teachers. The purpose of value clarification is to help us to choose the values we personally wish to live by. There are many exercises and strategies which we can use to determine what our values are, and this morning we'd like to spend some time on this. (For more information on value clarification confer Raths, Harmin, and Simon, *VALUES AND TEACHING*, Charles E. Merrill Publishing Co., Columbus Ohio, 1966. Brian Hall, Vol. 1 *VALUE CLARIFICATION AS A LEARNING PROCESS: A SOURCEBOOK*, Brian Hall & Maury Smith. Vol. 2 *VALUE CLARIFICATION AS A LEARNING PROCESS: A GUIDEBOOK*, Brian Hall & Maury Smith. Vol. 3, *VALUE CLARIFICATION AS LEARNING PROCESS: A HANDBOOK FOR CHRISTIAN EDUCATORS*, New York, Paulist Press, 1973.)

2) Value Clarification Strategies:

THEME:

The purpose of the strategies is to help individuals discover what values they hold and clarify what are partial values for them.

MATERIALS NEEDED:

Pencil & paper
A room where there are tables to write on, or clip boards.

DIRECTIONS:

1. Introduce the word association, which is really a warm up exercise to help the participants begin to think. The word associations show what a person tends to think about when certain key words are enunciated.

Word Association List:

Notre Dame
Peace Corps
Church
Drugs
Prayer
Change
Receiving

War
Sister
Christian
Suffering
Conflict
God
Death

Authority
Community
School
Loneliness
Career
Gift

Simply read off these words and let the sisters respond by writing next to the word whatever image or word first comes into their minds. Later on they will be given time to share what they discovered about themselves in this word association game.

Value Clarification Strategy #2:
Ask the participants to make a love list of ten items that are important to them. Give them approximately 10 minutes to make their love list. This is an open

ended direction. They can include anything they wish on their love list.

After the participants have made their love lists of 10 items, the leader will ask the following value clarification questions: (N.B. to leader: the questions are about the seven criteria of a value and value indications.)

1. Put a dollar sign by any item that costs three dollars or more.
2. Put a 10 by any item that you would have been doing 10 years ago.
3. Put an "a" by any item that you can do alone.
4. Put an "s" by any item that is a school activity.
5. Put a "c" by any item that is a community activity.
6. Put a minus sign by any activity that you would not be willing to share.
7. Put a date by each of the items, the last time that you actually did the item.

Value Clarification Exercise #3
"I Urge You Telegram"

Ask the participants to write an "I Urge You Telegram." They are to pick one of the values from their love list which they feel is important, and which they would want to communicate and urge others to pursue. Ask them to write a telegram either to their mother superior, or their congregation, asking her or them to take a stand on the particular issue or value. Give the participants approximately 5 minutes to do this. (N.B. to leader: this exercise is asking the person to publicly affirm their value.) Ask some of the members to share their telegrams.

Value Clarification Strategy #4:
"Hope to Accomplish List"

Ask the participants to make a list of ten items they hope to accomplish before they die. Give them approximately 5 minutes to make this list. Then ask the following value clarification questions:

1. Put a check by any of the items that you have talked about with others.
2. Put a star by any of the items that others could help you with.
3. Circle any of the items that you have done something about in the last 3 months.

After the participants have finished their hope to accomplish list, and you have asked the value clarification questions, then break them into small mixed groups. In this session the total group is mixed. Let them share with one another what they have discovered about their own values through these value clarification strategies. At this time introduce the idea that they are to share only as much as they would like to share. Part of their dignity as a person is that they have the freedom to share or not to share according to how they feel about what it is they have written.

Value Clarification Strategy #5: (Coat of Arms)

The next task will be to ask the participants to make themselves a coat of arms. This can be the coat of arms of the sisters according to their religious community, or the focus may be on the individual themselves, whichever the leaders feel will be most profitable for the group. See the example of the coat of arms on the next page. Ask the participants to make themselves a coat of arms in any shape they wish, dividing their apex in half vertically and then drawing two parallel lines horizontally, so that they end up with six areas. They are not to use any words but they are to use only symbols or draw pictures, they do not have to be artists or good drawers to do this. They may use stick men if they like. Encourage them to draw a picture or make a symbol for each of the areas you talk about. Then ask them to make the following pictures or symbols: 1.) draw a picture or a symbol of what you do best as a religious sister; 2.) what is the biggest success of the past year you have had as a religious sister?; 3.) what is the biggest failure of the past year that you have had as a religious sister?; 4.) what as a religious sister will you not budge on?; 5.) If you only had one year to live as a sister, what would you choose to do?; 6.) (you may humorously say to the group that since they have been doing so well with the drawing, as a reward they may now write some words. Then give them the following instructions) write three words to describe who you are as a religious sister. Emphasize that the words are to be about *who* you are, not merely functions or jobs. (Another option to this is to ask them to

SAMPLE: COAT OF ARMS

1) WHAT YOU DO BEST AS A RELIGIOUS SISTER:

2) YOUR BIGGEST SUCCESS AS A SISTER THE LAST YEAR.

3) YOUR BIGGEST FAILURE THIS YEAR AS A SISTER.

4) WHAT YOU WILL NOT BUDGE ON AS A SISTER.

5) AS A SISTER, WHAT WOULD YOU CHOOSE TO DO IF YOU HAD ONLY ONE MORE YEAR TO LIVE.

6) WRITE THREE WORDS THAT DESCRIBE *WHO* YOU ARE AS A SISTER.

print the epitaph that they would like to have on their tombstone, which would reflect the kind of person they have been as a sister.)

Ask the group to divide into small groups, mixing by city origin and including everyone in the group. The facilitators' task during these small group discussions is to be a resource person, to answer any questions that the group may have about the projects, and to get a feel for how interested the group is in what they are doing.

This will be followed by ten minutes for Journal Time and thirty minutes for Optional Dyadic Time.

PROCESS:

Generally speaking, the group will find these value clarification strategies very interesting and very stimulating. They will become aware of a clear focus of individual values, and will be discovering relationships to the values they hold. Usually, the small group discussions will literally be "Buzz Groups" as the participants get involved in exploring what their values are and sharing these values with one another. There are two items the leader should be aware of: 1.) The strategies demand serious thinking and as a result tend to be very tiring for the participants; and 2.) On occasion some individuals are disturbed by what they find out about their values, especially when they find a contradiction between what they have thought were their values and what the exercises show are actually their values. Frequently, participants will want to talk to the leaders and explore their values even more.

(An option to this session would be to use the *Penney Forum* issue on Value Clarification (Spring-Summer, 1972.) This particular issue has an excellent brief introduction to Value Clarification. Contact your closest Penney Store.)

3. STAGE THREE: **Identity Search**

The goal of this session is to help individuals discover more about themselves and where they stand on important issues in the religious life of a sister.

MATERIALS NEEDED:

Pencil, paper & pins.
You will need to make cards which have the answers on them.
Please refer the leader's identity search sheet given on the next page. For example, the question on #1. "What is your role in a new group of people?" You will need four cards, each card printed with one word: For example, one card will have "wall-flower," another "dominating," another "wait and see," another "critical." You can use simple 8 x 11 sheets of paper and a wide felt pen so that they can be easily read from across the room. Place a set of answered cards in each corner of the room, lined up in the order of the questions.

DIRECTIONS:

We will present the format using #1 as an example, continue this same format with all thirteen questions. The sisters need to be able to move their chairs around easily, and break up into the four corners of the room. Please refer to the leader's identity search sheet given on the next page. Begin by telling the sisters, "we are going to have an identity search by bringing up several issues important to the religious life. As you choose your answer to a particular question (even though it is a forced choice answer) write this answer on a sheet of paper with a felt pen, pin it to your chest, so others can see what your answers have been." At the end of the exercise they will have a list of decisions they have made about important issues in the religious life.

For example, begin with number 1 and say, to the sisters; "What is the role you usually play when you come into a new group of people?" Then point to the small posters in the four corners of the room. One corner will have the answer "wall-flower" on it, another corner the answer "domineering", and another corner "wait and see", and the fourth corner will have the answer "critical." Ask the sisters to choose which way they are most likely to answer this question and go to that corner, forming a small group. Then allow them anywhere from 10 minutes to ½ hour to discuss that particular question depending on how involved and how dynamic the discussion seems to be.

LEADER'S IDENTITY SEARCH SHEET

1. What is your role in a new group of people?:
   wall-flower—dominating—wait and see—critical
2. I am most like (or identify with):
   mother—sibling—outside family—father
3. What aspect of sisterhood appeals to me?:
   serve kingdom of God—community prayer—apostolic work
4. Who I'd like to be like (or my image of a great sister):
   Little Flower—Jacqueline Grennen—Sr. Anita Carberry—Sr. Frances Borgia
*5. The prayer model which makes the most sense to me:
   Father-daughter—Christ, my brother—Creator-Creature—One with the Cosmos
*6. How most of my students see me:
   Nun—Hard worker—Professional—Friend
*7. What is my attitude toward conflict situations?
   Hawk—Lamb—Ostrich—Chameleon
8. What is my basic attitude toward authority?
   Dependent—Counterdependent—Alienated—Indifferent
*9. In affectional relationships I. . . .
   Give more than I get—Don't get enough
   Get more than I give—Don't give enough
10. If religious life as you know it were disbanded, you would choose:
   bi-sexual celibate community—secular institute
   married couples religious community—marriage
*11. What I fear most about the future:
   Incompetency—Loneliness—Retirement—Being a slot-filler
*12. When others are angry at me, my usual response is to:
   feel hurt—withdraw—deny it—get angry myself
*13. What needs the most work right now?:
   Prayer life—Community—Job—Self

*(At this particular workshop, the stared questions were used.)

The leader should note that these questions are placed in hierarchy of difficulty, beginning with a very simple question and going to more difficult questions. There are several questions that are thorny issues and that the group will become much more involved in discussing other questions.

We are giving here all 13 questions that could be asked. These questions are somewhat arbitrary. The planning committee may well change questions and bring issues that are more important and relevant to that particular group at that time.

In the actual community building workshop we used only numbers 5,6,7,9,11,12, & 13. The leader should allow time for each of the questions according to the interest in the question by the group. Generally speaking, the first question or two is fairly light. The group within 5 or 10 minutes will have discussed that issue sufficiently. However, as you get into questions like number 11, the group may well spend a good ½ hour discussing. There is no need to cover all of the questions you have prepared: it is sufficient that you move with the group according to its interests and what catches the group's fascination. The principle here is that the group will tend to manifest what it needs to discuss by spending more time on one of the questions than on others. When you notice that the groups are, as it were, winding down it is time to move on to the next question.

Next ask the second question, for example, "I am most like." Have someone close to the corners pull off the first answer and reveal the second set of answered cards, one in each corner. In the first corner, "father", in the second corner "mother", in the third corner, "sibling", and in the fourth corner "outside family". Then ask the participants to decide which answer they would be most likely to choose, going to that corner and forming another discussion group.

On occasion the entire group may well split up into two large groups. On some of the other questions, most of the participants may well go to only three corners. If the leader sees that there is only one person in a corner, it is best that he join that person in order that the person does not feel left out, and has someone to discuss his viewpoint with.

PROCESS: By the end of this exercise each participant has a list of decisions on the sheet of paper on her chest. They have also had the opportunity to see how others have responded to these issues. Generally speaking, participants find this a very interesting and exciting exercise, and discover new things about themselves. It is important for the leader to flow with the group, and to keep the momentum by moving on when it seems there is not interest in a particular issue, (give them more time when it seems that the group is excited about a particular issue.). One option is to use only half of these questions. Or if you know of a particular issue the group is interested in, include a question about it.

AN OPTION TO THE IDENTITY SEARCH

In the event that the full day has been very tiring and the sisters are becoming tired of talking and thinking, then a delightful exercise dealing with the same issue would be to ask the sisters to make a collage expressing the kind of person that she would like to be as a sister. Provide crayons, paint, clay, and old magazines. Give the group approximately ½ hour to make their collages; break them into small groups to share what their collage means to them.

SUNDAY—THEME: **Community And Inter-Personal Relations**

4. STAGE FOUR: *Person and Community*

THEME: Individuals reflecting on themselves as persons in community, with the opportunity to discuss with one another what they think religious community is all about.

MATERIALS NEEDED: Pencil and paper

DIRECTIONS: Ask the sisters to take forty minutes to write at least one paragraph on what they think and feel about the following 10 issues of religious life. The topics:

Community
Authority/Obedience
Teaching
Prayer
Poverty
Recreation
Personal Apostolate
Friendship
Celibacy
Personal Fulfillment

Instruct the participants to spend forty minutes writing one paragraph about each of these important areas in their religious life, including both thoughts and feelings. At 10:00 they are to meet in small groups, dividing by cities of origin. The leaders may visit the groups, acting as resource persons to them and facilitating the discussions.

PROCESS: Generally speaking, the individual has an opportunity to reflect on and write out what she actually thinks and feels about these important areas of her religious life. Coming into the small groups, they are prepared to share and discover with one another, how they as a community feel about these important issues. The discussions are usually very lively. Allow the participants to spend whatever time they wish on each of the areas. Depending on the group, they will tend to spend more time discussing one area than another.

VALUE CLARIFICATION SHEET: PERSON & COMMUNITY

THEME: An opportunity for the sisters to focus more specifically on the areas needing change or upbuilding in their community. The previous session on the 10 areas of being a woman religious will provide background for this value clarification sheet.

Value Clarification Sheet: Person and Community

You are interested in building community, as well as in clarifying personal values. Building community has long been the goal of those striving to live a religious life modeled after the Gospel message. However, some people maintain that true community is always an elusive dream, never to be fully realized. That when the community becomes all important, the individual member is suffocated into a life of conformity to other people's expectations. The unique, personal identity of each person is of paramount importance and should never be sacrificed for any abstract ideal, however lofty.

1. Do you agree with the above statement? If not, change it so that it expresses your opinion.

2. List five or more qualities that should be present in any good community of religious:

3. List five or more specific areas of potential conflict between the individual and the community:

4. Enumerate those changes that you personally feel would be of benefit to your own community:

MATERIALS NEEDED: Pencils
Make copies of the form "Value Clarification Sheet: Person & Community" for each of the participants.

DIRECTIONS: Pass out the form asking the participants to read and answer the questions. Give them approximately 20 minutes to a ½ hour.
Then break them into the same small groups that they were in at the beginning of the session (their city groups) and ask them to discuss the answers.

PROCESS: Generally speaking, participants find the value clarification sheets help them to reflect and discuss the issues that the sheet presents. You will note it provides more focus to the issue; especially moving towards concrete approaches. On occasion, elderly people find that these sheets demand too much writing. It is best to allow them the freedom not to participate or to participate only as much as they wish in the discussions.

5. **STAGE FIVE:**   *Conflict/Change in Religious Life*

Focus on understanding and appreciation of conflict and change in the religious life today.

MATERIALS NEEDED: The film—"Is It Always Right to be Right?"

The broken squares exercise must be prepared. The directions are given below.

You will also need copies of the value sheet on Religious Life Today for each of the individuals.

Then—Show the film, "Is It Always Right to be Right?"

This film is self-explanatory. The leader may make a few comments on conflict and change in religious life today. There are three points he may make: One, the acceptance of conflict and change as a part of life. It is not our goal to dream of some kind of unrealistic Utopia, but rather to learn to better handle conflict and change in order that we might grow. We can see conflict as an opportunity for creativity; as an opportunity to grow and expand rather than a defeating event in our lives.

A second attitude that is helpful in dealing with conflict and change is what the behavioral sciences call a "win-win attitude." A win-win attitude is exemplified by cooperation with another person or persons in order that both are able to meet their needs. We try to work together and pull together rather than work against one another. It is very easy for us to get into a "win-lose" attitude in which we think someone must win and the other must lose. It is better to have a trade off in an issue, namely, that we do it your way this time, and my way the next time, than to have no compromise at all.

A third idea to mention to the group within this framework of acceptance of conflict and change, and of a win-win attitude that we can see one another as resource people. In the United States we tend to have a highly competitive attitude and even quickly develop the notion that the other is an enemy. Rather we should begin, especially within our religious communities, to realize we are working as a team, and all are resource people to each other. Each one of us has talents and gifts and special training that can be of help to the entire group. We can learn to appreciate the talents, abilities, and special training of each person and accept her as a resource person of whom we can make use.

Exercise: The Broken Squares (small groups according to city groups)

THEME: The goal of this broken squares exercise is to illustrate group behavior in problem solving, and to help the participants perceive the way their behavior contributes toward or obstructs the solving of a group problem.

MATERIALS NEEDED: They will need to make a set of broken squares according to the directions that are given below:

BROKEN SQUARES

Directions For Making a Set of Squares

A set of five envelopes containing pieces of cardboard which have been cut into different patterns and which when properly arranged will form five squares of equal size. One set should be provided for each group of five persons.

To prepare a set, cut out five cardboard squares of equal size, approximately six by six inches. Place the squares in a row and mark them as below, penciling the letters a, b, c, etc., lightly, so that they can later be erased.

The lines should be so drawn that when cut out, all pieces marked "a" will be of exactly the same size, all pieces marked "c" of the same size, etc. By using multiples of three inches, several combinations will be possible enabling partici-

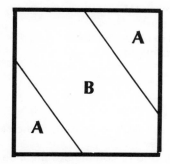

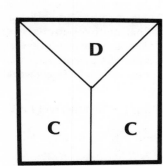

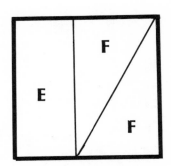

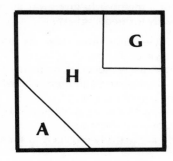

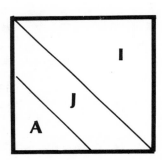

pants to form one or two squares, but only one combination is possible to form five squares six-by-six inches.

After drawing the lines on the six-by-six inch squares and labeling them with lower case letters, cut each square as marked into smaller pieces to make the parts of the puzzle.

Mark each of the five envelopes A,B,C,D, and E. Distribute the cardboard pieces in the five envelopes as follows:

Envelope A has pieces i,h,e
Envelope B has pieces a,a,a,c
Envelope C has pieces a,j
Envelope D has pieces d,f
Envelope E has pieces g,b,f,c

Erase the pencilled letter from each piece and write, instead, the appropriate envelope letter. This will make it easy to return the pieces to the proper envelope for subsequent use when a group has completed the task.

Instructions To The Group

In this packed there are five envelopes, each of which contains pieces of cardboard for forming squares. When the facilitator gives the signal to begin, the task of your group is to form five squares of equal size. The task will not be completed until each individual has before him a perfect square of the same size as that held by others.

Specific limitations are imposed upon your group during this exercise:

1. No member may speak.
2. No member may ask another member for a card or in any way signal that another person is to give him a card.
3. Members may, however, give cards to other members.

Are the instructions clear? (Questions are answered.)
Facilitator gives signal, "Begin working."

Instructions To The Observer Judge

OBSERVER: Your job is part observer and part judge. Make sure each participant observes the rules:

1. No talking, pointing, or any other kind of communicating among the five people in your group.
2. Participants may give pieces to other participants but may *not* take pieces from other members.
3. Participants may not simply throw their pieces into the center for others to take; they have to give the pieces directly to one individual.
4. It is permissible for a member to give away all the pieces to his puzzle, even if he has already formed a square.

Do your best to strictly enforce these rules. As an observer, you may want to look for some of the following:

1. Who is willing to give away pieces of the puzzle?
2. Did anyone finish their puzzle and then somewhat divorce himself from the struggles of the rest of the group?
3. Is there anyone who continually struggles with his pieces but yet is unwilling to give any or all of them away?
4. How many people are actively engaged in mentally putting the pieces together?
5. Periodically check the level of frustration and anxiety—who's pulling their hair out?
6. Was there any critical turning point at which time the group began to cooperate?
7. Did anyone try to violate the rules by talking or pointing as a means of helping fellow members solve their puzzle?

(Pfeiffer & Jones, *HANDBOOK OF STRUCTURED EXPERIENCES FOR HUMAN RELATIONS TRAINING*, Vol. 1, pages 24-29.)

DIRECTIONS: Set up a number of tables with 5 people at each table. Ask if any in the group have ever participated in this exercise before. If any have, then appoint them as observers and give them a copy of the instructions to the observers. It is always well to have observers. The facilitator of the group may emphasize the following ideas to the group: each individual must understand the total problem, each individual should understand how he can contribute toward solving the problem, each individual should be aware of the potential contribution of other individuals, and there is a need to recognize the problems of other individuals in order to aid them in making their maximum contributions.

Once the group is divided up into fives and the observers have been appointed, read very carefully the instructions to the participants. These instructions are given on the sample sheet which is called "Instructions to the Group." Make sure that all understand the instruction to work non-verbally. No one may speak. Meet privately with the observers. Give the observers their sheet and make sure that the observers understand their job. One of the co-leaders can meet with the observers in another room while the leader prepares the participants. Depending on the size of the group, try to have two or three observers.

It is important for the leaders and observers to enforce the rules in order for the exercise to be effective. The facilitator may visit the groups, answer any questions, and see how they are doing. If an individual asks a question, in fairness to all the groups, the leader should answer that question to the total group. Some groups may finish the project earlier than others. This presents an opportunity for the leader to sit with that group and to process with them the experience. When all the groups have completed the task, take some time to have a general discussion for at least 10 to 15 minutes in which they describe what the experience was like for them. If the opportunity presents itself, it is well to point out that the co-operativeness or lack of cooperation shown in this exercise is also probably present in their backhome situations. On occasion, a particular group may not be able to accomplish the task. For this kind of a workshop it is best that the leader sit with this group and explain the task to them and help them to discuss at least intellectually what the purpose of the task was. There are some people who are unable to benefit from an experiential learning task of this sort. Their mode of learning should be respected and the leader should prevent undue frustration which might cause hostility towards the total program. The leader should make it very clear to the group that they will not be punished, that he does not hold it against them if they are not doing the exercise, but rather that they are truly free not to engage in the exercise if they so desire. He can best do that by simply talking with them and explaining the reason for the exercise.

PROCESS:
This exercise focuses in very sharply on the cooperativeness of a group. In the event that a group shows a lot of cooperativeness there may be some aspects in which they learn to cooperate all the better. In the event that a group shows a lack of cooperativeness, this can be talked about, and they can come to some understanding of what would have been more helpful to them as a group. Though this exercise seems to be very simple, it can be a very intense experience for individuals. The leader should pay careful attention to the dynamics within the group, and help facilitate the discussion at the end in a constructive manner, and not allow the exercise to deteriorate into frustration and anger.

Exercise II—Value Clarification Sheet on Religious Life Today.

THEME:
To help focus on change in religious life today, providing a structure in which the sisters might analyze an approach to dealing with change in religious life today.

MATERIALS NEEDED:
Pencils
Copies of the Value Clarification Religious Life Today, for each participant.

DIRECTIONS:
Ask each of the individuals to answer the questions. Give the group approximately 15 minutes.

After the individuals have answered the questions, break them into their city groups for approximately 40 minutes to discuss. Or, bring the whole group together for a general report on what they have discovered as possible approaches to dealing with change and religious life today.

PROCESS:
This value clarification sheet helps to focus in on the issue of change. Since this is a very touchy issue, and a very important issue in religious life today, the discussions stimulated are usually intensive.
5:20—Show the film "Is It Always Right to be Right?" again. This is a 10 minute film. Groups profit from seeing it again. We choose on this particular occasion not to discuss the film itself, since the discussion time assured that the insight from the film would be shared. Also, we have found that the film is so stimulating it is discussed during free times and coffee breaks. An alternative is to use the value clarification sheet on "Is It Always Right to be Right?", providing a block of time to deal with the group's answers.

Value Clarification Sheet: Religious Life Today

Some say that the first thing a sister in religious life today must be is a flexible person, able to accept change and adapt. Personal growth always necessitates change. To live is to change, and to become perfect is to have changed often. However, this viewpoint overlooks the good values of the past that we already possess. Not all change is for the good. In fact, some change is regression to inferior values. Therefore, in religious life, to insure good change, superiors should always initiate the process of change.

1. Do you agree with the above statement? If not, what would you change to make this statement acceptable to you?

2. How would you describe the meaning of the word 'change'?

3. List those things that you feel should *not* be changed in religious life:

4. List specifically all the changes in religious life affecting you personally:

Value Clarification Sheet: Is It Always Right to be Right?

1. It takes courage to say "I may be wrong. You may be right."
2. Two "rights" can make a costly wrong.
3. The value of learning, as well as teaching, listening as well as telling. (Influence must be a two-way process)
4. The search for truth never ends.
5. Social problems are solved not by one group blaming another, but by two groups reaching for understanding.
6. Our complex age requires the spirit of a "Declaration of Interdependence."
7. The film gives a good solution.

1. It is easy to admit a mistake.
2. Stand fast when you are right.
3. People must be obedient to teachers and leaders.
4. Truth is absolute, eternal, and unchanging.
5. We need strong leaders who can force people to act right.
6. A man must learn to stand on his own two feet.
7. The film is too simplistic.

1. Choose which of the above statements you agree with and explain why.

2. How do you feel and act when you are talking with someone whose views are quite different from your own? Write down an example.

3. How do you think another person feels when you disagree with him?

4. Make a list of useful "do's" and "don't's" to change an argument into a discussion where both persons can learn from their differences.

5. Why is it hard for some people to say "I may be wrong?"

6. STAGE SIX: GROWTH IN COMMUNITY

THEME:

To help the participant come to a fuller realization of the good qualities she has, and that others see in her. It is also hoped that by having others point out the good qualities a person has, that person will come to appreciate her own dignity and self worth.

MATERIALS NEEDED:

It is best, if possible, that there be small rooms where the groups can have privacy for this exercise.

Pencil & paper is all that is necessary.

DIRECTIONS:

The leader gives an introduction, pointing out the influence of our puritan and stoic heritage in the United States, ensuring that many of us have a low self concept. He may say a few words about what humility truly is, not false humility which denies one's talents and abilities. You may refer to the gospel passage of how Christ is going to judge us by how we have used our talents. It is also well to speak about the ability to receive both positive and negative feed-back from others in order that others may help us to be more effective in our work and also help us to grow as persons.

At approximately 7:15 ask each participant to make a list of 10 good qualities she has. The ground rule is, acknowledge the qualities totally. There cannot be any modifying or qualifying statements that belittle or take away the good quality listed.

After the participants have their good qualities listed, they are to form a small group according to their home convents and to share their lists. Encourage them to be honest, sincere, and to only say what they truly feel and think. One of the other sisters is to be appointed secretary for that person. The person in the "love seat" gives her list of her good qualities. The secretary records these good qualities, and the rest of the members of the group then add to the list those qualities they appreciate about that person.

The participants may choose to simply go around the circle from left to right or they may choose to spontaneously volunteer to be the next one to be on the "love seat". Another sister is asked to take a turn at being the second sister's secretary.

This exercise should only be used towards the end of a workshop, because it demands a high degree of trust and cohesiveness in the group in order for it to be an effective experience. Used at an appropriate time most groups find this to be one of the highlights of their experience together. The members are especially moved when those with whom they live cry out to them their good qualities. Some members of the group find it to be a very emotional experience to receive a great deal of positive feed back at one time, but I have never found this experience to be harmful in any way to the participants.

A party should be prepared by one of the sub-committees for the sisters. In the planning of the workshop we felt that after two intensive days of working and especially after the love seat experience, it would be good for the community to have an opportunity to recreate together. This is not merely time wasted, but rather brings across the value of recreation together.

The love seat experience is taken from Herbert A. Otto, *GROUP METH-ODS TO ACTUALIZE HUMAN POTENTIAL*, Beverly Hills, California: The Holistic Press, 1970. Another alternative would be to ask the sisters to use crayons, paints, clay or to make a collage that would express the ideal self they are striving for. They would share these pictures of their ideal self, asking the group to help them overcome what is blocking the growth in potential and creativity. The decision of our planning committee was to use the love seat experience in this workshop, because of its positive thrust. The ideal self picture can take a negative thrust if not handled carefully. But it is a good and intensive experience for people who have the cohesiveness and trust to help one another by constructive feed-back.

7. STAGE SEVEN: BACK HOME APPLICATION

Dyadic Partner Closing Time

It is important to allow some time towards the end of the design to give the partners at least ½ hour to finish off the Dyadic Encounter. They will gain a feeling of it being closed and finished for them. Point out that closing the dyadic relationship is necessary, and that ½ hour is provided in the session.

Journals

Ask all of participants to make a list of their learnings from the spiritual renewal. Suggest they use their journals as an aid.

Grouping

At approximately 10:00, ask the sisters to move into their convent groups, share what they have learned from the experience, and plan how they will continue the community building at home.

An alternative: structure this back home application session with a questionnaire: 1.) Where are you now? What have you learned about yourself in the spiritual renewal experience, and about your relationship to your community? Can you specify these learnings in terms of personal assets and liabilities? 2.) What do you need to work on the most? What can you plan for back home that will help you to work on it? 3.) What in your community needs the most work? How can you as a community make plans to improve your community? 4.) Five years from now where do you want to be spiritually, psychologically, and physically? How can you plan to be where you want to be? What help do you need? 5.) Five years from now where would you like your community to be spiritually, psychologically? How can you plan to help your community reach this goal?

Another alternative would be to take a full session and do the Christian Growth project contained in this resource kit under the modern discussion week-end program.

Evaluation of the Spiritual Renewal

Gather the total group together facing the original newsprint listings of the expectations the group had of the workshop on Saturday morning. Ask the group to read over their expectations as they are on the newsprint, and evaluate whether or not the goals were met. Ask if any fears were realized. Whether the leaders in the group protected them adequately. It is important for the leaders to push honesty in this evaluation. The general goal of the workshop should have been accomplished. There may be some criticisms of the workshop, which will give the leaders an opportunity to model acceptance of constructive feed-back and receive help for their work with groups.

An alternative to this closing is to ask each participant to make a list of things she liked about the workshop, and a list of things she did not like about the workshop. *And* collate these.

Personal Journal Time

Give the participants the last few moments to celebrate the closing of the workshop by making a concluding entry into their personal journal. They can be told at this time they will be asked to place their journal on the Eucharistic altar at the time of the offertory, signifying their re-dedication to Christ.

Closing celebration of the Eucharist

Ask the liturgical committee to plan a special closing with a theme of their choice, but in the general area of rededicating to the religious life.

EVALUATION OF THE MODEL

This model was designed for a particular group of sisters. It is very easy to design a group dynamic and experiential learning approach for younger sisters or to take a traditional lecture approach with older sisters. The importance of this model is as an introduction to a group dynamic approach and value clarification for a group of sisters containing both young and old.

A goal of the model was to create a spirit of community and understanding and appreciation among the sisters. This goal was accomplished. The sisters asked to have a second phase workshop to build on the first one. All of the design of the workshop was toward putting the approach in such a manner that the older sisters would feel comfortable and participate, and at the same time that the younger sisters wouldn't be turned off by the approach. Anyone who has worked with sisters in recent times is very much aware of the problems of working with an intact community.

This workshop should be beneficial to any group of sisters similar to the original design group. However, it would demand an adaptation in order for it to be as effective with other kinds of groups of sisters. (One last point; in taking a group process approach, trying to move with a group as it is developing, sometimes a project you have planned simply doesn't click with a group. The group is not interested. When this occurs, it is best to have available another project to substitute. At times, especially toward the end of the second day, it may be that the group is simply low in energy, tired from the intensive work. Stop and give the group a break. Do not hesitate to let the group be part of that decision.

If you see the group seems to be dragging its feet, ask them about their energy level; whether they feel they need a rest. If they ask for the rest, give it to them. If they say their energy is up, but they are not interested in this project, then explore to find out what they are interested in and spontaneously provide for their needs at the time.)

E. MATERIALS/RESOURCES

MATERIALS NEEDED:

The following materials will be needed:

The Schedule (give them only the short schedule; the three page schedule is for the benefit of the leaders.)

Copies of the Value Clarification sheet on person and community.

Copies of the Value Clarification sheet on religious life today.

The parts for the broken squares exercise.

Pencils and papers for everyone.

The film "IS IT ALWAYS RIGHT TO BE RIGHT?"

Copies of the Dyadic Encounter for each person.

Remind the liturgical committee to prepare copies of whatever prayers or psalms they need. The prayer committee for morning and evening prayers should prepare whatever copies they need.

The identity search cards have to be made.

OPTIONAL MATERIALS NEEDED:

crayons
chalk
clay
poster paper
old magazines
scissors
paste, etc.

PART THREE:

RETREATS FOR RELIGIOUS COMMUNITIES

I. COMMUNITY GROWTH WEEKEND

by Donald Devaney, C.P.

and Raphael Domzall, C.P.

A. THEME/PARTICIPANTS

INTRODUCTION

The trend today among religious men and women is for their local communities to manage their affairs through shared responsibility. The members themselves desire to be fully involved in the decisions which affect their internal life and their external apostolic work. However, the functions of leadership cannot be eliminated. To grow into this new style of religious living, the members must have first hand experience of the understandings and skills that make this possible.

In brief, then, the individual members must understand the processes of group collaboration and experience their effects, grasp the importance of clarifying needs and goals, develop skills essential to creating and maintaining a climate for effective group decisions. Hence the exercises for brainstorming, interaction, consensus, priority sorting, conflict and collaboration.

This program has been designed for religious men and women in a local community setting. It envisions ten to twenty participants for best results. Two smaller communities could join together for the weekend. Much larger groupings would demand additional structuring.

Overall, the goal of the workshop is to enrich the lives of members in a local religious community. This workshop would help to accomplish this goal by emphasizing shared responsibility and developing the skills necessary to effectively exercise this responsibility.

B. OUTLINE/SCHEDULE AND GUIDE-LINES

1. Outline of Content

THEME: Community Growth through Interaction and Collaboration

INPUTS:
1. Religious Development (Historical)
2. Development Curve (Present Trends)
3. Brainstorming
4. Consensus
5. Intergroup competition

EXERCISES:
1. Then and now reflections
2. Generation of needs
3. Priority sorting
4. Conflict climate
5. Definition of Religious life
6. Action planning

2. Schedule and Leader's Outline

THEME: Community growth through interaction and collaboration

SESSION I: Friday Evening (7:30—9:00)

MATERIALS NEEDED:
Handout of Developmental Curve
Newsprint (3' x 5')
Wide felt pens (as many as there are groups of five)
Masking tape

INPUTS:
(30 minutes in the general assembly)
1. Orientation:
   a) procedures of the workshop:
      listening to inputs
      specific group tasks
      reports and reflections
   b) role of the workshop director:
      not doctor to patient
      not teacher to pupil
      not a prophet for the future, but give brief inputs, structure the exercises and assist in reporting
2. History of Religious Development (see appendix)
3. Developmental Curve (confer handout)

EXERCISE:
(30 minutes in small groups)

1. Divide the assembled group into smaller groups of five or six. Count off individuals across the rows to accord with the number of groups desired. For example, if twenty people are present and you wish to have four groups of five, count one to four across the rows of those seated so that those sitting in clusters will be distributed among all four groups. It is best if you let the individuals themselves call out their numbers—one, two, three, four and repeat. They will feel less

structured by reason of their participation.

    2. Set the task of generating "*Then* and *now*" experiences in religious life: those that were pre-Vatican II and present experiences. Four suggested areas of reflection to be assigned, one to each group are: Community Living, Spiritual Practices, Apostolic Works, and Government.

    3. Have each small group write out their results on the large newsprint sheets with the felt pens in one or two word phrases that describe or at least indicate the experience they're recording.

REPORTS AND REFLECTIONS: (30 minutes in general assembly)

    1. After the participants have returned to the general assembly with their lists of experiences "then and now" for each category, have the large sheets posted in front of the room. Ask a secretary from each group to report and explain their listings.

    2. Encourage all participants to reflect and react after each report.

    3. This exercise warms up the group since everyone will have something to say. Encourage the flow of conversation. It will leave the group for the evening on a high note and with a good bit of confidence about the workshop. It will help dissipate some of the initial anxiety about a growth weekend.

SESSION II: Saturday morning (9:30—11:00)

MATERIALS NEEDED: Handout on "Brainstorming"
Newsprint
Felt pens, chalkboard and chalk

INPUT: (15 minutes in general assembly)

    1. Introduction on brainstorming (follow outline of handout)

EXERCISE: (40 minutes in small groups)

    1. The small groups are asked to generate lists of needs of both individual members (personal needs) and of the community as a whole (group needs). Let half of the smaller groups address themselves to individual needs and the other half cover group needs.

    2. Initially using brainstorming techniques, they are to generate an exhaustive list of needs and only afterwards carefully sift through the list, eliminating similarities and items that do not seem significant to the group. Their final listing should describe personal and group needs in one or two word phrases.

    3. A secretary from each small group then prints this list on a large newsprint sheet for display and will eventually report the meaning of their listing to the assembly.

REPORTS AND REFLECTIONS: (30 minutes in general assembly)

    1. After the small groups have returned and their list of needs have been posted, a secretary reports their findings.

    2. As the secretaries report, encourage the participants to note items that are repetitious and synonymous. At times you will have to interject to reconcile semantic differences and move the sorting process along. Once you have eliminated items that are repetitious, make a final list of personal and group needs on the chalkboard in two separate columns.

    3. Then pointing to the listing, highlight what personal needs overlap the group needs (success, friendship, prayer), as well as what items are distinctively different (privacy/leadership). Have the group assist you in this clarification.

    4. The point to note in this exercise is that groups are made up of individuals and healthy group life does encompass many, many individual needs. This is the zone of stability between individual and group in which the needs of both and the goals of both can be met. It is one of the basic purposes for pooling resources. Inform the group that the list of needs they have generated will be the subject of the next exercise.

MATERIALS NEEDED: Handout on Consensus
Masking tape
Felt pens, index cards (3″ x 5″)

INPUT: (15 minutes in general assembly)
1. Introduction to the consensus process (follow outline of handout)

EXERCISE: (40 minutes in small groups)

1. Select 18 of the more important needs that were generated in the last exercise and have these printed on the index cards, one need to a card. You will need as many sets of 18 as there are small groups. Each group will have its own set.

2. Since they already have the experience of generating their own personal and community needs, they will next scale these needs according to *priorities* and do so in small groups by a *consensus process* that was just described to them. Give each small group a set of index cards so that they can spread them on a table or on the floor so as to be easily seen by all. First they are to sort the listing of needs into three sets of top, middle, and lower priorities, classifying the items in the order of importance as each group agrees to it consensually. See which items all agree to as top and which as bottom and then begin to work through their differences.

3. Then as a second step of the exercise have them take the resulting top set of priorities and put each need in a strict order of importance using the consensual approach. Once completed they will tape their top set of priorities together in sequence so they can be displayed.

REPORTS AND REFLECTIONS: (30 minutes in general assembly)

1. After the list of top priorities from each group has been displayed, the secretaries will make their reports. Let all the participants note the similarities and differences from group to group.

2. Ask each group to try to discover the point of view or frame of reference (from most pressing to least pressing need) they used in order to make their particular listing. Implicitly or explicitly they had to agree upon a certain point of view to begin the sorting, as for instance, by reason of urgency, cause and effect, the very nature of things, etc.

4. Now ask each group to reflect how closely they followed the consensus approach in doing their exercise. Let honesty be the policy. They can say whatever they want and comment on the exercise as they please. They will learn best from their own reflections.

5. The amazing result of this exercise is the vast similarities in their choices. A simple reflection about what other groups might do (e.g., husbands and wives, educators, women libbers, agnostics) heightens the similarity of their own evaluation. In the close living of local communities we fail to see that we are far more alike than we are different.

SESSION IV: Saturday Evening (7:30—9:00)

MATERIALS NEEDED: Handout on Consensus Exercise
Chalkboard or overhead projector for final tally

EXERCISE: (a four phase exercise; one hour duration)
Phase 1: Consensus in small groups (30 minutes)
   a. Distribute the prepared handout for the consensus exercise to all participants. (See appendix)
   b. Have them gather in the same small groups formed earlier in the day. The task now is to reach consensus on the two statements at the bottom of the handout following direction indicated there.
Phase 2: Debate by four representatives (20 minutes)

a. Two representatives will argue in favor of or defend the consensus position reached by their group with two opponents from another group.

b. No assignment of competing partners will be made. Each group must select its own two representatives and jointly plan a strategy to win the debate.

c. The two pairs of debators argue for their revision of the statements in the center of the room; all others will observe in silence.

Phase 3: Negotiation for points (5 minutes)

a. After the debate the debators return to their small groups to decide on the number of points they feel they deserve and wish to negotiate for. A hundred points are to be divided between the competing groups. No ties are allowed (No 50/50 split). Neither is an impasse allowed. Each group must decide for itself how many points it wants of the hundred.

b. Having decided how many points they want, each group must now select a representative to negotiate. Opposing negotiators will meet in private for five minutes. They must determine the point distribution between their two groups. An impasse will be resolved at the final tally.

Phase 4: Final tally (5 minutes)

a. After five minutes of negotiation, the two negotiators will report the results to the whole assembly. Let the results be posted on a chalkboard or overhead projector so as to be visible to all.

b. An impasse will be settled by the flip of a coin giving the total points (100) to one or the other of the two competing groups.

c. The winning groups will be announced in a "broadcast" style.

REPORTS AND REFLECTIONS:

(30 minutes in the general assembly)

1. By means of this conflict exercise participants are to experience the full effect of win/lose situations. (Note the paper on the dynamics of conflict—see appendix)

2. Elicit reflections from each group of how they felt about their initial consensus in modifying the two statements.

3. Ask the debating pairs to reflect their feelings before, during, and after the debate.

4. Check on how the negotiators felt about their resulting success or failure to gain points for their team.

5. Elicit reflections from the whole assembly about the final tally and announcement of the winners.

INPUT:

(10 minutes)

Explain the paper on the dynamics of conflict (See appendix). This will conclude the evening session.

SESSION V: Sunday Morning (9:30—11:00)

MATERIALS NEEDED:

Large newsprint sheets
Felt pens
Masking tape

EXERCISE:

(45 minutes)

Definition of Religious Life

1. The following is a small group exercise to assist participants in clarifying their present ideals and goals.

2. Instruct each small group to write a single sentence describing the religious ideals of their community. It is suggested that the group first brainstorm the essential elements of their life and work. Then, compose these elements into a single sentence beginning with the words: "We religious are . . ." Once again let the group use the consensual approach in carrying out this assignment. It will

give participants a better awareness of their community's operative ideals and goals.

3. Have a secretary write the final definition on a large newsprint paper and post it in the general assembly.

REPORTS AND REFLECTIONS:

(30 minutes in the general assembly)

1. Because religious life is bound in, with, and for others, it is helpful to analyze the definitions on the basis of the relationships they express or fail to express. List the following on the chalkboard or overhead projector and then direct the group to be active listeners, looking for indications of the following:

Relationships expressed:
a. to God in faith
b. to Church in professed mission
c. to one another in community
d. to others in service
e. to their special charism (those distinctive characteristics that give them a corporate identity).

2. As the secretaries make their reports and compare them to the outline on the chalkboard, ask for clarifications and comments from each group. Everyone should feel free to question the definitions of the other groups. This kind of interchange will help to achieve a better understanding of the perceptions of their operative ideals and goals.

3. Though not all differences can and will be reconciled in this session, the community members should be encouraged to work out the areas of disagreement as an ongoing responsibility, and at the same time to respect the different views held by community members. This is a good time to reflect on what consensus implies—not total unanimity, but a working basis generally recognized as important to the needs of the community.

SESSION VI: Sunday Afternoon (2:00—3:30)

MATERIALS NEEDED:

Newsprint sheets
Felt pens
Masking tape

EXERCISE:

(1 hour in small groups)
Action Planning

1. Indicate that this exercise will bring into focus all the major areas of the workshop. This will consist in developing action plans for the local community that will be both practical and acceptable. This exercise will help them meet needs through implementation.

2. Introduce the exercise by instructing the small groups that the action plan should be developed by a consensus discussion so that it will represent the best thinking of all the members. It is best, of course, to begin by brainstorming. A secretary should write the plans on the large newsprint sheets for later posting and reporting.

3. On the chalkboard or overhead projector write a list of the following topics:

a. What procedures would improve the running of local house meetings?
b. How can you bridge the diversity of differences within your group?
c. In what ways can you build up your mutual trust and support?
d. How can you endorse special interests and talents of members and give them greater recognition and esteem?
e. How can you provide adequate time for leisure?
f. What better ways are there of sharing decision making?
g. How can you effectively raise the morale of the community and create a climate for growth and development?
h. What programs are needed at the local level for sound religious renewal?

i. How cultivate a positive attitude toward experimentation? Design one in life style.

j. How practically motivate and integrate members who are threatened by their differences, rigidity and excessive independence?

4. Ask the question of the general assembly: "Which of these areas of community living are most in need of attention in your actual community?" When you've received some comments from the floor: select as many topics as there are small groups and assign one topic to each group.

REPORTS AND REFLECTIONS:

(30 minutes in the general assembly)

1. Ask a secretary from each small group to report the action plan and give any necessary explanations.

2. Allow for comments from the floor. Ask the question: "Are these action plans feasible?" "Can we put them into action?"

3. Try to get a general agreement from the workshop participants that they will attempt to follow through on the plans.

INPUT:

(5 minutes)

Conclusion

"The basic theological understanding upon which this workshop is built is the truth that 'grace builds on nature'. We must always remember that religious life is life. Life is always changing, always growing. Life is a process as we respond to the circumstances we meet from day to day.

Since we are living in a period of rapid change we can never be sure that the answers of today will fit the questions that will be asked of us tomorrow.

We have had the opportunity of working closely together for two days. During these hours we have worked hard. Maybe it is not possible to remember all that we have heard, but hearing has been reinforced by experience. That in itself proves that we can discuss our problems and try together to find answers."

C. TALKS/EXERCISES

1. Historical Survey Of Religious Traditions

Spirituality and Structure

KEY:

"At any given time and place in history, society challenges men differently and therefore, challenges men to respond to God differently." . . Bernard Cooke, *CHRISTIAN SPIRITUALITY*

Spirituality is shaped culturally
Structure and religious expression parallel
Spirit and form

I. First fervor of faith and practice
Take the beginnings that were fresh to the sources of faith.
ACTS OF THE APOSTLES: Seven different structures at least.
1. *Disciple system:* core group of twelve and sixty disciples.
2. *Council battle-collegiality:* Paul rebukes Peter, "Holy Spirit and Us"
3. *Strong headed center* (autocratic): James at Jerusalem; Matthew's gospel at Antioch to the North.
4. *Schools of thought*: Johannine school at Ephesus; Alexandrian school later
5. *Charismatic figures*: Itinerant missionaries: Paul, Cephas, Apollo, Barnabas and Mark, Mark's gospel.
6. *Communes:* Shared live-ins
Ananias and Sapphira—Acts 4,31
7. *Desert Separatists:* Christian Qumranese
Desert fathers.
Therefore, the point is, no one structure could contain the life. The followers of Jesus tried to lay down interpretations of what the gospel (good news) implied for human living (written gospels).

II. The Sweep of Religious History—Counter-Culture:
1. *Athanasius* (Matthew 10:37)
Hermitage in protest
anti-world; anti-clerical political
Martyrs for Christ vs. toleration of Christian compromises in cities
2nd, 3rd, and 4th centuries
2. *Origenist School* (Alexandrian)
Spirit vs. matter
emptying body and mind
dualism of evil and intellectualism
Apatheia and Gnosis
3rd and 4th centuries
3. *Benedictine Tradition*
Self sufficient (stable-spirituality)
Community life in a castle with prayer, work, scripture ordered
Stability vs. social flux, disorders, barbarian invasions
4. *Mendicant Transition*
Apostolic, order of social labors;
Going about doing good vs. new middle class and universities
Question of active-passive life
Thomas Aquinas: "Contemplata aliis tradere"
5. *Devotional practices and High Mysticism*
Council of Constance (1414)

Visions
Purifications, and gift of God
Sacred Heart devotion vs. Jansenism (17th century)
14th, 15th century phenomena
6. *Trent vs. Reformers*
Orthodox structure vs. spontaneous innovators
Law is chosen to protect the uneducated
300 year law tradition
Canon law 1917: revision of all rules a must
7. *Ignatian Spirituality*
Prayer as a style of life;
Finding God in all things (magnalia Dei)
Meditation at work;
Spiritual exercises—decision for Christ;
"In actione contemplativa"
8. *Institutionalized Spirituality* (19th & 20th centuries)
Ultra mechanical piety—Mortification of the eyes!
Formal meditation . . . "Ignatian" method
Spiritual directors and masters and customs
9. *Divine Milieu*—Teilhard de Chardin
Life as a process from the Alpha to the Omega
Where we are now—"process"
Exhortation to religious (para. 12)
The chief problem of any kind of renewal, adaptation and updating is:
—how to balance the changing with the changeless
—how to balance the demands of being contemporary with the treasures of the past
—how to be vital for the times if solidly grounded in the sources of Christian life
—how to be sure of a way of life with more democratic procedures.

THE DEVELOPMENT CURVE

This graph traces the growth of population through all recorded history, and projects it into the future to the year 2000 A.D. The reason why one curve fits so many and such varied factors of modern life is that what it really measures is the passage of the human race from one kind of history to another: from Subsistence to what is now called Development. This passage and its implications constitute the single most important clue to an understanding of our civilization—and of all history before it.

Here are only a few examples of the elements of our civilization which follow this decisive curve:

The expansion and specialization of knowledge
Books and articles in publication
The speed and facility of communications
The increase in educational opportunities
The speed and volume of data processing
The growth of socialization and complexity
The understanding of psychology & motivation
The desire of self-determination in peoples
The growth of social conscience (racial justice)
The speed and depth of social change
The generalization of Western technology
The practical applications of science
The "expansion" of the known Universe
The speed and range of travel
The command of the power of explosives
The utilization of sources of energy
The growth in control over the forces of nature
The penetration of the secrets of life

THE DEVELOPMENT CURVE

If the political divisions of the world at this moment were distributed according to their degree of Development they would be strung out along the same curve, with the United States at the top of the curve, the Western and Westernized countries below it on the "vertical" leg, the more advanced Communist countries on the rounded corner, and most Communist and all "developing" countries along the bottom.

DEVELOPED

HISTORY

Development Revolution

Information Revolution

Technological Revolution

Socio-Structural Revolution
(Quadragesimo Anno)

Second Industrial Revolution

Managerial Revolution

Capitalist Revolution
(Rerum Novarum)

Industrial Revolution

Agricultural Revolution

Medico-Sanitary Revolution

Geographical Revolution

SUBSISTENCE HISTORY

6000 mils.

5000

4000

3000

2000

1000

2000 AD

1000 AD

1 AD

1000 BC

2000 BC

3000 BC

4000 BC

2. Brainstorming

WHAT IS BRAINSTORMING?

As defined by Webster, Brainstorming is "a technique by which a group attempts to find a solution for a specific problem by amassing all the ideas spontaneously contributed by its members."

The brainstorming session is nothing more than a creative dynamic for the sole purpose of producing a checklist of ideas. These ideas must be further processed and evaluated, but this is subsequent to the brainstorming session.

WHY DOES IT WORK?

Social facilitation is a principle contributing to the success of brainstorming. Tests have demonstrated the "free associations" on the part of adults are from 65 to 93 percent more numerous in group activity than when working alone. There is also a stimulative effect in the rivalry and competition in dealing with the group task. The positive reinforcement principle is also operative since all suggestions and ideas are received and rewarded, and there is no criticism or judgment to hinder the free flowing process of ideas.

WHAT ARE THE RULES?

1. *Criticism is Ruled Out.* Adverse judgment of ideas must be withheld until later.
2. *"Free Wheeling" is Welcome.* The wilder the idea, the better; it is easier to tame down than to think up.
3. *Quantity is Wanted.* The greater the number of ideas, the more the likelihood of useful ideas.
4. *Combination and Improvement Are Sought.* In addition to contributing ideas of their own, participants should suggest how ideas of others can be turned into better ideas; or how two or more ideas can be joined into still another idea.

WHEN CAN YOU USE IT?

The problem should be specific rather than general, it should be narrowed down so that the members can shoot their ideas at a single target. Group brainstorming is indicated for problems which primarily depend on idea-finding, not for problems which primarily depend on judgment. Brainstorming can't be helpful for any problem for which there are only two or three alternative solutions. If the solution to a problem is a yes or no, then list the pros and cons and use analytical judgment. Weigh and evaluate each pro and con by comparative judgment to seek the solution. Imagination rarely comes into the judicial process, so brainstorming can be of no help.

WHAT ABOUT THE PARTICIPANTS?

Education and experience have trained most adults to think judicially rather than creatively. As a result they tend to impede their fluency of ideas by applying their critical power too soon. By deferring their judgment during a brainstorming session they find they can think up substantially more good ideas. The participants must be convinced of the harm of criticism and judgment during the brainstorming session.

In brainstorming, quantity helps breed quality. In most sessions the quality of the last 20 ideas in a session are much higher than the ideas produced early in the session.

It's good to have a core group who are acquainted with the problem to work in a brainstorming session with some outsiders. The outsiders pump fresh ideas into the session. A group left together for a long period of time tends to develop rigid patterns of thinking, so that one member can almost anticipate the reactions of another.

If it is an all male group, it's a good idea to have a woman brought into the session. This sets up rivalry and increases the flow of ideas. People in the group should be substantially of the same rank so there will be no feelings of inferiority between the members.

The ideal number for a session is about a dozen. If the group has had no previous experience with brainstorming, it would be good to have an orientation and a little practice session.

The "chairman" of the brainstorming session should go over the problem and make sure that it is a simple and specific topic and not an umbrella problem like how to win the cold war. The chairman should have some kind of direction and suggested solutions to the problem already. Then if the stream of ideas slows down the leader can prime the joint flow by interpolating suggestions of his own. But he should always hold back whenever any of the group is waiting to be heard. The chairman should let the participants think about the topic of the brainstorming session for a few days in advance to let incubation enhance the workings of association.

HOW DO YOU CONDUCT AN ACTUAL SESSION?

Have a placard in full view of the participants displaying the four rules for conducting the session.

The chairman recognizes those who raise their hands to signify they have ideas to offer. Sometimes so many hands go up that he simply goes around the table and lets each person present one idea in turn. Participants should never be allowed to read off lists of ideas which they have brought into the meeting. These can be handed to the leader before the session. Only one idea at a time should be offered, otherwise the pace would be badly impeded and the opportunity for hitch-hiking ideas would be precluded.

The leader should especially encourage ideas that are directly sparked by a previous idea. This chain reaction is worthy of immediate attention so the panelists are asked to snap their fingers as well as raise hands when they have a hitch-hiker idea to offer. Each panelist should have a note pad before him to write his ideas down so when called he won't forget what he wanted to say.

A recording secretary sits next to the leader and in direct line of conversation between him and the others. Ideas are taken down organizationally, not word-for-word. No idea is identified by the name of its suggestor.

The optimum time for a session is about 30 minutes.

The time after the session is the time to evaluate and develop the ideas created during the brainstorming session. The basic aim of brainstorming is to pile up a quantity of alternative ideas. Brainstorming should not be used on problems requiring value judgments.

3. Consensus Exercise

DIRECTIONS:

Each group has a half hour in which to reach consensus on the following two statements.

You can accept them as stated or you can modify them by addition, subtraction or rephrasing.

The accepted (and/or amended) statements should express the ideas of each member of the group and each one should be ready to defend them.

STATEMENTS:

A. Individuals make the most effective decisions. Groups are cumbersome and ineffectual in making decisions.

B. A superior is necessary if a group is to accomplish anything.

CONSENSUS:

Whenever two or more are gathered to make a decision, the net result is not necessarily unrelieved bad news. There can be strength in group problem solving. A disgruntled group member once defined a camel as a horse put together by a committee. Group decisions often are frustrating and inadequate. All members want agreement, but they also want to make their own points heard. So they bargain, they compromise, and the final product is often a potpourri that no group member really believes in. Consensus is a technique in group problem solving.

1. WHAT IS CONSENSUS?

Consensus is a decision process for making full use of available resources and for resolving conflicts creatively. Consensus is difficult to reach, and it will not always meet with everyone's complete approval. Complete unanimity is not the goal, and it is rarely achieved. But each individual should be able to accept the position or proposal on the basis of logic and feasibility. When all the group members feel this way you have reached consensus. You can function as a group because you have reached operational agreement. This means, in effect, that a single person can block the group if he thinks it necessary, but this option should be rarely used.

2. WHAT ARE SOME GUIDELINES?

A. *Avoid arguing.* Present your position as lucidly and logically as possible. Listen to what the other members of the group say and consider what they say carefully before you press your point. You may be able to say to yourself, "Although I can't accept everything fully, I can agree with the basic idea. Although I'm not completely convinced, I can live with it. I see the validity and the truth of their statements."

B. *Do not assume that someone must win and someone must lose* when discussion reaches a stalemate. Instead, look for the next most acceptable alternative for the group.

C. *Don't change your mind simply to avoid conflict and to reach agreement* and harmony. When agreement seems to come too quickly and easily, be suspicious. Explore the reasons and be sure everyone accepts the solution for basically similar or complementary reasons. Yield only to positions that have objective and logically sound foundations.

D. *Avoid conflict reducing tchniques such as majority vote*, averages, coin flips and bargaining. When a dissenting member finally agrees, don't feel that he must be rewarded by having his own way at some later point.

E. *Differences of opinion are natural and expected.* Seek them out and try to involve everyone in the decision process. Disagreements can help the group's decision because with a wide range of information and opinions, there is a greater chance that the group will hit upon more adequate solutions.

F. *If consensus does not occur* after this process has been gone through and sufficient time has been spent in discussion, *table the matter* and move on. It could be that the matter needs more research, or that more data must be gathered, or that the matter is not sufficiently mature and needs additional time for reflection.

G. *The members of the group should be more committed* to reaching a good decision *than to committing themselves* to the decision they have reached.

3. BEST USE OF CONSENSUS

The diagram on the next page illustrates the relationship between degree of uncertainty of the task, and the need for group consensus. Where uncertainty is low the need for group consensus is low, partly because the solution can be developed easily by someone who has the expert knowledge needed, and partly because these reasons and justifications for the solution can be readily understood and accepted by the whole group.

On the other hand, where the degree of uncertainty is high, the need for group consensus is high. This is partly because no one has the expert knowledge to reach a solution, and partly because everyone's reasons and knowledge are necessary to reach the best decision and to develop acceptance of and commitment to the decision when it is reached.

4. THE ADVANTAGES OF CONSENSUS

A. The individuals are heard. There is true participation in the group.

B. The group achieves creativity because, believe it or not, two heads are better than one. At times the group can achieve synergism, the ability of a group to out-perform even its own best individual resource.

C. A sense of unity, an esprit de corps or community grows in the group.

D. The individuals in the group feel more committed to the decision that the group has arrived at and will work harder to make it a reality.

5. CONCLUSION

Studies on consensus have found, (1) groups function as their members make them function and, (2) that conflict effectively managed, is a necessary precondition for creativity. Thus, decision-making groups can be expected to do better than even their best members. There is nothing in group process that makes committees, boards, and panels inherently inept. Ineffective solutions to problems are the product of groups that are pessimistic about their own potential, and have imperfect ways of dealing with conflict.

The horse that is put together by a group that understands group dynamics won't turn out to be a camel. It may be a thoroughbred filly fit for the Triple Crown.

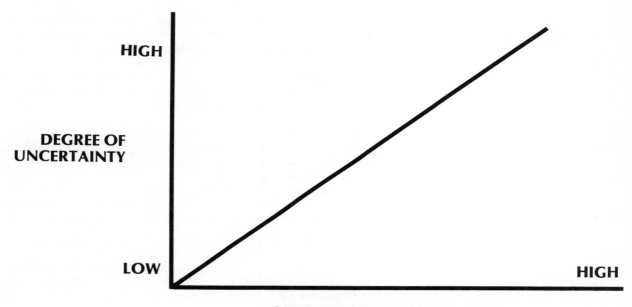

4. Competition In Groups

The simulation you have just experienced has been replicated many times with a variety of groups. The results have been surprisingly constant so it is now possible to predict, with relative certainty, what will generally happen as a consequence of intergroup competition. These predictions are summarized here.

1. WHAT HAPPENS WITHIN GROUPS?

The members of each of two competing groups begin to close ranks and quickly experience increased feelings of group loyalty and pride. Each group sees itself as the best and the other group as the enemy. Under the pressure of time and task deadlines, the group willingly accepts more structure and autocratic leadership. The group climate is characterized by work, as opposed to play or fight, task as opposed to maintenance. Conformity is stressed and there is little tolerance for individual deviation.

2. WHAT HAPPENS BETWEEN GROUPS?

Whatever interaction there was between the members of the two groups before the competition decreases and becomes more hostile. What communication there is becomes very selective—each group hearing only comments that confirm its stereotype of the other and support its own position.

3. WHAT HAPPENS TO THE WINNER?

The winning group climate can be called "fat and happy." Tension is released; there is little desire to get on to work. People would prefer to play and rest on their laurels. There is little desire to explore earlier conflicts and possibly learn from them.

Generally, the winners not only retain their prior cohesion but become more cohesive. The exception is when the group really does not feel as if it won or when the decision is close and they did not win decisively. Under these conditions, winners often act like losers.

4. WHAT HAPPENS TO THE LOSERS?

The members, initially, deal with having lost in one of two ways. Some groups deny reality—"We didn't really lose. It was a moral victory." Other groups seek a scapegoat, someone other than themselves to blame for the defeat. The scapegoat can be the judges, the representative, or the rules. Cohesion is low and fights are prevalent.

A losing group is, however, also a "lean and hungry" group. Tension increases, old conflicts are re-examined, and the group really digs in and learns a lot about itself in preparation for the next task.

5. WHAT HAPPENS TO THE REPRESENTATIVE?

People seldom realize how much responsibility a person feels when he is asked to represent his group and the tension that results from being put in such a position. In addition, it is often unclear just how free a representative really is to be himself as opposed to being what the group expects him to be. How flexible is he to deviate from the group's mandate in response to changes in the situation? Finally, if his group loses, the representative often feels guilty and responsible.

Given the difficulties of reducing intergroup competition, strategies for eliminating it in the first place may be desirable.

a. Relatively greater emphasis is given to total organizational effectiveness and the role of departments in contributing to it; departments are measured and rewarded on the basis of their contribution to the total effort rather than on their individual effectiveness.

b. High interaction and frequent communication are stimulated between groups to work on problems of intergroup coordination and help; reward given partly on the basis of help that groups give to each other.

c. There is frequent rotation of members among groups or departments to stimulate high degrees of mutual understanding and empathy for one another's problems.

d. Win-lose situations are avoided; groups should never be put into the position of competing for the same organizational reward; emphasis is always placed on pooling resources to maximize organizational effectiveness; rewards are shared equally with all the groups or departments.

D. MATERIALS/RESOURCES

References

BOOKS: George Lane, *CHRISTIAN SPIRITUALITY*, Argus Communications, Chicago, Illinois, 1968, passim.
Kolb, Rubin, McIntyre, *ORGANIZATIONAL PSYCHOLOGY*, Prentiss Hall Publication, New Jersey, pp. 258-262.
Devaney, Domzall, Overman, *LOCAL COMMUNITY LIVING*, Management Concepts, Dayton, Ohio, 1972, pp. 25-33.

PERIODICALS: George Charrier, "Cog's Ladder; a model of group growth," *ADVANCED MANAGEMENT JOURNAL*, Vol. 37, 1, Jan. 1972.

E. LITURGIES/HOMILIES

SUGGESTED LITURGY: **Mass of Christian Unity**

1. Readings: #812—5th reading New Testament
              813—5th responsorial
              815—7th reading—Gospel
2. Hymns: All of My Life
              Take Our Bread
              Peace, My Friends
              Christians
3. Homily: Christians are called to and respond in community.
   a. Life from God flows in a triangle which involves others as well as ourselves in relation to him.
   b. The Gospel message directs us to go to the Father TOGETHER.
   c. Therefore, we must be a priestly people tying two worlds together . . . bridge builders.

II. A PRAYER CLARIFICATION DAY

by Donald Devaney, C.P.

and Raphael Domzoll, C.P.

A. THEME/PARTICIPANTS

INTRODUCTION

    The theme of this clarification day is search, grow and share through prayer. It enables a religious community to clarify the meaning and operative value that prayer has in its life.

    The prayer clarification day provides an opportunity for members of the community to share the more significant values of their lives, to cultivate an awareness and respect for each other and finally lead them, rather gently, into experiences of shared prayer. These experiences are designed to encourage them to participate actively. A prayer clarification day would make an excellent day of recollection.

B. OUTLINE/SCHEDULE AND GUIDE-LINES

1. Outline of Content

THEME: Search, grow and share through prayer

INPUTS:
1) Theological virtues are incarnational
2) People are gifts of God
3) Johari Window
4) Communication levels
5) Needs and values are correlative
6) Christians are called to and respond in community

EXERCISES:
1) Personal response to religious living (small groups)
2) Prayer clarification (paper and pencil)
3) Personal experiences of God (small groups)
4) Liturgy . . . Mass of Christian Unity

2. Schedule and Leader's Outline

THEME: Search, grow and share through prayer

SESSION I: *9:30 a.m.—11:00 a.m.*

Inputs: (to the general assembly)
Theological virtues are incarnational (10 min.—see appended outline)
People are gifts of God (10 min.—see appended outline)

Exercise: Personal Response to Religious living (1 hour in small groups)
Gospel model . . . Matt. 11:2-10
Divide the assembled group into small groups of no more than ten in a group
Instruct the small groups to share in a round robin discussion of the following points:
1) What were you looking for when you joined this religious group?
2) What has your religious life meant to you over the years?
3) How are you responding to religious living today?
After all have shared in a small group, ask them to join hands and pray aloud for what they really want their religious life to be.

Inputs: (11:00 a.m.—in the general assembly)
Brief group reports of special points of interest from the last exercise; volunteered on the floor. (10 min.)
Opening one's window on the world of reality. (15 min.) Johari Window and levels of communication explained and applied. (See periodical references)
Jesus with the woman at the well. (10 min.) (See periodical references)

SESSION II: *1:30 p.m.—General Assembly*

Exercise: Prayer Clarification
Paper and pencil exercise for individual recording and reflection.
1) Ask each individual to record ten activities he enjoys most of all—that they like to do most of all.

2) Tell them to record how frequently they do this activity—for example: once a month, once a week, once a day, once a year, etc.
3) Let them note when they last did the activity.
4) Ask them to place a star on the three most enjoyable activities of those listed.
5) Pose the question: "Where is prayer on your list?"
6) Commentary:
   a) If you don't enjoy something, like prayer, it isn't a full value yet. What is of worth, value, or good to a person, once possessed, gives joy.
   b) Basic Psychology: "What you want is what you get." Basically people do what they want . . . even subconsciously.
   c) Need-Value correlation (see appended outline).

Second paper and pencil exercise:
1) Instructions: Now ask the assembled group to make three columns on a page of paper and head each column, Column I—Before entering Religious Life; Column II—During formation of Religious Life; Column III—Now.
2) Ask them to respond to the following questions by writing their answer in each column for that period of time. The questions are:
a) What different *kinds* of prayer did you make? . . . at the three different stages of time in your life.
b) With *whom* did you pray, or was it alone?
c) *How much* prayer did you make?
d) *Why* did you pray at those times?
e) Did you *enjoy* praying? What period most?
3) Give them a few minutes to personally reflect on what they have recorded under the three periods of time.
4) Write a paragraph: "I would like my prayer to be . . ."

Small group experience (2 p.m.)
Instruction: Gather in the same small groups as before to share the following ideas in a round robin discussion.
1) Share the paragraph you have written on what you want your prayer to be.
2) Share your idea of God; what kind of person is He for you?
3) Did you ever have an experience of feeling especially close to Him? Share this.

C. TALKS/EXERCISES

Outlines Of Inputs

THEME: Theological virtues are incarnational

Jesus Christ was a relational person. He related to the Father and to all of us. He grew in wisdom and age before God and man. He grew in faith and trust and especially love.

By a religious profession we are especially dedicated to practice faith, hope and charity in our relations to God. But these virtues must also be incarnational, that is, begin with relating to others. (Confer I John 4:19-21)

We relate to God in faith, hope and charity having first realistically grown in faith, trust and love of others. To the degree that we have developed our capacity to believe and trust and love others, only to that degree are we capable of turning and relating to God in faith, hope and charity.

THEME: People are a gift of God

In the Old Testament Abraham was chosen to be a blessing to his people.

Isaac, Jacob, and Joseph: The nation of Israel was blessed because of these leaders.

Mary at the Annunciation "All nations shall see me as a blessing."

Jesus was saviour, a blessing to his people.

We are to be a blessing to one another; people are gifts of God.

THEME: Needs and Values are correlative to each other

We value that which appears good to us.

Needs are indicative of our values at any given moment of time or level of growth.

What we value is determined by our pressing needs.

Once we possess the good that we need, we experience satisfaction.

D. MATERIALS/RESOURCES

References

BOOKS:

Raths, Harmin, Simon, *VALUES AND TEACHING*, Merrill Pub. Co., Columbus, Ohio, 1966.

Bernard Cooke, *CHRISTIAN COMMUNITY: RESPONSE TO REALITY*, Holt, Rinehart, Winston, N.Y., 1970.

Gregory Baum, *MAN BECOMING*, Herder and Herder, N.Y., 1970.

"Communication" and The Johari Window", *LOCAL COMMUNITY LIVING: PARTICIPANT'S MANUAL*, Management Concepts, Inc., Dayton, Ohio, 1972.

PERIODICALS:

"The Johari Window"—The *REVIEW FOR RELIGIOUS*, April, 1971.

"Communication: The Invitation to Live and Grow,"—*SISTERS TODAY*, Dec., 1972.

E. LITURGIES/HOMILIES

LITURGY: *(3 p.m.) Mass of Christian Unity*

    A. Readings: No. 812—5th reading New Testament
                         813—5th responsorial
                         815—7th reading—Gospel
    B. Hymns: All of my life
               Take our bread
               Peace, my friends
               Christians
    C. Homily: Christians are called to and respond in community.
        1) Life from God flows in a triangle which involves others as well as ourselves in relation to him.
        2) The Gospel message directs us to go to the Father TOGETHER.
        3) Therefore, we must be a priestly people tying two worlds together . . . bridge builders . . . Pontifex.

ACTIVITIES INDEX

LITURGY INDEX